THE SLAYER COLLECTION
VOLUME 1

TITAN

WWW.TITAN-COMICS.COM

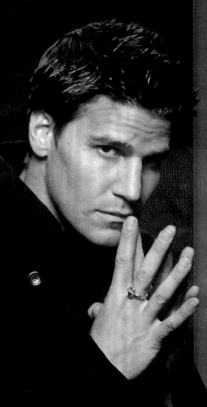

**Buffy the Vampire Slayer
The Slayer Collection Volume One**
ISBN: 9781782763642

Published by Titan
A division of Titan Publishing Group Ltd.,
144 Southwark Street,
London
SE1 0UP.

Collecting material previously published in the
Official Buffy the Vampire Slayer Magazine and
the Official Angel Magazine, 1997-2007.

A CIP catalogue record for this title is available
from the British Library.

First Edition October 2015
10 9 8 7 6 5 4 3 2 1

Printed in China.
Titan.

Editor Natalie Clubb
Senior Art Editor Rob Farmer
Additional Design Dan Bura

Art Director Oz Browne
Acting Studio Manager Selina Juneja
Publishing Manager Darryl Tothill
Publishing Director Chris Teather
Operations Director Leigh Baulch
Executive Director Vivian Cheung
Publisher Nick Landau

Acknowledgments
Titan Would Like to Thank...
The cast and crew of *Buffy* for giving up their
time to be interviewed, and Josh Izzo and Nicole
Spiegel at Fox for all their help in putting this
volume together.

WELCOME TO THE HELLMOUTH...

"Into every generation a Slayer is born: one girl in all the world, a chosen one. She alone will wield the strength and skill to fight the vampires, demons, and the forces of darkness; to stop the spread of their evil and the swell of their number. She is the Slayer."

With these fateful words, one of the most iconic, ground-breaking genre shows of all time, screamed onto TV screens. For seven seasons, *Buffy the Vampire Slayer* captivated audiences around the world with its intoxicating mix of horror, comedy, drama, tragedy, and award-winning writing - and changed the face of genre TV forever.

Now, in this first special collection celebrating the TV phenomenon, the best of the official *Buffy the Vampire Slayer Magazine* revisits the Slayer, her world and her legacy, and delves deep into the mythology of the Slayers, the Watchers, and the trusted Scoobies.

Slayers

Scoobies

CONTENTS

Watchers

CLASSIC SCENE

"welcome to the Hellmouth"

"Why can't you people just leave me alone?"

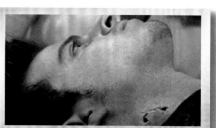

The Story so far...

Having moved from Los Angeles to Sunnydale with her mother, Buffy's first day at her new school doesn't exactly go to plan when she discovers evidence of vampire activity on the campus.

The Scene...

THE LIBRARY, SUNNYDALE HIGH SCHOOL.
(Buffy confronts Giles after discovering an ex-student dead in a locker, completely drained of blood...)

GILES: You really have no idea what's going on, do you? You think it's coincidence, your being here? That boy was just the beginning.

BUFFY: Oh, why can't you people just leave me alone?

GILES: Because you are the Slayer. Into each generation a Slayer is born, one girl in all the world, a Chosen One, one born with the strength and skill to hunt the vampires...

BUFFY: ...with the strength and skill to hunt the vampires, to stop the spread of their evil, blah, blah, blah... I've heard it, okay?

GILES: I really don't understand this attitude. You, you've accepted your duty, you, you've slain vampires before...

BUFFY: Yeah, and I've both been there and done that, and I'm moving on.

GILES: What do you know about this town?

BUFFY: It's two hours on the freeway from Neiman Marcus?

GILES: Dig a bit in the history of this place, you'll find a steady stream of fairly odd occurrences. Now, I believe this whole area is a center of mystical energy, that things gravitate towards it that that, that, that you might not find elsewhere.

BUFFY: Like vampires.

GILES: Like zombies, werewolves, incubi, succubi, everything you've ever dreaded was under your bed, but told yourself couldn't be by the light of day. They're all real!

BUFFY: What? You, like, sent away for the Time-Life series?

GILES: Ah, w-w-w-yes.

BUFFY: Did you get the free phone?

GILES: Um, the calendar.

BUFFY: Cool! But, okay, first of all, I'm a Vampire Slayer. And secondly, I'm retired. Hey, I know! Why don't you kill 'em?

GILES: I'm a Watcher, I haven't the skill...

BUFFY: Oh, come on, stake through the heart, a little sunlight... It's like falling off a log.

GILES: A, a Slayer slays, a Watcher...

BUFFY: ...watches?

GILES: Yes. No! He, he trains her, he, he, he prepares her...

BUFFY: Prepares me for what? For getting kicked out of school? For losing all of my friends? For having to spend all of my time fighting for my life and never getting to tell anyone because I might endanger them? Go ahead! Prepare me.

EPISODE CREDITS

Buffy Season One, Episode One

first aired: 03/10/97 (U.S.) & 01/03/98 (U.K.)

written by: Joss Whedon
directed by: Charles Martin Smith

Main actors this scene:
Buffy: Sarah Michelle Gellar
Rupert Giles: Anthony Stewart Head

WHY SO COOL?

This early scene is a revealing, insightful glimpse into the Slayer/Watcher relationship, which, from day one, was a fundamental ingredient to the show's success.

EPISODE TRIVIA

 "Welcome to the Hellmouth" was broadcast in New Zealand some six weeks before the series made its debut in the U.S.

 Sarah Michelle Gellar's lines in this scene were actually shot eight months after the rest of the episode. It was reshot because she had apparently come across as a bit too angry.

Compiled by Kate Anderson

Slay Belles

It's a centuries-long ritual, but the role of the Vampire Slayer is shrouded in its own mysteries. Buffy Magazine examines the mythology of the Slayer.

{ "I'M THE THING THAT MONSTERS HAVE NIGHTMARES ABOUT. AND RIGHT NOW, YOU AND ME ARE GOING TO SHOW 'EM WHY." BUFFY TO THE TUROK-HAN, "SHOWTIME." }

by K. Stoddard Hayes

overhears Giles and Angel discussing the prophecy that the Master will kill her. At first, she doesn't handle it very well:

"I quit," she says. "I resign, I'm fired, you can find someone else to stop the Master from taking over."

Giles tries to intervene: "Buffy, if the Master rises—"

"I don't care! I don't care. Giles, I'm 16 years old. I don't want to die," she says, and runs off.

Giles actually doesn't handle it very well, either. One would expect an experienced Watcher to have accepted the reality that his Slayer is more likely to die than not. Instead, Giles prepares to do battle with the Master himself, determined that he's not going to let his young Slayer be killed. Fortunately for him and the world, Buffy quickly comes to terms with her calling and her fate, and returns to do battle. And even though she dies for a few seconds, she also destroys the Master. It's not the last time she will run away, but because she is the Slayer, she always comes back.

THE WATCHER GUIDE

The Slayer is supposed to have this total commitment to her calling. Traditionally, she is also supposed to be totally disciplined and obedient to her Watcher and the Watcher's Council. Kendra is the embodiment of this traditional type of Slayer. Raised by her Watcher, she lives apart from her family, and has no friends, no hobbies, and no life apart from being the Slayer. She has learned to suppress her emotions, seeing them as a distraction and a weakness. She

The Vampire Slayer is the champion of the human world against the forces of evil, the one girl in all the world born with the strength and skill to hunt the vampire. In many ways, she's a lot like a classic superhero: young, pretty, gifted with hero-sized powers, and a hero's mission to save lives daily and save the world at least once a year. Unlike many superheroes, though, the Slayer is not one of a kind, but part of a long and ancient tradition. Each individual Slayer is just a link in a chain of lives that has spanned thousands of years.

The Slayer's notoriously short life span is the most poignant aspect of Slayer mythology. While vampires can live for centuries, Slayers don't usually live to be 20, as Giles reveals when he tells Buffy that the Slayer rite of passage occurs *if* the Slayer reaches her 18th birthday ("Helpless"). Every Slayer has to live with the certainty that someday in the not-too-distant future, some demon will kill her. Buffy confronts her mortality for the first time in "Prophecy Girl", when she

studies hard, and she does whatever her Watcher tells her; indeed, her solution to every new situation is to go to the Watcher for new instructions. She is, in fact, the Council's ideal of what a Slayer should be. She is also quite dead, having survived as the Slayer for less than a year. So much for the Council's ideals.

In contrast to Kendra, Buffy makes clear to Giles on their very first day that she is not the obedient type. Though she has learned to depend on Giles' knowledge, wisdom and friendship, she is the Slayer, and she makes her own decisions about slaying. Giles learns to respect Buffy's independence, but the Council never accepts it. At first, Buffy submits to the Council's authority. She endures their frightening coming-of-age rite, which strips her of her power and almost gets her mother killed; she accepts – well, tolerates – the replacement of Giles with a new (and completely incompetent) Watcher (Wesley); she even submits to the Council's "review" when she needs their help to fight Glory. However, Buffy quickly realizes that the Council need her more than she needs them.

In truth, although the Watchers provide a vital role for Buffy when she is first called as the Slayer, problems eventually crop up in the relationship. The Council believes that its methods are the best, and they dislike any indication that they are wrong. Every time she asks for help, the Council either refuses to cooperate, or tries to bargain or blackmail her into acknowledging their authority. It's not the best way to get along with a Slayer who has never liked being told what to do. When Buffy realizes in "Checkpoint" that she, not the Council, holds the real power, she rejects their authority entirely and orders them to stay out of her way.

Who Watches The Watchers ?

We take a look at some of the Watchers we've encountered so far.

The Watchers' Council, though not nearly as old as the line of Slayers, existed for many centuries (one tradition is at least 1200 years old). The Council tracked all Potential Slayers, trained and assigned a Watcher to each Slayer and Potential, and regulated the entire tradition of the Slayer. The Council also kept a vast library of scholarship on Slayer tradition and all kinds of evil beings. Virtually all the Council were killed and the library destroyed in an explosion ordered by the First Evil during its campaign to wipe out the Slayer tradition.

RUPERT GILES is Buffy's second Watcher (the first, Merrick, was killed before she came to Sunnydale – also check out his brief flashback appearance in "Becoming, Part One"). Though he seems no more than a scholar, he is in fact a seasoned and ruthless demon fighter as well. The Council fires him because his close relationship with his Slayer leads him to rebel against the Council's traditions to protect her. Buffy forces them to reinstate him a couple of years later. Giles serves actively as Buffy's Watcher until he moves back to England, and remains her mentor and ally at all times.

WESLEY WYNDHAM-PRYCE Giles' replacement, is the Council's ideal Watcher: scholarly, slavishly obedient to all Council rules and traditions, and completely inexperienced in the real world. The conflicts with the Mayor and Faith give him his baptism of blood. After being fired by the Council, he becomes a rogue demon hunter, then goes to work for Angel Investigations.

GWENDOLYN POST Faith's new Watcher, was actually an imposter, a rogue Watcher who came to Sunnydale to trick the Slayers into leading her to a mystic Glove. She was fried by the Glove's energy when Buffy cut it from her hand. ("Revelations")

QUENTIN TRAVERS the head of the Watchers' Council, demonstrates with his every word and action his determination to make sure that the Council controls the Slayer and her Watcher, and that everyone follows the Council's orders, rules and traditions. He genuinely believes that rules, traditions and obedience are the best way to fight evil. Ultimately, the First sets out to destroy the Watchers' Council – and succeeds. ✤

POWER GIRL

So you wanna be the Slayer? Well, okay... but you'd need these abilities...

Superhero physical powers allow the Slayer to fight vampires and demons on equal terms. We're so used to seeing Buffy throw large monsters overhead, catch arrows in mid-air and leap tall buildings (or at least tall monsters), that we forget how remarkable these powers are, until she goes against real world human warriors. When she joins the commandos of the Initiative in a combat drill, she cleans them up in less than a minute.

The Slayer can thank her supernatural healing abilities for letting her take many blows before she shows so much as a bruise – and a good thing, too: how would Buffy explain a never-ending succession of black eyes and fat lips? Wounds that would cripple or kill an ordinary human will only slow her down a bit. A stake wound in the belly just needs a little combat first aid; a bullet to the chest is more serious, but even without Willow's healing spell, it probably would have only kept her in the hospital for a while.

The blood of the Slayer has special powers, both magical and medical. The Master needs a drink of Buffy's blood to release him into the world; and when Faith poisons Angel in "Graduation Day", only the blood of a Slayer can save his life. Spike claims that the blood of a Slayer is a potent vamp aphrodisiac, but since any sort of violence seems to be a vamp aphrodisiac, especially to Spike, we can't take this claim as fact. ✦

FIGHTING TALK

The Slayer has supernatural strength, speed and agility to fight and kill; death is indeed her gift and her art, as Spike and the First Slayer have told her. And this
gift and this power are a huge responsibility. Not every Slayer handles it well. Faith is (or was) the anti-Buffy, the Slayer who recognizes no rules, and revels only in her power.

The first time Buffy and Faith fight a gang of vamps together, Faith beats one vamp for several minutes just for the pleasure of the violence. When Buffy reminds her that their purpose is to kill vampires, not beat them up, she retorts, "If doing violence to vampires upsets you, I think you're in the wrong line of work."

When Faith accidentally kills a man, mistaking him for a vampire in the heat of battle, Buffy learns just how irresponsible Faith can be. She not only conceals the murder, she won't even admit that she has done anything wrong.

"You're still not seeing the big picture, B. Something made us different. We're warriors. We were built to kill," she insists.

"To kill demons," Buffy argues, "But that does not mean we get to pass judgement on people, like we're better than everyone else."

"We are better! That's right. Better! People need us to survive. In the balance, nobody's going to cry over some random bystander who got caught in the crossfire."

Faith has her own rationalization for why Buffy wants her to own up to the murder; she believes that Buffy, like her, feels the seduction of power without responsibility.

"You need me to tow the line because you're afraid you'll go over it, aren't you, B? You can't handle watching me living my own way, having a blast, because it tempts you. You know it could be you."

And she wants Buffy to come over to her side. "The life of a Slayer's very simple, B. Want, take, have," she explains to Buffy as she plunders a weapons store.

It's true that Buffy feels the temptation of violence and power; she knows the thrill of a good kill. But unlike Faith, Buffy is always on her guard against this temptation, and even more on guard against losing her humanity, her heart, in the harshness and violence of her life.

"I feel like being the Slayer is starting to turn me to stone," she tells Giles. "To slay, to kill, it means being hard on the inside. Maybe being the perfect Slayer means being too hard to love at all."

Giles sends her on a spirit quest to find out if being the Slayer requires her to give up love. Instead, her vision of the First Slayer tells her that she is, "full of love. You love with all your soul. It's brighter than the fire, blinding. That's why you pull away from it... Love is pain and the Slayer forges strength from pain." ("Intervention")

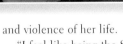

BUFFY SUMMERS

The Slayer is supposed to work in secret, her identity known only to her Watcher and to the Council. Buffy's secret identity was history the moment Xander overheard her Slaying chat with Giles on her first day at Sunnydale High. And despite Slayer tradition and the Council's open disapproval, Buffy's friends are a key factor in her relative longevity. Most Slayers fight alone and die alone. Buffy fights beside her friends, and the Scoobies' assistance has helped her beat the monsters and save the world, too many times to count. They have even saved her life a few times. In a world with only one Slayer to fight a whole universe of badness, the Slayer can use all the help she can get.

And that's without even mentioning the sanity factor; Buffy's friends are her emotional refuge whenever the life of the Slayer becomes too violent, too scary, too painful. This, too, is critical to Buffy's survival, as Spike explains in "Fool for Love". When Buffy asks him how he was able to kill two Slayers, he explains that any Slayer's fatal weakness is not a failure of strength or skill; it's her secret fascination with Death.

"Every day you wake up to the same bloody question that haunts you: 'Is today the day I'm gonna die?' Death is on your heels, baby, and sooner or later it's gonna catch you. Part of you wants it, not only to stop the fear and uncertainty, but because you're just a little bit in love with it. Death is your art. You make it with your hands day after day… Part of you is desperate to know – what's it like, where does it lead you? Every Slayer has a death wish. Even you."

And Spike recognizes that Buffy has something to offset that secret death wish: "The only reason you've lasted as long as you have, is you've got ties to the world – your mum, brat kid sister, the Scoobies. They all tie you here."

Unlike every other Slayer we know, Buffy has a life in the world. And she has fought to maintain that life – school, work, friendships, family. When all is said and done, her life is what she's fighting for – not the destruction of evil, but the preservation of the things she loves. It's what she's willing to die for, as she does when she throws herself into the void to save Dawn and stop Glory. And it's what she's willing to live for, when her friends pull her out of Heaven back to the cold, cruel world.

Above all, the Slayer is invincible – not as an individual, but as an ancient force for good, which is renewed with every death. Kill a Slayer and another rises – or even, in Buffy's case, the same Slayer rises again. Beat the Slayer down with terror and pain, and she'll get back up again, and keep fighting until she wins.

Buffy reveals the Slayer's true power when she and her friends are looking for a way to stop the First Evil. The First seems invincible – indeed, it is literally the root of all evil. Its champion, the Turok-Han, has beaten Buffy so badly that her friends aren't sure she'll recover her nerve.

"The First predates everything we've ever known or can know," says Giles. "It's everywhere, it's pure. I don't know if we can fight it."

"You're right," says Buffy, "we don't know how to fight it. We don't know when it'll come. We can't run, can't hide, can't pretend it's not the end, 'cause it is… I'm beyond tired. I'm beyond scared. I'm standing on the mouth of Hell and it is going to swallow me whole," she says, and the others stare at her, fearing that their Slayer has been

beaten at last. Then Buffy finishes her sentence: "And it'll choke on me." And she declares war on the First, promising the Potential Slayers, and the Scoobies that, "From now on we won't just face our worst fears, we will seek them out. We will find them and cut out their hearts one by one, until the First shows itself for what it really is. Then I'll kill it myself. There is only one thing on this earth more powerful than evil. And that's us." ✢

A COMPANY OF SLAYERS

Buffy's not the only Vampire Slayer we've met in the show's history — here are some of the others we've become acquainted with...

THE FIRST SLAYER. Buffy meets this primeval woman in a shared dream after a spell affronts the source of the Slayer's power; and later in a vision quest ("Restless", "Intervention"). Of herself, the First Slayer says, "I have no speech, no name. I live in the action of death. The blood cry, the penetrating wound. I am destruction, absolute, alone."

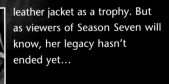

KENDRA. Activated when Buffy dies for a few seconds in "Prophecy Girl", Kendra is highly trained, focused and disciplined, knowing no life but that of the Slayer. Drusilla kills her in "Becoming, Part 1".

FAITH. Kendra's successor, she becomes the anti-Slayer, reveling in power and lawlessness, turning rogue and committing a whole series of crimes, until she is finally redeemed by Angel in the *Angel* episode, "Sanctuary".

NIKKI, the New York City Slayer. In the graphic novel *Tales of the Slayers*, Nikki lives in Harlem and battles a monstrous vampire bat and the crime lord who brought in the bat and killed her man, a New York police officer. In "Fool for Love" Spike tells Buffy about fighting Nikki on a subway in 1977 (she's not actually named in the episode). After a long battle, he breaks her neck then takes her black leather jacket as a trophy. But as viewers of Season Seven will know, her legacy hasn't ended yet...

THE CHINESE SLAYER also appears in a flashback in "Fool for Love." She fights like a Hong Kong martial arts master, but she still dies at Spike's fangs in a temple during the Boxer Rebellion, 1900. Spike and Dru taste her blood and make love next to her body.

TALES OF THE SLAYERS tells the stories of eight Slayers from throughout history. Along with Nikki and the First Slayer, we meet Slayers from medieval Europe, Revolutionary Paris, 19th Century England, and Nazi Germany. Then there's the Native American Slayer whose killing ground is the future site of Sunnydale; and a Slayer from the future named Melaka Fray, who finds a library of Slayer history. (Melaka is also the focus of Joss Whedon's limited series *Fray*, published by Dark Horse Comics.)

Some characters to look out for (maybe) in the future include the Potential Slayers who appear in Season Seven. One of the season's main storylines involves the fact that Potential Slayers are being hunted down and slaughtered by minions of the First – for example, we see Potentials being murdered in Frankfurt, Germany and Istanbul. Some of the surviving Potentials, including Molly, Annabelle, Kennedy, Rona, Eve and Amanda, eventually turn up in Sunnydale. These Potentials are trained by Giles and Buffy, although Annabelle and Eve are eventually killed by the First and the Turok-Han. Buffy informs the Potentials that, while they do not possess the full power of the Slayer, they do contain certain powerful abilities – a small fraction of the power, along with a Slayer's instinct. ✦

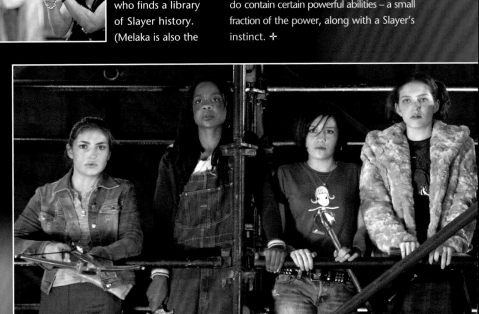

J oss Whedon is feeling sentimental. His television baby, *Buffy the Vampire Slayer*, has grown up and moved out of the house. And now he, the proud daddy/creator/executive producer is sitting back and reminiscing. It really is the day some people hoped would never come, the day when Joss would look back on *Buffy* rather than forward. But the show signed off on May 20, 2003, with a series finale entitled "Chosen," which – for now, anyway – brought to an end the adventures of the Slayer, Buffy Summers, and such friends, allies, nuisances and enemies as Willow, Xander, Giles, Dawn, Spike, Anya, Faith, Kennedy, Amanda, Indigo, Principal Wood, Caleb, Andrew and The First.

"*Buffy* has been very close to what

I envisioned, except it grew up a lot more," Joss says of his show, which ran for seven years, five on the WB and two on UPN. "When I started the show, I didn't know its full potential because I just sort of had the basic notion, and [I knew] that it'd be funny and evolving and scary and really hit on things that people can relate to. I didn't know how good my actors would be. I didn't know how long we'd go, and how much they'd grow and change and how far we could go with the medium, how much the network would let us do – or networks, I guess I

FAREWELL TO THE HELLM

OUTH

JOHN STOKES

should say. Did I know that I was going to make a musical ["Once More, With Feeling"], or did I know that Buffy was going to sleep with Angel and he would go bad? No. It just kept growing. So, the basic idea – that I think that we're very true to, especially in the last episode, with the empowerment of the girls and the toughness of this life – was always there, but it grew beyond my best imagination."

The finale gave fans the sight of Buffy at long last defeating The First, but not without a huge fight, a lot of blood and a few deaths that hit close to home. Anya perished, as did Spike. Angel returned to lend a hand against the greatest ever threat to Sunnydale and its most fearsome Slayer. But bringing down the Big Bad really boiled down to teamwork and Buffy sharing her power with the Potentials. That last point, Joss acknowledges was paramount in his mind while crafting the finale.

"We've dealt with all of these Potential Slayers, and Buffy's attempt to lead and Willow dealing with her fear of everyone sort of dealing with their insecurity of their place," Joss says. "The season has really been about power or, at least, that's what we started out talking about. And the mission statement of the show was, 'This girl has power. No one knows. No one sees it. They don't respect her. They don't get it, but she has enormous power.' And this [last] episode was about that as well. The episode dealt very specifically with how she decided to use that power and what she thinks of it and what it's really for and that, to me, was very important."

Building to the finale meant turning to some familiar faces, though the word familiar is a relative thing. Joss resurrect-

ed The First, an enemy of yore, for the final season, and he turned to Nathan Fillion, late of *Firefly*, to play Caleb. And since Gina Torres from *Firefly* was available, Joss actually brought her over for a several-episode stint as Jasmine on *Angel* as that show neared the end of its fourth season. "I used The First as a device solely to tell the story about Buffy and Angel that I wanted to tell, but that's what happened on the show," Joss explains. "You're looking for something and you suddenly realize that it's sitting in your lap, that everything you need is right there. The First seemed like the perfect villain for the series finale because it's all of them, it's all of what they've been through personified. So, it just seemed serendipitous. Sometimes it just happens.

"[As for Nathan Fillion and Gina Torres], it was very simply a case of we had created the characters, and in both cases, [the casting] didn't come from me. I was worried that it would seem too incestuous, but they were like, 'Look, we have the people, we know them, we know their names, and we have their

phone numbers.' These guys, both Nathan and Gina are bigger than life, and we knew that they would bring up the storytelling and give it an epic quality and give us performances that we could count on, that are very different than the ones that they gave in *Firefly*. And I thought, 'Who cares if it's incestuous? Most people didn't watch *Firefly* anyway.' Hell, I did, but if you have an actor that you know can get the job done and you haven't seen them do it 400 times [you go with them]. Nathan had never played a villain and when Gina was playing Zoe [on *Firefly*], she didn't get to be all pretty and smile all of the time. So, it was stuff that we knew that they had in them, that they hadn't shown us on screen. It was a good opportunity for them and I'm not stupid. If I've got the guys, and I know that they can do it, then, that's the guy. Besides, they're wonderful people that make the set an even

better place to be around."

Finales serve multiple purposes: they're designed to close out a series on a high note, to bring an end to the storylines of the main and supporting characters, to put a bow on relationships and inside jokes, and to, depending on the situation, permanently wrap things up or put the characters on the road to their next adventure. But then there's the question of for whom a finale is intended. Is it the viewer? The cast and crew? Its creators? "The finale is for the viewer," Joss replies. "I honor this cast, and this crew who America hasn't seen, enormously, but at the end of the day, the finale has to be for the viewers. Will there be little shout-outs to things? Yeah, but usually, they're old episodes or things that long-time viewers will understand. It's never about anyone but the viewers. Now, the writer, obviously, it comes from him or them in some cases, and it has to reflect what they believe that they want, but the fact of the matter is, I write as a fan. I write as someone who wants to know what's going to happen next on *Buffy*, not just as, 'Oh, what do I feel like talking about today?'"

Buffy the Vampire Slayer ended when it did for several reasons. Sarah Michelle Gellar wanted to move on, the ratings had dropped a bit, though not precipitously, and everyone involved with the show wanted to call it a day before the quality started to suffer. Still, fans are asking if Joss would have returned had Sarah agreed to do so. "No, no," Joss insists. "I knew that this was my last season before Sarah made it official. Sarah and I had talked about it a lot and I was pretty certain that this was her last season too, but I had already told the people close to me, even if Sarah suddenly got

offered a trunkload of money and decided to come back, or whatever it was that would've changed her mind, that I was done. That's not for lack of love or lack of stories or anything, [but rather] just pure physical exhaustion, just the grind of turning out stories one by one. I was afraid that I was going to start to flip and compromise and not care as much, and once you start doing that, it shows. It always shows. So, no, I knew that this was my last year."

Joss laughs when asked if he foresees himself plagued by phantom pains, the sort of psychological ailment exhibited by a soldier who's lost his leg. In other

words, it might be tough for him to come up with a great *Buffy* tale and have no outlet in which to tell it. "Phantom story-making," he says. "I think that, inevitably, things will occur to me. 'Oh, you could do this. Oh, they could go here.' But you know, I'm constantly in the process of figuring out stories and thinking up movies and stuff and a lot of them aren't *Buffy*-related, and because I have *Angel*, that's going to be 22 stories that I'm going to have make up in the same basic genre. I think that I'll be able to put [*Buffy*] to rest for a while anyway… But we did not destroy the entire fabric of the *Buffy* universe at the end of the last episode and some people even lived. So, there's definitely an open door for more series or a movie, you name it."

As for future *Buffy*-related projects, no news is bad news, unfortunately. Other than Spike leaping over to take a bite out of *Angel* on a regular basis starting next season, that show's fifth, there's nothing to report on the animated *Buffy* and *Buffy* spin-off fronts. "Everything is pretty much in limbo right now," he says. "The animated series; there's no one out there who's got enough interest and enough money to make it look as good as it would have to. I don't want to make a cheesy version. There could be a spin-off sometime, but there's no talk of one besides *Angel* right now. So, nothing for the fall."

Angel, however, will be back in the Fall. The WB renewed the series, which was thought to be "on the bubble" and in danger of being canceled. Even better, the WB gave *Angel* the best possible timeslot, positioning it after their red-hot juggernaut series, *Smallville*. Joss confirms that when *Angel* returns to the airwaves for the 2003-2004 season, it will

{ "I KNEW THAT THIS WAS MY LAST [*BUFFY*] SEASON BEFORE SARAH MADE IT OFFICIAL. I HAD ALREADY TOLD THE PEOPLE CLOSE TO ME, EVEN IF SARAH SUDDENLY GOT OFFERED A TRUNKLOAD OF MONEY AND DECIDED TO COME BACK, THAT I WAS DONE." }

be a lighter and leaner series. "We're entering a whole new arena, a whole new way of telling these stories next season and so, there's a huge amount of license," says Joss, who will write and direct several episodes. "[Season Four was] a strange season because the whole thing took place over approximately two weeks, but the intensity never let up and I really do feel like we kind of pulled it off. But next season, we're going to hope to keep that extraordinary, over-the-top melodrama and action that defines this show in one way that *Buffy* didn't. But we're also going to take it to a new place, a way to generate stories that is not so totally internal. So, it won't be like one giant two-week adventure, [and that's] as a way to let people know who've never seen it, sort of get into it a little bit more."

Joss has said over the years that he wanted to put something out there that was as good as the shows he loved, shows

like *Masterpiece Theater* and *Hill Street Blues*, which are considered classics. A lot of people would put *Buffy* in the classic category, but relatively speaking, not nearly as many people ever tuned into *Buffy* as tuned into *Masterpiece Theater* or *Hill Street Blues*. *Buffy* evolved into a cult favorite with a modest, but incredi-

easier.' At the same time, *Buffy* was not a show that some people were going to switch on to, and that's just the way it is. And that doesn't bother me."

So, will *Buffy* grow in status over the years, perhaps in ways that even *Masterpiece Theater* and *Hill Street Blues* didn't? "Well, it has an opportunity that they didn't have, which is that it's out on DVD," Joss replies. "And it's out now, before it looks wicked dated, although some of the outfits from Season One are pretty funny. The thing that we were trying to do was tell epic, timeless stories on a small, emotional scale. And that sort of thing, if it's done right, certainly can live on. Will it? I don't know. I do know that the character and the concept have affected the way that people think about heroines and heroes and who can front a show and what boys will watch and a lot of different things, and that's a more important legacy to me than, 'They're still watching the episodes.'"

> "WE DID NOT DESTROY THE ENTIRE FABRIC OF THE *BUFFY* UNIVERSE AT THE END OF THE LAST [*BUFFY*] EPISODE AND SOME PEOPLE EVEN LIVED. SO, THERE'S DEFINITELY AN OPEN DOOR FOR MORE SERIES OR A MOVIE, YOU NAME IT."

bly loyal and ardent following. "'*Buffy* was designed to be a pop culture icon, she became that, and so, she exists beyond her ratings," Joss states. "And it's true, we've never found an enormous audience. We've never been on one of the bigger networks. But at the same time, we've retained our sort of cult status in that our viewership has never been as large as the awareness of us. But *Buffy* certainly was not designed to exclude anyone, because I don't believe in exclusion. I didn't want to make a teen show that said, 'Look how stupid grown-ups are.' I wanted to make a teen show that said, 'Look how hard it is to do this, to live through this, and by the way, when you get to be a grown up, it doesn't get

All of which is to say that *Buffy the Vampire Slayer* far surpassed any expectations Joss himself ever had for it or for himself. "I decided to create a TV show practically out of film school," concludes Joss, who plans to spend whatever newfound free time he's got working on movie scripts, prepping *Angel* for Season Five and relaxing with his wife, Kai, and their young son. "No one would hire me to direct, and I wanted to direct. And I thought, 'I'll hire myself. And in the process, I'll sort of learn.'

"I've been able to do that, but I've also learned more about writing in the last seven years than I did in the 30 years before that. *Buffy* has been a huge education." ✛

EPISODE SPOTLIGHT

SEASON 1
EPISODE 12

"Prophecy Girl"

First US airdate
02.06.97

First UK airdate
21.03.98

Synopsis

It's Sunnydale High's school prom, and Buffy is left with no date after turning down poor Xander! But being dateless is the least of her problems – Giles has uncovered a book of infallible prophecies which predicts that Buffy is destined to fight the Master in a battle to the death which she won't survive. Oh, and the Hellmouth is about to be opened, bringing forth the apocalypse. Eek!

Initially, Buffy doesn't take the news well (would you?) and quits, telling Giles she doesn't want to be the Slayer anymore; that she's only 16 and doesn't want to die (go Buffy!). But the murder of some students at the hands of the Master's hungry vamps prompts her to face her destiny...

Guest Star Info

Robia LaMorte, who plays Jenny Calendar, paired up with another dancer, Lori Elle, to form the well-known group Diamand and Pearl (right), who had a string of hits with The Artist Formerly Known as Prince in the 1980s.

Trivia

 "Prophecy" was cut due to length. In the original script it rained stones right after the scene in which Buffy turns down Xander's invitation to the prom.

 The tentacles of the massive demon which comes up out of the Hellmouth at the end are actually just humans in costumes. Optic Nerve put the actors into tentacle costumes which they could manipulate from within to save on the episode's budget!

Memorable Dialogue

The Master: "You were destined to die! It was written!"
Buffy: "What can I say? I flunked the written."

Xander: "That's okay. I don't wanna go. I'm just gonna go home, lie down and listen to country music. The music of pain."

Buffy: "Sure! We saved the world. I say we party!"

Statistics

 No. of times Buffy gets to kick ass: 3

 No. of times Buffy gets her ass kicked: 2

 No. of vamps killed: 2

 No. of screams: 7+

EPISODE CREDITS

Written & Directed by Joss Whedon

Buffy Summers	Sarah Michelle Gellar	Angel	David Boreanaz
Xander Harris	Nicholas Brendon	Joyce Summers	Kristine Sutherland
Willow Rosenberg	Alyson Hannigan	Jenny Calendar	Robia LaMorte
Cordelia Chase	Charisma Carpenter	The Master	Mark Metcalf
Rupert Giles	Anthony S. Head	The Anointed One	Andrew J. Ferchland

Compiled by Kate Anderson

A

CELEBRATING THE LIFE

SLAYER LIFE

BY K. STODDARD HAYES

Buffy Anne Summers grew up in Los Angeles, the only child (remember that?) of Hank and Joyce Summers. While she was a student at Hemery High School, a rather strange man named Merrick told her that she was the Vampire Slayer, the Chosen One, one girl in all the world (remember that, too?) born with the strength and skill to hunt vampires. Merrick, her Watcher, introduced the reluctant former cheerleader to the traditions of the Slayer. After he was murdered by vampires, Buffy cleaned out a nest of vampires from the school gym, with the help of a hot motorcycle jockey named Pike. She also burned down the gym in the process, and was expelled from the school.

WELCOME TO THE HELLMOUTH

Buffy's parents were already splitsville, so Buffy's mother moved to Sunnydale to give her daughter a fresh start in a new school.

On Buffy's first day of school, Joyce's only motherly advice is, "Try not to get kicked out!" The last thing Buffy wants is to continue her career as a Slayer, and when her new Watcher, Rupert Giles, tries to introduce himself, Buffy runs out of the room as fast as she can.

The bad side of moving to Sunnydale: it's on the Hellmouth, a serious magnet for all things bad and bloodthirsty. So for Buffy, escaping her destiny as the Slayer was never on the cards. In no time at all, she is up to her stakes in cheerleading witches, boy-eating substitute teachers, and principal-eating hyenas. Then there are the Big Bads: Principal Snyder, the bane of every kid who's not a star athlete; and the Master, an ancient vampire with big and nasty plans.

The good side is the friends Buffy makes – although Slayers are traditionally not supposed to have friends. Willow, Xander, Giles, and even Cordelia help Buffy have a piece of what she wants most of all: a

R'S
E

normal high school life. They also give her something to fight for as she tries to protect them from the baddies; and they in turn watch her back, and sometimes even save her life. Above all it's thanks to the Scooby Gang that Buffy, alone of all the Slayers before her, survives being the Chosen One.

Then there's Angel – a vampire in love with the Vampire Slayer. What could be more perfect? He and Buffy try to keep their distance, but passion and destiny are just too strong. With help from him and the rest of her friends, Buffy takes on the Master, confronting, along the way, a prophecy that he will kill her. He may indeed kill her, but at least she knows she can take him with her. In fact, she sends him to hell alone, and survives to plan a trip to the mall with her friends.

WHEN HE WAS BAD!

With the Master's bones crunched to dust, everything in Sunnydale should be

Buffy Face/Offs

The most memorable confrontations between Buffy and her friends, family, enemies...

Buffy vs. Joyce, "Becoming, Part Two"
Never ask a Slayer to choose between her mom and her calling when the world is at stake.

Buffy vs. Angelus, "Becoming, Part Two"
To hurt this girl, you have to love her, and make her love you.

Buffy vs. Faith, "Consequences"
Is Buffy scared of Faith because she's bad, or because she reminds Buffy of her own secret wish to be bad?

Buffy vs. Dr. Walsh, "The I in Team"
Never assume a Slayer is dead until you've actually seen the body!

UberBuffy vs. Adam, "Primeval"
What's a little uranium against the ancient power of the Slayers?

Buffy vs. Bad Willow, "Two to Go"
Buffy's still too close to the dark to be able to lead Willow out of it.

Buffy vs. Holden, "Conversations with Dead People"
A stake is a sure-fire way to guarantee doctor-patient confidentiality.

Buffy vs. Caleb, "Dirty Girls"
What else you got? Big trouble, until Buffy finds a big Scythe!

Buffy vs. everyone, "Empty Places"
Not even the Slayer herself can order obedience without trust.

hunky-dory, right? Wrong! Angel's old vampire pals, Spike and Drusilla, arrive with big plans to kill the Slayer (that's after they've dealt with the 'Annoying' One). Buffy and her friends have Spike and Dru pretty much in hand until the gruesome twosome get the most surprising and deadly ally of all: Angelus. A single night of love with Buffy and a single moment of perfect happiness strips Angel of his soul, and turns him into the cruelest of enemies who knows every soft spot in Buffy's heart. He spends weeks tormenting her and her friends, until she resolves to kill him, even though it means killing all hope that her beloved Angel might return. When Willow finds the spell to re-ensoul him, Buffy has to make the hardest choice of all. She stabs Angel just as his soul returns, because only his blood can close the portal into Hell that Angelus opened. Then she flees Sunnydale, her family and her destiny.

Bad Girls

After the war over Angel's soul, senior year should be a snap. Buffy finds the courage to return home, and discovers that Angel has returned from a hell dimension. Her only Big Bad opponent is the Mayor, who simply wants to turn himself into a giant demon serpent and eat the whole graduating class. And he should be easy to handle, with the help of the new Slayer in town, Faith. Except for the fact that Faith's Slaying values are more than a few degrees off centre. She loves the power and the

violence, and she's seriously into teaching Buffy to enjoy the bad side of Slaying, as well. But then she takes things too far by killing a man and signing on with the Mayor.

After that, it's war between the Slayers, until Buffy puts Faith in a coma for trying to kill Angel. The Scoobies train the entire graduating class to fight the Mayor's minions, and a little high explosive – or rather, a LOT of high explosive – takes care of the Mayor, and adds another demolished high school to Buffy's permanent record. But most important of all, Buffy and her friends have survived high school...

Where the Wild Things Are

While Willow takes to college like a geek to a computer, Buffy can't seem to handle being a freshman. Roommate problems, dating problems and a psych professor from Hell all figure into the mix. She does meet a cute guy, Riley, who seems refreshingly normal and wholesome – until Buffy learns that he's part of the Initiative, a secret government operation that's moved into Sunnydale to capture 'subhumans' and do nasty experiments on them, and Buffy's psych professor, Maggie Walsh, is the chief experimenter.

When she's not putting Buffy down, Maggie is secretly building a super-soldier, Adam, out of a nuclear power cell and spare demon parts. Among the captured demons are Spike and Willow's former werewolf boyfriend, Oz. Buffy and the Scoobies rescue both, and Spike actually starts helping out the good guys – well, sort of. Finally, Buffy has to go head to head with Adam, who's been turning soldiers and scientists into zombies for his army. To fight him, she and her friends cast a spell which gives her the power of all the Slayers – a spell which helps her destroy Adam, but also wakens the spirit of the First Slayer to walk in Buffy's dreams.

Family

There's nothing like waking up one morning to find you've got a bratty teenage kid sister ('only child', remember?). Although Dawn is actually a mystic energy 'key', some monks turned her human and made her Buffy's sister so that the Slayer could protect her, even going so far as to change history so that everyone would think she's been there all along.

Dawn's arrival brings the focus back to Buffy's family relationships. With Joyce diagnosed with a brain tumour, Buffy now has more to worry about than just her mother's health; she also has a kid sister to look after. Joyce's death forces Buffy to become an adult a lot sooner than she wanted to. Trying to fill her mother's shoes is, in some ways, even more difficult for Buffy than fighting off the conceited god, Glory, who will do anything to get her 'key' back. As if that's not enough, Buffy's worried that being the Slayer has made her too hard inside to love at all. She goes on a spirit quest to meet the First Slayer, who tells her she's full of love and that her gift is Death.

But love doesn't seem to be enough when Glory captures Dawn. Buffy's so guilt-stricken for failing to protect her sister – the one thing her mother asked of her before she died – that she becomes catatonic, and only Willow can bring her out of her own head. When Glory's followers complete the ritual using Dawn's blood to open the portal between dimensions, Buffy closes it in the only way she can – by sacrificing her own life to save her sister and the world.

Entropy

So Buffy's dead, and without the Slayer around, everything in Sunnydale goes to hell faster than you can say, "Hellmouth". Except Buffy is not in any kind of hell. She's actually in heaven, at peace and at rest for the first time. "Death is your gift" turns out to be the exact truth – until Willow works some dark magic to bring her back.

Although the Scoobies and Dawn are overjoyed to see her, Buffy is miserable being back in the world. She can hardly cope with everyday life. She doesn't even notice that Dawn and Willow, her sister and her best friend, are both in serious emotional trouble; and she starts a hot affair with Spike because she needs to feel something, anything besides complete numbness. Although she finds her way back to life, her despair gets in the way when Willow needs a friend to call her back from utter evil. Buffy is too close to darkness to get Willow to listen. All she can do is fight to keep Dawn alive, while Xander gets to take his turn at saving the world.

End of Days

Dawn's in high school, Buffy gets a new job as school counsellor, and there's a hot new principal, Robin Wood, who knows all about vampires because his mother was a Slayer. Both Willow and Spike are back, Spike with a shiny new soul to make him worthy of Buffy's love, and Willow with a lot of training in how to use her witchy powers without getting all dark and scary. Unfortunately, Evil is also back – The First Evil, the source of all badness in the world, and he or she (depending on whose face it's using today) is determined to destroy the Slayer tradition and overrun the world with evil.

When The First destroys the Watchers Council (no great loss), Buffy and her friends round up all the Potential Slayers they can find in the hope of protecting them. The First has two allies – Spike, who's under a hypnotic trigger, and Caleb, a very nasty preacher. While Spike is freed from his trigger, with a little help from Robin, Caleb

"CLARK KENT HAS A JOB. I JUST WANNA GO ON A DATE."
"NEVER KILL A BOY ON THE FIRST DATE"

The Weirdness File

Charting the most bizarre, far-fetched and funny experiences in Buffy's supernatural life...

A living ventriloquists' dummy chats her up, "The Puppet Show"

A spell turns Buffy into a helpless 18th Century lady, "Halloween"

A spell makes her (and everyone else) fall madly in love with Xander, "Bewitched, Bothered and Bewildered"

Faith switches bodies with her, "This Year's Girl"/"Who Are You?"

Buffy gets the ability to read minds, including – ewww! – Giles and her mother recalling their "Band Candy" liaison, "Earshot"

Her mother dates a robot who's not good stepdad material, "Ted"

Buffy and Spike get engaged (not really that weird considering their recent actions), "Something Blue"

Spike makes a robot double of Buffy, "Intervention"

The Nerd Trio accidentally makes Buffy invisible, "Gone"

A demon makes her and all the Scoobies break out into song and dance, "Once More, With Feeling"

nearly crushes the Slayer and her friends by killing several Potentials and maiming Xander. When Buffy tries to lead another attack on him, presuming on her authority as the Slayer, her friends blow her off her pedestal and out the door. Sure, they're lost without her, but she's lost too, until she earns back their trust by letting go of her fears and winning the Scythe, a mystic weapon only a Slayer can wield.

After that, no evil in the world can stop her and her friends. Willow's power draws on the Scythe to turn all Potentials into Slayers – an unstoppable army that, with a little help from Spike and a magic amulet, devastates the First's army of Ubervamps, and closes the Hellmouth once and for all. And Buffy is no longer the "one girl in all the world". She's just one in a world full of Slayers, and no longer has to carry the burden alone. She can finally have what she's always wanted – a normal life... whatever *that* means. ✛

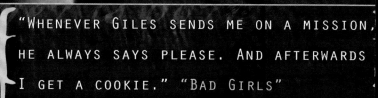

BUFFY Episode Checklist

Caption????!!!!!!

YOUR HANDY ONE-STOP GUIDE TO THE ENTIRE SERIES OF *Buffy the Vampire Slayer*

SEASON ONE

EPISODE 1: "WELCOME TO THE HELLMOUTH"
Buffy Summers arrives in Sunnydale and meets up with Willow, Xander and Giles.
EPISODE 2: "THE HARVEST"
Buffy and her new friends face The Master.
EPISODE 3: "THE WITCH"
Someone's up to no good as Buffy tries out for the school cheerleader trials.
EPISODE 4: "TEACHER'S PET"
Xander gets a crush on his new schoolteacher – but all she wants to do is crush him…
EPISODE 5: "NEVER KILL A BOY ON THE FIRST DATE"
Buffy learns that dating and slaying don't really mix.
EPISODE 6: "THE PACK"
Xander starts mixing with the wrong crowd – the possessed-by-evil-hyena-demons crowd…
EPISODE 7: "ANGEL"
As Buffy's feelings for Angel deepen, she discovers the shocking truth about him.
EPISODE 8: "I ROBOT… YOU, JANE"
Willow starts emailing an admirer – unaware that he is a cyber-demon!
EPISODE 9: "THE PUPPET SHOW"
Buffy teams up with a possessed puppet to track a killer.
EPISODE 10: "NIGHTMARES"
The Scoobies' worst nightmares start coming true.
EPISODE 11: "OUT OF MIND, OUT OF SIGHT"
An invisible girl seeks revenge on her classmates.
EPISODE 12: "PROPHECY GIRL"
Buffy is shaken when she hears a prophecy that The Master will kill her – will it come true?

SEASON TWO

EPISODE 1: "WHEN SHE WAS BAD"
The Gang must prevent the Anointed One from resurrecting The Master.
EPISODE 2: "SOME ASSEMBLY REQUIRED"
Two schoolkids want to use Cordy's head to complete their Frankenstein's monster.
EPISODE 3: "SCHOOL HARD"
Spike and Drusilla arrive in Sunnydale and cause trouble at the Parent-Teacher Night.
EPISODE 4: "INCA MUMMY GIRL"
Xander falls for a foreign exchange student who turns out to be a mummified princess!
EPISODE 5: "REPTILE BOY"
Buffy discovers she's to be sacrificed to a snake demon.
EPISODE 6 "HALLOWEEN"
The Scoobies face danger on Halloween after purchasing their costumes from sorcerer Ethan Rayne…
EPISODE 7: "LIE TO ME"
An old school pal of Buffy's has an unhealthy interest in vampires.
EPISODE 8: "THE DARK AGE"
A demon from Giles' past catches up with him.
EPISODE 9: "WHAT'S MY LINE, PART ONE"
Buffy is on the hitlist of a group of supernatural assassins known as The Order of Taraka. Plus, meet Kendra the Vampire Slayer!
EPISODE 10: "WHAT'S MY LINE, PART TWO"
Buffy and Kendra face the Order of Taraka, and Spike kidnaps Angel.
EPISODE 11: "TED"
Joyce's new boyfriend isn't quite all that he seems…
EPISODE 12: "BAD EGGS"
Buffy faces the Gorch brothers, and the students of Sunnydale High become slaves of a creature living under the school.
EPISODE 13: "SURPRISE"
On Buffy's birthday, her relationship with Angel reaches a new level…
EPISODE 14: "INNOCENCE"
Angelus is back – and mega-demon The Judge is also causing major trouble.
EPISODE 15: "PHASES"
There's a werewolf on the loose in Sunnydale…
EPISODE 16: "BEWITCHED, BOTHERED AND BEWILDERED"
Thanks to a magical spell, Xander becomes a love magnet!
EPISODE 17: "PASSION"
Angelus murders an ally of the Scoobies.
EPISODE 18: "KILLED BY DEATH"
Buffy gets a very deadly dose of the flu.
EPISODE 19: "I ONLY HAVE EYES FOR YOU"
Angel and Buffy become entangled in the fate of two Sunnydale High ghosts.
EPISODE 20: "GO FISH"
The Sunnydale swim-team start metamorphosing into fishlike monsters.
EPISODE 21: "BECOMING, PART ONE"
Angelus attempts to bring about Hell on Earth, and Drusilla murders Kendra.
EPISODE 22: "BECOMING, PART TWO"
It's up to Buffy to stop Angelus' evil plan.

SEASON THREE

EPISODE 1: "ANNE"
While working in LA, Buffy pays a visit to Hell.
EPISODE 2: "DEAD MAN'S PARTY"
A welcome home party for Buffy doesn't go to plan.
EPISODE 3: "FAITH, HOPE AND TRICK"
There's trouble in store for Buffy as Mr Trick, Faith and Kakistos all arrive in Sunnydale.
EPISODE 4: "BEAUTY AND THE BEASTS"
Oz is suspected of a series of maulings that occurred during a full moon.

EPISODE 5: "HOMECOMING"
SlayerFest '98 spells trouble for Buffy and Cordy, and Willow and Xander get closer.
EPISODE 6: "BAND CANDY"
Ethan Rayne is back – this time to cause trouble with a rejuvenating candy bar.
EPISODE 7: "REVELATIONS"
Faith's new Watcher, Gwendolyn Post, arrives.
EPISODE 8: "LOVERS WALK"
Willow is kidnapped by Spike who wants her to cast a spell to reunite him with Drusilla.
EPISODE 9: "THE WISH"
Cordy unwittingly makes a request of Vengeance Demon Anyanka – resulting in disastrous consequences for the whole of Sunnydale.
EPISODE 10: "AMENDS"
The First Evil causes Angel to contemplate suicide.
EPISODE 11: "GINGERBREAD"
The mothers of Sunnydale band together against witchcraft – but is something more sinister afoot?
EPISODE 12: "HELPLESS"
On her 18th birthday, Buffy undergoes a deadly ritual – but Giles isn't happy about it.
EPISODE 13: "THE ZEPPO"
The Scooby Gang are dealing with the latest apocalypse – but Xander has problems of his own…
EPISODE 14: "BAD GIRLS"
There's a new Watcher in town – Wesley – and Faith accidentally kills an innocent.
EPISODE 15: "CONSEQUENCES"
Faith shows her true colours, and the Mayor invites her to join forces with him.
EPISODE 16: "DOPPELGANGLAND"
Vampire Willow from "The Wish" pays a visit to our Sunnydale.
EPISODE 17: "ENEMIES"
Faith turns Angel into Angelus. Or does she…?
EPISODE 18: "EARSHOT"
Buffy gains telepathic powers and starts to hear things she really doesn't want to.
EPISODE 19: "CHOICES"
Willow is kidnapped by The Mayor.
EPISODE 20: "THE PROM"
Angel breaks up with Buffy, and the Slayer must save the school prom from a pack of Hellhounds.
EPISODE 21: "GRADUATION DAY, PART ONE"
When Faith poisons Angel, Buffy goes after the rogue Slayer's blood – literally.
EPISODE 22: "GRADUATION DAY, PART TWO"
The Mayor unleashes his master-plan at the school graduation ceremony.

SEASON FOUR

EPISODE 1: "THE FRESHMAN"
With Sunnydale High a thing of the past, the Scoobies begin their new lives.
EPISODE 2: "LIVING CONDITIONS"
Buffy's got the room-mate from Hell – complete with Celine Dion posters and possessed toe-nails…
EPISODE 3: "THE HARSH LIGHT OF DAY"
Buffy and Spike fight over the Gem of Amarra – an amulet which enables vampires to survive in daylight.
EPISODE 4: "FEAR, ITSELF"
Chaos breaks out at a frat-house Halloween party.
EPISODE 5: "BEER BAD"
Things start to get a bit primitive when Buffy's beer is spiked by a warlock.
EPISODE 6: "WILD AT HEART"
Oz gets involved with a fellow werewolf.
EPISODE 7: "THE INITIATIVE"
Spike escapes from The Initiative and attacks Willow.
EPISODE 8: "PANGS"
Angel returns to Sunnydale as Buffy is attacked by some Indian spirits.

EPISODE 9: "SOMETHING BLUE"
Willow accidentally casts a spell which causes havoc in the lives of her friends.

EPISODE 10: "HUSH"
The ghoulish Gentlemen terrorise Sunnydale and steal everyone's voices.

EPISODE 11: "DOOMED"
Buffy and Riley attempt to come to terms with each other's moonlighting activities.

EPISODE 12: "A NEW MAN"
Ethan Rayne turns Giles into a demon.

EPISODE 13: "THE I IN TEAM"
Buffy joins the Initiative – but if Professor Walsh has her way it won't be for long...

EPISODE 14: "GOODBYE IOWA"
Professor Walsh's monstrous creation, Adam, is on the loose.

EPISODE 15: "THIS YEAR'S GIRL"
Faith returns to Sunnydale and switches bodies with Buffy thanks to one of the Mayor's little devices.

EPISODE 16: "WHO ARE YOU?"
Faith has fun in Buffy's body, while Buffy (in Faith's body) is captured by the Watchers.

EPISODE 17: "SUPERSTAR"
Everyone's hero, Jonathan, leads the troops into battle against Adam. Er, hang on…

EPISODE 18: "WHERE THE WILD THINGS ARE"
Everyone in Riley's dorm starts acting very strangely, although Buffy and Riley are too busy being otherwise engaged to notice...

EPISODE 19: "NEW MOON RISING"
Oz returns to Sunnydale, and Willow is forced to choose between him and new love interest Tara.

EPISODE 20: "THE YOKO FACTOR"
Angel and Riley clash, and Spike and Adam are up to no good.

EPISODE 21: "PRIMEVAL"
The Scoobies cast a unification spell to defeat Adam.

EPISODE 22: "RESTLESS"
The Scoobies experience some very peculiar dreams.

SEASON FIVE

EPISODE 1: "BUFFY VS. DRACULA"
Buffy meets the most famous vampire of them all.

EPISODE 2: "REAL ME"
Harmony's got her own gang – will she prove to be this season's Big Bad?

EPISODE 3: "THE REPLACEMENT"
Xander is split into two halves – a cool version and a nerdy version.

EPISODE 4: "OUT OF MY MIND"
Spike tries to get the Initiative's chip removed.

EPISODE 5: "NO PLACE LIKE HOME"
Buffy comes face to face with Glorificus.

EPISODE 6: "FAMILY"
Tara's family visits Sunnydale, threatening to expose her 'secret'.

EPISODE 7: "FOOL FOR LOVE"
An insecure Buffy asks Spike for information about the Slayers he's killed.

EPISODE 8: "SHADOW"
Joyce's condition deteriorates, and Glory sends a minion out for information on the Key.

EPISODE 9: "LISTENING TO FEAR"
A deadly alien murders some Sunnydale mental patients – and his next target is Joyce.

EPISODE 10: "INTO THE WOODS"
It's make or break time for Riley and Buffy – and things are looking pretty broken.

EPISODE 11: "TRIANGLE"
Willow and Anya fight when they are left in charge of the Magic Box, and Olaf the Troll pays a visit.

EPISODE 12: "CHECKPOINT"
The Watchers Council return to Sunnydale to cause more problems for Buffy.

EPISODE 13: "BLOOD TIES"
Dawn discovers her true identity.

EPISODE 14: "CRUSH"
Drusilla returns to Sunnydale, and finds that she has some rivals for her affections.

EPISODE 15: "I WAS MADE TO LOVE YOU"
Who is the mysterious young girl who's desperate to find Warren?

EPISODE 16: "THE BODY"
Buffy and her friends must deal with Joyce's death.

EPISODE 17: "FOREVER"
Dawn attempts to bring her mother back from beyond the grave.

EPISODE 18: "INTERVENTION"
Glory kidnaps Spike, thinking he is the Key.

EPISODE 19: "TOUGH LOVE"
It seems that Glory is finally close to discovering who the Key is...

EPISODE 20: "SPIRAL"
The Scoobies go on the run from Glory.

EPISODE 21: "THE WEIGHT OF THE WORLD"
Unable to cope with Dawn's capture, Buffy withdraws into herself.

EPISODE 22: "THE GIFT"
It's the final showdown between Glory and Buffy.

SEASON SIX

EPISODE 1: "BARGAINING, PART ONE"
Willow prepares to cast her biggest spell yet – to resurrect Buffy.

EPISODE 2: "BARGAINING, PART TWO"
Buffy returns, as Demon bikers invade Sunnydale.

EPISODE 3: "AFTERLIFE"
It looks like Buffy brought something evil back with her from the dead.

EPISODE 4: "FLOODED"
Warren, Jonathan and Andrew team up to become Buffy's new arch-nemeses.

EPISODE 5: "LIFE SERIAL"
The Nerds scupper Buffy's attempts to get a job.

EPISODE 6: "ALL THE WAY"
Dawn has a deadly new friend.

EPISODE 7: "ONCE MORE, WITH FEELING"
Everyone in Sunnydale keeps bursting into song-and-dance routines – what's going on??!

EPISODE 8: "TABULA RASA"
The Scoobies lose their memories thanks to one of Willow's spells after she has a fight with Tara.

EPISODE 9: "SMASHED"
A lonely Willow de-rats Amy, and Spike discovers something unusual about Buffy.

EPISODE 10: "WRECKED"
Willow meets a dangerous warlock known as Rack.

EPISODE 11: "GONE"
The Nerds turn Buffy invisible – but is she bothered?

EPISODE 12: "DOUBLEMEAT PALACE"
Buffy gets herself a job at a burger joint – watch out for the Wig Lady!!

EPISODE 13: "DEAD THINGS"
The Nerds accidentally kill Warren's ex-girlfriend and try to pin it on Buffy.

EPISODE 14: "OLDER AND FAR AWAY"
The Gang become trapped in the Summers' house, thanks to Dawn, and Anya's friend Halfrek.

EPISODE 15: "AS YOU WERE"
Riley makes a surprising visit to Sunnydale – accompanied by Mrs Finn!

EPISODE 16: "HELL'S BELLS"
It's the wedding day of Xander and Anya! What could possibly go wrong?!

EPISODE 17: "NORMAL AGAIN"
Buffy hallucinates that Sunnydale is an illusion and that her parents are still together and alive – put her in a s mental hospital.

EPISODE 18: "ENTROPY"
Anya and Spike seek solace in each other's arms.

EPISODE 19: "SEEING RED"
Warren and Buffy face off, but someone else gets in the firing line. Literally.

EPISODE 20: "VILLAINS"
A grief-stricken, enraged Willow hunts Warren down.

EPISODE 21: "TWO TO GO"
Buffy, Xander and Dawn try to protect Andrew and Jonathan from Dark Willow.

EPISODE 22: "GRAVE"
Willow sets about destroying the Earth.

SEASON SEVEN

EPISODE 1: "LESSONS"
Buffy and Dawn have some ghostly encounters at the new Sunnydale High.

EPISODE 2: "BENEATH YOU"
Spike and Buffy have a heart to heart, and Anya's up to her old vengeance tricks.

EPISODE 3: "SAME TIME, SAME PLACE"
Willow returns to Sunnydale, but doesn't quite get the welcome she had hoped for.

EPISODE 4: "HELP"
Buffy meets Cassie, a schoolgirl who claims she has only one week to live.

EPISODE 5: "SELFLESS"
All you ever wanted to know about Anya – but were justifiably too afraid to ask…

EPISODE 6: "HIM"
The Scooby Girls (including Willow!) find themselves strangely attracted to one of Dawn's schoolfriends.

EPISODE 7: "CONVERSATIONS WITH DEAD PEOPLE"
Willow and Dawn encounter The First and Andrew murders Jonathan.

EPISODE 8: "SLEEPER"
Buffy confronts Spike about the fact that he's killing humans again.

EPISODE 9: "NEVER LEAVE ME"
The First has Spike kidnapped and the Watchers Council is destroyed.

EPISODE 10: "BRING ON THE NIGHT"
Giles returns to Sunnydale along with three Potentials, and the group meet their first Ubervamp.

EPISODE 11: "SHOWTIME"
Buffy and the Ubervamp face off in a deadly battle.

EPISODE 12: "POTENTIAL"
Willow detects a new Potential in Sunnydale – could it be Dawn?

EPISODE 13: "THE KILLER IN ME"
Willow and Kennedy's first date doesn't quite go according to plan…

EPISODE 14: "FIRST DATE"
Will Xander's new date turn out to be a demon priestess? Er, probably.

EPISODE 15: "GET IT DONE"
Buffy visits the past to discover secrets about the very first Slayer.

EPISODE 16: "STORYTELLER"
Andrew decides to make a documentary on Buffy, his own life and Xander's craftsmanship.

EPISODE 17: "LIES MY PARENTS TOLD ME"
Spike versus Principal Wood. 'Nuff said.

EPISODE 18: "DIRTY GIRLS"
Faith joins the fight. And so does Caleb…

EPISODE 19: "EMPTY PLACES"
The Scoobies come to a dramatic decision regarding Buffy's leadership.

EPISODE 20: "TOUCHED"
In the quiet before battle, various couples get closer – including Spike and Buffy.

EPISODE 21: "END OF DAYS"
Buffy acquires a mystical scythe and Angel returns to Sunnydale.

EPISODE 22: "CHOSEN"
The final battle with The First – and not everyone is going to walk away from it.

How to Slay a Slayer

Many have tried, but none have succeeded. It's nearly impossible to stop the Slayer. You can slow her down for a while, but like a certain bunny representing a certain battery company, she just keeps going and going and going.

That's not to say that she doesn't have vulnerabilities, however. In order to offer equal time to the villains and beasts in Sunnydale, we've consulted a number of Buffy's greatest foes and compiled a handy guide on how you might go about trying to stop the Chosen One and her Scooby gang, should you ever take up a life of crime and villainy.

But seriously, if you do go toe-to-toe with Buffy, good luck. You're going to need it.

HAIRY SITUATIONS
Though her career as a Slayer has hardened her somewhat, she's still vulnerable to the occasional bad hair day. Messing up her 'do is certain to distract her.

FACE OFF
Before you tangle with the Slayer, check out the look on her face. If she's smiling, you may survive a loss. If she's having a bad day, her scowl means you're dust.

IN THE NECK OF TIME
It might be the most sought-after neck in the world. There isn't a vamp alive (or dead) who wouldn't want to sip from Buffy's jugular.

HARDEN MY HEART
The chick's got heart, and while it can be her greatest weakness (see chart at the right), it's also her greatest strength, and what sets her apart from the Slayers who came—and died—before her.

BODY BLOWS
A powerful kick to the stomach won't stop Buffy, but it has sent her flying many times.

HANDS OF FATE
Since Buffy's stakes are often crudely fashioned or improvised, weapons providing a perfect grip are few and far between. But vamps be warned: if you try to knock the stake out of her hand and you miss, the next sound you'll hear is the broom sweeping up what's left of your carcass.

SHE'S GOT LEGS
Though Buffy's quite a puncher, kicking is her physical violence forté. She's also well-trained in many forms of physical combat, so watch out for leg sweeps.

TIPTOE THROUGH THE EVIL
You can take the girl out of the mall, but you can't take the mall out of the girl. In spite of her rough-and-tumble destiny, Buffy remains a slave to fashion, so as long as steel-toed shoes are out of style, a foot stomp will slow down even the toughest foe. Also beware of spike heels—especially wooden ones.

Heart Attacks
To Get to the Slayer, Get to Her Friends

JOYCE SUMMERS
Despite nearly burning Buffy at the stake, the Slayer loves her mother very much. Getting to Joyce will get you the Slayer's undivided attention, but that's rarely good. Anyone who comes close is quickly dusted.

GILES
The librarian is like a father figure to Buffy, and while easy to knock out, he's significantly beefed-up his fighting skills over the years. His soft spot for jelly donuts might be worth exploiting.

ANGEL
The power of a vampire and the soul of a human—Angel is one bad man in black. It's hard to spot any weaknesses, but it's a sure bet that if you harm Buffy, all bets are off. Don't mess with this dude.

WILLOW
The Slayer's best friend is also a practicing witch, but if you can keep her from casting spells—and away from her laptop—the Slayer will do just about anything to keep her out of harm's way.

XANDER
Twinkies, Ho-Hos, moon pies—anything sweet and bad for you offers a certain path to his weakest side. Be careful—his loyalty to the Slayer is as unflappable as his odd sense of humor.

CORDELIA
Mr. Pfister found her greatest weakness: free cosmetics. But with this reluctant member of the gang, flattery will also get you everywhere. She may also still have a soft spot for Xander.

OZ
Write a song featuring the E-flat, diminished ninth chord. It will either distract Oz enough to make him easily beatable, or result in the mangling of several of his fingers. Avoid him during full moons.

FAITH
Activated as a Slayer when Kendra died, she has an angry, emotional fighting style that hurts her technique. The best way to get close to her is to hang around after a fight. She'll find you.

By Kate Anderson

How to Cut It as a Vampire Slayer

Do you think you have what it takes to be the perfect Vampire Slayer? Could you replace Buffy Summers if someone needed to step into her stilettos in double quick time? Test yourself against these simple rules and find out…

#1 (Slayer Rules)
No. 1 — Be, er, female

You know the score: into each generation, a slayer is born (yadda, yadda, yadda). When the forces of good created the Slayer legacy, they chose the best man for the job… a woman. Sorry guys, but when it comes to vampire slaying, this is one occasion where the female of the species is definitely more deadly than the male. It just goes to prove that women are indeed the stronger sex. But then that's nothing we didn't already know, right girls?!

No. 2 (Slayer Rules)
Don't be squeamish

Let's get one thing straight: fainting at the sight of blood is not an option. When it comes to battling the likes of vampires, demons and monsters, this isn't a job for the faint-hearted. If you're a fan of *ER*, then you'll be well prepared for what's in store, but if the sight of the red stuff makes you gag, maybe you'd be better off staying at home knitting.

No. 3 (Slayer Rules)

KNOW YOUR STAKE FROM YOUR CROSSBOW

TO BE A GOOD SLAYER, you have to be master of all kinds of weaponry. You name it, you have to be able to use it in combat. Of course, there's the obligatory stake (a slayer's favourite *modus operandi*); the quarterstaff and the crossbow. And, in line with modern technology… a rocket launcher! A good slayer should also be able to improvise when fighting the undead; random items such as pool cues and tennis rackets can be easily transformed into substitute stakes.

No. 4 (Slayer Rules)

BE ABLE TO KICK ASS WITH STYLE

A PUNCH HERE… a kick there… then a back flip, rounded off by a high kick. When it comes to kicking ass slayer-style, it takes a certain finesse – so leave name-calling and hair-pulling for the playground. A slayer must be strong and athletic; in other words, super fit! So, dust off that tracksuit and those trainers and go join a gym!

No. 5 (Slayer Rules)

HAVE YOUR VERY OWN SCOOBY GANG

EVEN THE CHOSEN ONE needs a helping hand every now and again, which is why it's vital to have your own support system around you. In other words, behind every good slayer are her friends. Pivotal members of your 'gang' include the clever, loyal, reliable best friend, who just happens to be the brainiest girl in college; and the dedicated self-styled 'loser', who constantly

underestimates his abilities. Throw in an annoying ex-demon and your posse is just about complete.

No. 6 (Slayer Rules)

BE ABLE TO RUN IN HIGH HEELS

OKAY, YOU'RE AT A PARTY, dancing with a really cute guy – and you look a million dollars. But you notice one of the partygoers' awful taste in clothes and you realize he must be a vampire. Suddenly, he takes off and you wish you'd worn sneakers instead of stilettos. They may be the latest thing in fashion, but let's face it, your Jimmy Choo shoes just weren't designed for vampire slaying. So, if you want to look good whilst on the job, you need to learn how to run in heels.

No. 7 (Slayer Rules)

AVOID ANY SORT OF SOCIAL LIFE

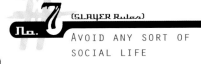

WHICHEVER WAY YOU LOOK at it, fighting the forces of evil is never going to be a 9 to 5 job. There's no contract, no minimum wage and certainly no paid overtime. Always on call, never off duty, maintaining any kind of normal social life is problematic in the extreme. Besides, what with your Slayer duties and the need to go out and earn money, it's not as if you're going to have much free time anyway.

No. 8 (Slayer Rules)

GET USED TO BEING A NIGHT OWL

ARE YOU MISERABLE in the mornings or do you come to life at night? If it's the latter, then you were born to be a slayer. But if you need at least eight hours sleep, then perhaps you should have a rethink. A slayer must exist on minimal sleep, what with those late nighters you have to pull. After all, falling asleep during night-time patrol is likely to get you killed!

No. 9 (Slayer Rules)

HAVE A HIGH ANGST LEVEL

ON A SCALE OF 1 TO 10, being a slayer must surely be at least a 15. It's a very stressful job fighting the undead. You have the weight of the world on your shoulders – not to mention its sheer existence! And as if that alone isn't enough to cause high blood pressure, slayers don't historically have a very long life. Plus, safeguarding your identity as the Slayer can ruin your love life. Superman/Clark Kent had it easy!

No. 10 (Slayer Rules)

ALWAYS BE PREPARED

LAST BUT BY NO MEANS LEAST, always remember to pack those Slayer essentials: a vial of holy water; a stake; and a crucifix. ✚

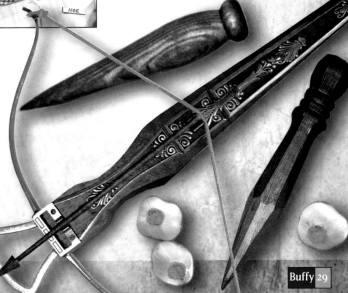

By Kate Anderson

SLAYING. DUSTING.
KICKING VAMPIRE ASS.
IT'S ALL IN A DAY'S WORK FOR
A VAMPIRE SLAYER. AND OVER
THE COURSE OF SEVEN
SEASONS, WE'VE SEEN PLENTY
OF VAMPIRES BITING THE DUST
– PARDON THE PUN! WHILST
IT'S NIGH-ON IMPOSSIBLE TO
PICK A MERE 10 OF THE BEST
VAMPIRE SLAYINGS, AFTER
MUCH DELIBERATION (AND
DISAGREEMENT!) WE'VE
COME UP WITH OUR TOP
TEN COOLEST VAMPIRE
SLAYING MOMENTS...

10 "BUFFY VS DRACULA"

What's Happened: Buffy and the Scooby Gang face off against the world's most infamous vampire when Dracula turns up in Sunnydale. Initially, Buffy seems to fall under the dark prince's spell, but thankfully, she eventually comes to her senses! After a pretty evenly matched fight, Buffy finally gets the better of Dracula and stakes him – but he doesn't stay dead...

Why It's Cool: Well, for starters, it would be downright rude not to include Buffy's slaying of the most famous of all vampires! The fight between Slayer and vampire is very energetic – it wears you out just watching it! – and culminates in not one but two stakings. Who'd have thought Buffy would have outsmarted old Drac? Nice try with the old vanishing act, though!

9 "ANGEL"

What's Happened: After heaps of unresolved sexual tension, Buffy and Angel finally do it – kiss, that is. But one snog later and Buffy discovers that the hunky young man is in fact a vampire. Shock! Horror! Angel tries to explain everything to Buffy, but their deep and meaningful is rudely interrupted by Angel's ex-lover and one time partner in crime, Darla, who tries to kill the Slayer. However, it's Darla who ends up being dusted. By Angel!

Why It's Cool: Boy, we certainly didn't see that one coming! Proving his loyalty to Buffy – not to mention the greater good – Angel kills his former love and sire. And a vampire staking a vampire is fabulous in an ironic way.

"Digging on the undead doesn't exactly do wonders for your social life."

8 "CONSEQUENCES"

What's Happened: Buffy's feeling terribly guilty about Faith killing the poor old deputy mayor. Faith, on the other hand, wouldn't know what a conscience was if it bit her on the butt. Buffy eventually decides to offload her guilt and tells Giles. But Faith's already pointed the finger of blame at Buffy for the deputy mayor's murder.

Why It's Cool: After doing the dirty on Buffy, Faith redeems herself – slightly – when she saves Buffy from getting it in the neck (get it?!) and stakes Mr Trick before he can snack on the Slayer. A snappy dresser like Mr Trick deserved to go out in style, and he sure did. His last line, "Oh no, this is no good at all," rocks!

7 "PROPHECY GIRL"

What's Happened: After Giles comes across an infallible prophecy that predicts that Buffy is destined to fight The Master – and die – Buffy decides that she doesn't want to be a Slayer anymore. But after some Sunnydale High students are brutally murdered by The Master's vampires, Buffy decides that it's time to face her destiny once and for all.

Why It's Cool: An amazing good vs evil battle as Buffy takes on The Master in an intense and exhilarating confrontation. Thankfully, Buffy manages to defeat The Master by throwing him through a glass roof and onto a wooden stake below. Ouch! That had to hurt!

6 "BECOMING, PART TWO"

What's Happened: After Angelus plans to awaken the demon Acathla and bring about Hell on Earth, Buffy is forced to face off against her former lover to save the world. Whilst Willow manages to restore the vampire's soul, it's too little too late. The only way Buffy can close the portal to Hell is to kill Angel.

Why It's Cool: Okay, so maybe it's not quite technically a vampire slaying. But Angel is a vampire. Buffy's a Slayer. And she kills him. (Okay, sends him to Hell!) But let's not get picky. It's dramatic; shocking; and sad. It deserves inclusion. Just don't get us started on Sarah McLachlan's hauntingly beautiful accompanying music or there will be tears!

5 "THE FRESHMAN"

What's Happened: Buffy's having a hard time settling into college life. To make matters worse, she also has to contend with the presence of a gang of vampires who rule the campus of UC Sunnydale. It seems as though Buffy may have met her match in the leader of the gang – the blonde, sarcastic and bossy vampire, Sunday.

Why It's Cool: Buffy hunts down Sunday and her gang to their lair and stakes them, one by one. Although the Scoobies arrive to help, Buffy has it covered. In one of the show's coolest dustings, Buffy throws the stake at Sunday who turns to dust. Now that's one classy staking! Sunday was a character with such huge potential, and it was a real surprise to see her go.

DOS AND DON'TS OF VAMPIRE SLAYING

DON'T wear your best clothes. Okay, so you want to look good, but remember, whatever you wear is likely to get ripped or covered in dust. It's advisable to wear something durable – and washable. Silk and linen are definitely out. Think of the dry-cleaning bill!

DO pack a few snacks. You never know how long you're gonna be out on patrol. Slaying can make you feel pretty hungry, so take an apple and a healthy nutritious snack bar to keep those munchies at bay. (And some chocolate and chips!)

DON'T take your Ipod. It's never a good idea to listen to music whilst on patrol. Yes, it can be boring waiting for vampires to show up. But a sneaky vamp just might jump you from behind. Not to mention steal your Ipod!

DO remember to take all those handy Slayer essentials with you. A good Slayer is a well-prepared Slayer. So don't forget to pack some holy water, a crucifix and a few stakes.

DO practise your slaying "chat-up lines." Good verbal banter helps to keep those nasty vamps on their feet. And besides, trading verbal blows makes the whole experience a lot more fun.

DO know your anatomy. To dust a vampire successfully, you need to know exactly where their heart is. Prepare yourself by watching back-to-back reruns of *ER*. (The ones with George Clooney, of course!)

4 "CONVERSATIONS WITH DEAD PEOPLE"

What's Happened: During a typical night out on patrol, Buffy bumps into a former classmate, Holden Webster. It turns out that Holden is now a vampire, and he's revelling in his newfound powers and immortal status.

Why It's Cool: What makes this more than just another Slayer and vampire face-off is the wonderful and insightful conversation that takes place between Buffy and Holden. Whilst trading blows, the former psychology student manages to get Buffy to totally open up and explore her feelings like never before. The mock therapy session ends when Buffy does what she does best – kills the vampire.

3 "BAD GIRLS"

What's Happened: Bad girl Faith continues to be a bad influence on Buffy, with the pair playing hooky from training, not to mention partying and dusting vamps for the fun of it. But their fun is put on hold thanks to the arrival of the demon Balthazar; the very large and very ugly leader of a vampire sect.

Why It's Cool: Faith and Buffy make such a great team, with their synchronized slaying in the cemetery whilst having a "girlie" conversation about boys. They may be complete opposites, but it's fun to see them working well together. The moment where Faith thrusts a stake into the back of a vampire, who screams, throws up his hands, and crumbles to ash is awesome. A top quality dusting moment!

2 "CHOSEN"

What's Happened: It's the biggest of all battles when Buffy and the Potentials face off against The First and its army of ubervamps. Aided by Willow's spell to imbue all of the Potentials with full Slayer powers, the fierce battle ends with The First being destroyed and the Hellmouth collapsing – taking Sunnydale with it.

Why It's Cool: Wow! It's the ultimate face-off between Slayers and thousands of those ugly, nasty ubervamps. Throw in some slow-mo and dramatic music for good measure and this vampire slaying *en masse* is edge-of-your-seat, kick-ass entertainment. Just don't try to count the number of vampires slayed!

1 "WHO ARE YOU?"

What's Happened: After Faith and Buffy have switched bodies, Faith – as Buffy – has an attack of conscience. She decides to do something selfless (for once) and risks her life to save the day when a group of vampires takes innocent people hostage at a local church.

Why It's Cool: The whole concept of Faith living Buffy's life is wicked fun. It's an eye-opening experience for Faith, when she gets a taste of what her life could have been like if she'd had a family and friends who loved and supported her, like Buffy had. The face-off with the vamps in the church is vampire slaying on full throttle, particularly the part where Faith (as Buffy) stakes a vampire, flips him over, and he disintegrates in mid air!

The Pun Is Mightier Than The SWORD

The Pun Is Mighti

OVER SEVEN YEARS OF *BUFFY* WE'VE SEEN SOME PRETTY IMPRESSIVE BATTLES — AND AN IMPRESSIVE ARTILLERY TO MATCH! WE TAKE A LOOK AT 10 OF THE BEST!

Buffy doesn't need weapons. Unlike other Slayers who relied on a specific weapon (Kendra with her Mr Pointy, Faith with her special knife) or the rest of the Scoobies, Buffy's combat versatility and resourcefulness are so great that, as time goes by, she more and more often heads into battle unarmed. She is able to master most of the 'physical' weapons (axes, crossbows, swords and knives) so quickly and effortlessly that she will pick up whatever is to hand and – not so much *make do and mend* as – make do and stab! She admitted as much, when instructing the potential Slayers in Season Seven. "In the hands of a Slayer, everything is a potential weapon – if you know how to see it." By this stage, Buffy had long since abandoned the weapons bag of early episodes in favor of improvizing (but maybe it wouldn't hurt to have a stake about her person, just in case…).

For the rest of the Scooby Gang, however, weapons are a must, so here for your delectation are the Top Ten Weapons no Slayer or Scooby should be without…

2. THE CROSSBOW

The Crossbow is another hotshot favorite for the whole gang. Better for long-range action than the stake but slower because it requires reloading, think medieval missile launcher – it can be used to penetrate armor and vamps from up to 150 feet away. Buffy carried a basic wooden one with her into final battle against The Master (in Season One's "Prophecy Girl"), while in Season Three's "The Wish," alternate universe Buffy did likewise with an updated, smaller, metal version.

3. THE QUARTERSTAFF

The Quarterstaff is one of the less-used items in Giles' arsenal of antique weaponry – a two-handed, six-foot long, wooden pole, perfect for Slayer basic training in combat techniques before moving on to the crossbow. At least, that's Giles' theory (in Season One's "Angel" episode) until La Buff gives him a 30-second practical demonstration as to who's the daddy when it comes to combat. After that, it's arrows all the way, though at least the practice came in handy for her broom-bashing of two vamps in Season Three's "Lover's Walk."

4. THE CROSS

The Cross or crucifix is another wooden implement with a history of limited effectiveness against the undead. It burns them when in contact with their flesh, and can destroy them eventually. That's unless they knock it away first. Better to treat it as a neck accessory or second line of defence to ward off vamps, or for exorcizing demons from human victims. Buffy sometimes wore hers around her neck in the early days, with spares in her weapons chest. In many ways, it's about as useful as…

5. HOLY WATER

…Like the cross, Holy Water's rep is bigger than its night-to-night effectiveness. It too will burn the undead if it touches them, and in sufficient quantity can slay them, as when a powerless Buffy conned the crazed vampire Zackary Kralick into drinking a glass of the sanctified squash in Season Three's "Helpless." Any H2O can be rendered h2oly so long as it has been blessed by a priest, and it's totally safe for the user (unless they're a vamp, that is!). Mostly it's carried for protection, but apart from that, it's a bit of a damp squib.

1. THE STAKE

The Stake is everybody's battlefield weapon of first choice: after all, there's nothing like poking vamps with a sharp stick to make them go poof! Simple, effective, and the traditional means of kissing bye-bye to the undead, nothing speaks imminent slayage like a stake. Only two things matter: it has to be made of wood, and sharpened at one end to form a point. Beyond that, anything can be improvized for staking duties: pencils, broken pool cues, tree branches, the remains of a wooden desk. Slayer Kendra loved hers so much she even named it Mr Pointy. Never leave the library without one.

By Alan Woollcombe

6. KNOWLEDGE

Knowledge is perhaps the group's greatest weapon, with Giles as the Merlin wizard figure. While he has an array of ancient physical weapons, his real arsenal lies in his storehouse of knowledge, the library, where the Scoobies assemble to plan strategies. It's no accident that the library is their HQ – despite their grumbling about schoolwork, all of them respect knowledge deeply. Indeed, it's just that love of knowledge that leads Willow down the slippery slope of dark magic. Now get back to your homework!

7. LANGUAGE

Language is Buffy's one constant personal weapon: not as a means of communication to coordinate an attack (she never carries a mobile, for starters), but more as an expression of who she is. Simply, to walk the Slayer's walk, Buffy has to talk the talk while she stamps the vamps. It's more than just a girl thing: it's part-psyching herself and the gang up, part-outpsyching the bad guys. Both before and during showdowns, Buffy and the Scoobies banter incessantly: the faster the quips, the harder the hits – and equally, if she's feeling off-color, she stumbles verbally or falls silent. Exactly what she says matters less than how she says it. It ain't a party without repartee.

Guns are generally a big no-no for the gang, mostly because they're no good against bloodsuckers (though if you're being picky, they can kill demons, like Billy Blim in the *Angel* episode, "Billy"). Sometimes, though, nothing but the biggest bang will do, as in Season Two's "Innocence," when Buffy blows big stiff The Judge into tiny pieces with the aid of a rocket launcher. And then in the very next episode ("Phases") the team sport tranquilizer guns to calm down werewolf Oz when he's having a hairy moment. Apart from that, guns make a rare appearance in the Slayer's studies – and after the devastating events of "Seeing Red," is it any surprise? When Warren shoots Buffy and accidentally kills Tara with a stray bullet, it just goes to show what dangerous weapons guns are – especially when they fall into the wrong hands.

8. FIREARMS

One item that might have been tailor-made to be La Buff's standard weapon *du jour* is the Hunga Munga, a war/hunting weapon from Central Africa. When hurled, it's a lethal cross between a throwing knife, an axe and a boomerang with several projecting blades, and it spins through the air like a baby buzz saw. Buffy only used one once in the entire series (in the Season Three opener, "Anne") though she did spot one in Giles' armory. Plus, of course, it's Joss Whedon's *objet d'amour*: "I am terribly in love with it," he confessed online in October '98. "In times of excitement I am known to shout HUNGA MUNGA in an irritating fashion." Who said love hurts?

9. THE HUNGA MUNGA!!!

The Slayer's Scythe is a mystical axe forged by the Guardians specifically for a Slayer "to defeat the last pure demon who walked the Earth," and left entombed in a crypt, ready for when Ms Summers drops in centuries later. Or put another way: it's Buffy's Excalibur. Sure enough, in Season Seven's penultimate episode, "End Of Days," our heroine pries the blade out of the solid rock in time to slice three über-vamps and dice demon vicar Caleb. Then, in "Chosen," she up-ends the whole One-girl-in-all-the-world tradition by getting Willow to magically zap Potentials all over the world with Slayer essence from the Scythe and – *Voila!* – an army of full-blown Slayers is born to stomp the forces of the Big Bad for good. Hurrah!

10. THE SCYTHE

EPISODE SPOTLIGHT

SEASON 5

EPISODE 22

"The Gift"

First US airdate
22/05/01

First UK airdate
02/06/01

Synopsis

Buffy faces her biggest, most challenging battle ever – facing off against a god to save her sister. As Glory prepares to use Dawn to unleash Hell on Earth, things have never looked quite so bleak. That is until Anya comes up with a cunning plan to use the Dagon Sphere and troll hammer to defeat Glory. Way to go, Anya!

While Dawn remains helpless, tied to the top of the tower waiting to die, Buffy (and the Buffybot) and Glory go head to head in a final confrontation. Buffy uses the troll hammer to overpower Glory, who suddenly morphs back into Ben. Although Buffy cannot take his life, Giles is on hand to finish the job! Spike tries to save Dawn but is stabbed by Doc and thrown from the tower. Buffy arrives just in time and pushes him to his death. But unfortunately, Dawn's blood has already started to open the portal. Just as Dawn prepares to sacrifice herself, Buffy realises that Dawn isn't the only one capable of preventing the dimensional walls from crumbling, and she throws herself into the portal. Can someone pass me a tissue?

Trivia

- **This is the show's** 100th episode.
- **At the Nocturnal** N3K *Buffy* Convention, Joss Whedon teased fans, saying that he had originally planned to kill Anya during "The Gift"'s climactic final battle. Luckily for fans – and Emma – he decided not to kill off the character.
- **Acclaimed stage actor** Joel Grey (Doc) is perhaps better known for his role in the musical *Cabaret* – for which he won a prestigious Tony Award. He also went on to win a Best Supporting Actor Oscar for the movie adaptation. He is the father of Jennifer '*Dirty Dancing*' Grey.

Guest Star Info

Charlie Weber (a.k.a. Ben) was born Charles Alan Weber, Jr on 20 September in Jefferson City, Missouri, and moved to New York to study acting when he was just 19. With his good looks, he managed to pick up a few modelling jobs to make ends meet, appearing in ads for the likes of *Vanity Fair* and Ralph Lauren. Weber has starred in several movies, including the romantic comedy *The Broken Hearts Club*, horror flick *Director's Cut*, and more recently *Dead Above Ground*, *The Kiss* and *The Crawl Space*. He plays the guitar, and likes to surf in his spare time.

Memorable Dialogue

Glory: "You're just a mortal. You couldn't understand my pain."

Buffy: "Then I'll just have to settle for causing it."

Spike: "I know you'll never love me. I know that I'm a monster. But you treat me like a man…"

Buffy: "Dawn, the hardest thing in this world is to live in it. Be brave. Live… for me."

Statistics

No. of times Buffy gets to kick ass: 2

No. of screams: a lot!

No. of deaths: 5

No. of tear-jerking moments: 5

EPISODE CREDITS

Written & Directed by Joss Whedon

Buffy Summers	Sarah Michelle Gellar	Dawn Summers	Michelle Trachtenberg
Xander Harris	Nicholas Brendon	Spike	James Marsters
Willow Rosenberg	Alyson Hannigan	Glory	Clare Kramer
Rupert Giles	Anthony Stewart Head	Ben	Charlie Weber
Anya	Emma Caulfield	Doc	Joel Grey
Tara	Amber Benson	Murk	Todd Duffey

Compiled by Kate Anderson

TRU TALL

IT'S NO BIG SECRET THAT WE'RE ALL MASSIVE FAITH FANS HERE AT TITAN TOWERS, SO WE'RE THRILLED THAT WE FINALLY MANAGED TO TRACK ACTRESS ELIZA DUSHKU DOWN TO TALK ABOUT HER FINAL EXPERIENCES ON *BUFFY* AND *ANGEL*. FIVE BY FIVE!!!

BY IAN SPELLING

ou've just gotta have faith. Eliza Dushku promised that she'd find some time for an interview with the official *Buffy the Vampire Slayer Magazine*, but right now everyone wants a chunk of her increasingly limited time. She's just started production on her new series, *Tru Calling*, which is filmed in Canada. And today, she's in Los Angeles attempting to juggle meetings with Fox, who will launch *Tru Calling* in the fall, several pending interviews and a magazine photo shoot. This very instant, in fact, she's sitting in a chair as a make-up artist and hair stylist dab, tease and primp her to perfection. True to her word, however, Eliza finds time to chat. And chat she does, for a full half-hour, albeit with frequent pauses – caused by a blow dryer – and apologies for those pauses.

First on the agenda is Eliza's new gig, *Tru Calling*. The upcoming series casts the raven-haired actress as Tru Davies, a young woman with a special gift/curse: she can relive any day. As such, Tru can turn back the clock and prevent murders, suicides and accidents from ever happening. And working in a morgue provides Tru with plenty of opportunities to try her hand at playing God, an activity that could backfire if saving one life costs others theirs. Tru also spends way too much of her time coming to the aid of her siblings, gambler

"I LOVED [*BUFFY*] AND I LOVED WHAT WE CREATED THERE, BUT I WANTED TO DO SOMETHING DIFFERENT. I STARTED PLAYING FAITH PROBABLY FIVE YEARS AGO, AND I THOUGHT, 'I WANT TO DO SOMETHING MAYBE A LITTLE DIFFERENT.'"

Harrison (played by Shawn Reaves) and drug addicted Meredith (Jessica Collins). "What intrigued me about the show?" Eliza asks, repeating the question posed to her. "It was everything, really; the script, obviously, right off of the bat, and the people involved. I'd been familiar with some of the things that they'd done. It was the whole package. I just figured, why not go for it. And right now, with *Buffy* having ended, there aren't a lot of shows out there with a female heroine. Maybe people would be missing one and are looking for one, and I think that these kinds of shows are almost like therapy for teenage girls and young girls going through kind of what's up in their own lives. So, I think that it's important to have that there."

Fox went all out on the *Tru Calling* pilot, recruiting Phillip Noyce to direct it. The respected filmmaker's credits include the features *Dead Calm*, *Patriot Games*, *Rabbit-Proof Fence* and *The Quiet American*. He's also called the shots on a couple of television series before, helming episodes of *The Hitchhiker* and *Nightmare Café*. "It was pretty cool because he's a genius and he made one of the best movies of the last year, *The Quiet American*," Eliza enthuses. "He's just super-talented and he's a trip. It's fun hanging out with him on set because he's really got a different, crazy,

but completely interesting personality. So, it was a lot of fun. He's an Aussie and so he's brutally honest. I think that I'm a little bit the same way being a Boston girl. I think that he'll be one of the executive producers. If not, I think – I'm hoping – he's going to keep some title on the side."

The pilot includes a line of dialogue that's sure to provoke knowing chuckles from members of the *Buffy* fanbase. At one point, Tru looks at her brother and says, "Have a little faith in your sister." Eliza laughs when that particular nugget is brought to her attention. "I don't know how that got in there," she says. "I think that it wasn't even meant to be a joke and then it just kind of happened. And now, obviously, it comes across as an in-joke. It's funny because a lot of people have kind of given me grief. I've got *Buffy* fans saying, 'I really loved Faith,' and they're

upset I didn't do more [in a proposed Faith spin-off series]. I loved the show and I loved the characters and I loved Joss [Whedon] and I loved what we created there, but I wanted to do something different. I started playing Faith probably five years ago, and when you're on a new show, that can run seven years. I thought, 'I don't know. I want to do something maybe a little different.' I also didn't want to be following in Buffy's footsteps and being compared to that the whole time. So, I hope that people can grow along with me and appreciate this new character I'm playing."

All of that makes perfect sense, but some people still might wonder about Eliza's choice of material. Not *Tru Calling*'s quality or prospects, but rather that now seemed as good a time as any for her to pursue a film career. Remember, she managed to squeeze in *Bring It On*, *Jay*

"DAVID [BOREANAZ] IS MY BROTHER, MAN. HE'S MY BOY, AND WE JUST HAVE SO MUCH FUN. WE REALLY JUST HIT IT OFF FROM THE BEGINNING, WAY BACK WHEN, AND I REALLY LOVE GOING AND WORKING WITH THOSE GUYS [ON *ANGEL*]."

and *Silent Bob Strike Back*, *Soul Survivors*, *The New Guy*, *City by the Sea* and *Wrong Turn* before, during and after her stints on *Buffy* and/or *Angel*. Also, *Tru Calling* definitely falls into the genre realm, and some might assume that she'd seek a comedy or romance or straight drama. Eliza sees no reason to second-guess her decisions. "I just felt like I had done a number of movies in the past couple of years," she notes. "Movies are great, and you get to move around and you get to go shoot here and there, but at the same time, I was also feeling like, 'Well, maybe I want something a little bit more consistent, something where I'll have my home nearby and I'll know where I'm going to work every day.' I kind of wanted something like that, and I just felt like, 'Why not?' I'm 22 years old, and if the show were to go six years, I'd be 28 when it ended. It just seemed like it was in my gut. Also, the bar between television and film has really been lifted with really great shows like *Sex and the City*. If the writing is there, I don't think that it's looked down on as much as it was in the past, when people would go, 'Oh, TV is B-acting and films are A-acting.' I feel like a lot of the TV out there on the air right now is almost better than the stuff on film. So, I wasn't really concerned with people going, 'Oh, television.'"

Buffy the Vampire Slayer will no doubt go down in history as a television classic. And as Faith, Eliza was a huge part of the show's heart, soul and success. Over the years, she kicked ass, displayed sass, battled against and alongside Buffy, matured and evolved. Her most recent, and perhaps last, stint as Faith began late last winter when Eliza turned up in three fourth-season episodes of *Angel*, namely "Salvage," "Release" and "Orpheus."

"Oh, I loved it," she enthuses. "David [Boreanaz] is my brother, man. He's my boy, and we just have so much fun. We really just hit it off from the beginning, way back when, and I really love going and working with those guys. People always ask what made me go back, and it's because it's so fun and the writing is always 100 percent, 150 percent, and it's just such a pleasure. David and I goof off and then, when we get a dramatic scene, he's really, really great to play off. You want to surround yourself with good people and that's exactly what I know I'm doing when I go over there. And I thought the way they got Faith out of prison was cute. 'Step away from the glass.' I thought that it was good. It was strong and it was kind of crazy and I thought that it was just right."

Following her trio of *Angel* engagements, Eliza wended her way over to *Buffy* for the final five episodes – "Dirty Girls," "Empty Places," "Touched," "End of Days" and the capper, "Chosen." As the last arc played out, Buffy seemed unable to reach out to, or win the confidence of, the Potential Slayers. They considered her too serious, too insular and intractable, and, in fact, they – with the approval of Giles, Dawn and the rest of the Scooby Gang – essentially appointed Faith as their leader. And even as she led the troops, she found time to romance Principal Wood, a burgeoning relationship that got its pay-off with the touching, then amusing moment when he appeared to die, only to cough and recover. "I was just excited to go back and be there because the show was a phenomenon and it is a part of history," she agrees. "I had no idea how they were going to end it, but I assumed that Joss would pick a fun thing and I was so impressed with the way that he cast it off.

I remember getting the last script and thinking, 'How is he going to do this? How do you end something like that?' And then, by the last page, I was like, 'Oh, like that! That's how you do it.' The way he writes, there's just so much blood in each character. The [Faith-Wood] relationship was good. He was fine. She was used to being this girl who had her boy toys, but they started to connect and by the end of it I thought that they had a really nice connection." And no, Eliza adds, she never for a moment thought that Faith would be among the familiar faces who kicked the bucket. "I hadn't heard any word on that, and so, no, I wasn't too concerned," she says. "I figure that if Joss was going to kill me, he would have let me in on the secret early on."

Waves of emotional highs and lows washed over the *Buffy* production team during its last few weeks. For a time it appeared that the show might return for an eighth season. For a period it looked as if a spin-off of some nature might come together. Then, finally, the show's fate was decided. It was to end; there'd be no next season nor any spin-off featuring Faith, Spike or anyone else (for the time being, anyway). Eliza reports that once the decision came down she picked up on a we-see-the-light-at-the-end-of-the-tunnel vibe bouncing around the *Buffy* set. "It

Eliza discusses her recent big screen outing, *Wrong Turn*

Buffy and *Angel* fans who can't get enough of their favorite actress need not look far to see Eliza. She recently starred in the film *Wrong Turn*. The horror flick, about a group of young adults stranded in the woods and murdered one by one, resembled a hardcore 1970s outing along the lines of *The Hills Have Eyes*. Unfortunately, audiences seemed to turn elsewhere when the film arrived in theaters this past summer. "I liked it," Eliza says. "I enjoyed it, my friends enjoyed it and I don't know why [it didn't catch on]. And I don't really give a sh*t about what other people thought. In terms of box office, it was an independent movie and you can't really have expectations. We were just glad that it made it into the theaters and got any audience. We made a horror movie for fans of horror movies. [Creature effects maestro] Stan Winston and Rob Schmidt, our director, both said, 'We want to make a horror movie that doesn't wink at the audience.' So, it was what it was, just a no holds barred, in your face, gruesome horror movie. It was a good experience and something that I had never done before. I like doing things that are different and mixing it up." *Wrong Turn* recently aired as a pay-per-view cable option, and DVD and home video releases are in the works. And just before starting in earnest on *Tru Calling*, Eliza wrapped production on another big screen project. "It's a movie with Terence Stamp," Eliza says eagerly. "It's kind of a romantic comedy, which was a nice change of pace. It's called *The Kiss*."

was just such a mixture of emotions because they really are a family, through all of the good and the bad," she says. "They were together for seven years and that's a lot. I think that they were ready to go, but at the same time, they were leaving their family. So, I think that it was joyful and also sad at the same time. I'm really proud of them all. Every time that I got back there I'd feel like I was going back and seeing my high school friends again, because we'd all been such good friends over the years. I'll miss not being able to go back and shoot with them, but they really turned it out for the finale and

they worked their asses off, and I'm just really proud of all of it."

Of course, the *Buffy*verse being the *Buffy*verse and the *Angel* gang still cranking it out over on The WB, there's no reason to think Joss won't call upon his old *Buffy* employees and friends to make guest appearances on *Angel*. Eliza knows full well that that's a genuine possibility. "I would never rule that out," she says. "I mean, I love it, playing Faith. It's so much fun and, absolutely, if they'd have me and if time permits, then, I'd love to go over and do some of that stuff again on *Angel*." ✦

"EVERY TIME THAT I GOT BACK [ON *BUFFY*] I'D FEEL LIKE I WAS GOING BACK AND SEEING MY HIGH SCHOOL FRIENDS AGAIN. I'LL MISS NOT BEING ABLE TO GO BACK AND SHOOT WITH THEM."

Good Clean PUN

"I've always been amazed with how Buffy fought, but... in a way, I feel like we took her punning for granted." Here, here, Xander Harris – you couldn't have said it better! Buffy Summers is unequivocally one of the greatest kick-ass heroines of any generation, but her prowess with a turn of phrase is a lesser appreciated gift that often pales in comparison to her handy skills with a stake. But for those that appreciate a cutting remark or the perfect pun to be as effective as a mortal strike, then Buffy's language skills are just one more unique tool in her already eclectic arsenal. Throwing puns as part of her verbal assaults became synonymous with Buffy's legendary fighting style – a fabulous roundhouse kick, followed by one hell of a quip.

But what if you're sitting there thinking, "Uhm…what the heck is a pun?" No problem, we can explain. Take a stroll with *Buffy & Angel Magazine* as we walk you through the world of punnage by highlighting classic examples from Buffy and her Scoobies, and even a few of her villainous foes, so maybe you too can stake your claim (See! There's one.) to verbal glory.

According to Dictionary.com, a pun is a noun and means: "A play on words, sometimes on different senses of the same word and sometimes on the similar sense or sound of different words." The pun has become a comedy staple, often used as a cheap joke because of the relative ease of creating one for just about any situation. In the case of *Buffy the Vampire Slayer*, the mythology is crazy fertile with material to create some truly worthy puns… and some groaners, too. There's blood, stakes, death, vampires, moon cycles, fighting, high school, and the list goes on and on for inspirational themes to craft the funny. Joss Whedon loved the pun and his writers, including Jane Espenson and David Fury, took the punnage to new heights on the show with all the characters. So first, let's take a look at some puns used by characters other than Buffy, shall we?

"THAT'S IT? THAT'S ALL I GET? ONE LAME-ASS VAMP WITH NO APPRECIATION FOR MY PAINSTAKINGLY THOUGHT-OUT PUNS. I DON'T THINK THE FORCES OF DARKNESS ARE EVEN TRYING. I MEAN, YOU COULD MAKE A LITTLE EFFORT HERE, YOU KNOW? GIVE ME SOMETHING TO WORK WITH."

By Tara DiLullo Bennett

Willow, with her shy and awkward ways, loved to use more subtle humor

Xander Harris and Willow Rosenberg

The natural class clown, Xander was always appreciative of giving and receiving a funny line. But at the other end of the spectrum, Willow, with her shy and awkward ways, loved to use more subtle humor to deflect or protect herself as she matured and came into her own over the years. Both truly admired Buffy's clever turn of phrase, and over time used her as a guide to their own puns – with varying success over the years.

"Anne"

Willow: "That's right, Big Boy. Come and get it."
Xander: "Come and get it, Big Boy?"
Willow: "W-well, the Slayer always says a pun or-or a witty play on words, and I think it throws the vampires off, and, and it makes them frightened because I'm wise-cracking. Okay, I didn't really have a chance to work on that one, but *you* try it every time."

"Go Fish"

Coach Marin: "Oh! Harris. Uh... how you feelin'?"
Xander: "Little dry. Nothing a lemon butter sauce won't cure."

"Killed By Death"

Xander to Angelus:
"Take a walk, overbite."

"Phases"

Xander: (about werewolf Oz) "Quite the party animal."

"What's My Line, Part Two"

Xander: "Hey, larvae boy! Yeah, that's right, I'm talkin' to you, ya big cootie!"

"Something Blue"

Willow: "'Cause you had your hands full with the undead English Patient?"

"Phases"

Willow: (to Oz) "Well, I like you. You're nice and you're funny. And you don't smoke. Yeah, okay, werewolf, but that's not all the time. I mean, three days out of the month I'm not much fun to be around either."

Foes

And it wasn't just the good guys that got all the good lines – plenty of vampires and villains got their shots in on the heroes – both physically and verbally.

"Goodbye Iowa"

Spike: (to Buffy) "Gotta hand it to you, Goldilocks. You do have bleeding, tragic taste in men. I got a cousin married to a regurgitating frovalox demon that's got better instincts than you."

"Bad Girls"

The Mayor (about some Boy Scouts): "Backbone of America, those little guys. Seeing the hope and courage on their bright little faces, I swear I could just, I... I could just eat 'em up."

"Conversations With Dead People"

Holden: "And I thought I was diabolical or, at least I plan to be. You do have a superiority complex. And you've got an inferiority complex about it."

"Homecoming"

Mr. Trick: "Have a Nice Death!"

"Blood Ties"

Glory: "Hey. Hey! This doesn't have to be a complete waste of my precious time. I've been meaning to send the Slayer a message. And I could use a little pick-me-up. Two birds, one stone, and... boom – you have yummy dead birds."

Buffybot

Programmed according to Spike's specifications (and then upgraded by Willow), the Buffybot was a life-like robot made to look and act just like the real Slayer – right down to her puns. But, without the real Buffy's personality, the Bot came off more like a bad stand-up comedian. Here are some prime examples of when Buffy + a pun = a bad time.

Time to Slay!

"Oh Spike. You're the big bad. You're the BIG bad!"

"That'll put marzipan in your pie plate, bingo!"

Buffy Summers

Buffy's fighting skills were one thing, but she also took pride in her ability to come up with the right quip during the heat of battle. Stung when her efforts weren't truly appreciated, now's the time to give the Slayer her due and rank some of her best alternate work.

"Wild at Heart"

"That's it? That's all I get? One lame-ass vamp with no appreciation for my pain-stakingly thought-out puns. I don't think the forces of darkness are even trying. I mean, you could make a little effort here, you know? Give me something to work with."

"Never Kill a Boy on the First Date"

"We haven't been properly introduced. I'm Buffy, and you're history!"

"Prophecy Girl"

"You're that amped about Hell... go there"

"Graduation Day Part Two"

"You want to get it back from me, Dick?"

"Wild at Heart"

"You know very well, you eat this late... you're gonna get heartburn. Get it? Heartburn?"

"Fear, Itself"

Giles (about killing Gachnar): "No, it's just – tacky. Be that as it may, Buffy, when it comes to slaying..."
Buffy: "...Size doesn't matter?"

"I Was Made to Love You"

"Oh, no. Love Doctor Buffy is not in. I am not qualified to give dating advice. I've had exactly two boyfriends, and they both left. Really left. Left town left."

"The Gift"

"You ever heard the expression, 'biting off more than you can chew'? Okay, um, how about the expression, 'Vampire Slayer'? Wow! Never heard that one? Okay, how about, 'Oh God, my leg, my leg?'"

"Conversations With Dead People"

"I commit. I'm committed. I'm a committee!"

"Chosen"

Caleb: "Stupid girl. You'll never stop me. You don't have the ba...?" (*Buffy swings the axe low in an upward arc and buries the blade between Caleb's legs.*) Buffy: "Who does nowadays?"

• Now you've passed the test, try your hand at some Buffy-style fun that will make Buffy proud!

CLASSIC SCENE

"Bad Girls"

"Is he evil?"

The Story so far...

After the Gwendolyn Post affair, Buffy and Faith's new Watcher arrives in Sunnydale, in the form of the straight-laced and pompous Wesley Wyndam-Pryce.

The Scene...

THE LIBRARY, SUNNYDALE HIGH SCHOOL.

(Giles is sitting on the table, looking bored, while a smartly dressed young man goes through a box of books...)

WESLEY: Of course, training procedures have been updated quite a bit since your day. Much greater emphasis on fieldwork.
GILES: Really?
WESLEY: Oh, yes. Not all books and theory nowadays. I have, in fact, faced two vampires myself. Under controlled circumstances, of course.
GILES: Well, no danger of finding those here.
WESLEY: Vampires?
GILES: Controlled circumstances. (Sees Buffy enter.) Hello, Buffy.
WESLEY: (Looking at Buffy.) Well... Hello. (Smiles smugly.)

(Buffy gives him a quick look up and down.)

BUFFY: (To Giles.) New Watcher?
GILES: New Watcher.
WESLEY: (Holding out his hand.) Wesley Wyndam-Pryce... It's very nice to meet you.

(Buffy just continues to eye him critically.)

BUFFY: Is he evil?
WESLEY: (Perplexed.) Evil?
BUFFY: The last one was evil.
WESLEY: Oh, yes. Gwendolyn Post. We all heard.

No. Mr. Giles has checked my credentials rather thoroughly and phoned the Council, but I'm glad to see you're on the ball as well. A good Slayer is a cautious Slayer.
BUFFY: (To Giles.) Is he evil?
GILES: Not in the strictest sense.
WESLEY: Well, I'm glad that's cleared up. As I'm sure none of us is anxious to waste any time on pleasantries, (picking up his Watcher diary) why don't you tell me everything about last night's patrol.
BUFFY: Vampires.
WESLEY: Yes?
BUFFY: Killed 'em.
WESLEY: Anything else you can tell me?
BUFFY: Uh... One of them had swords. I don't think he was with the other two.
WESLEY: Swords?

(He goes back to his box of books and begins to rifle through them.)

WESLEY: Swords... One long, one short?
BUFFY: Mmm. Both pointy. With, like, jewels and things.
GILES: Sounds familiar.
WESLEY: It should. (He hands a book to Giles.)
GILES: El Eliminati. 15th Century...
WESLEY: (Rudely interrupting.) 15th Century duellist cult, deadly in their day. Their numbers dwindled in later centuries due to an increase in anti-vampire activity and a lot of pointless duelling. They eventually became the acolytes of a demon called Balthazar, who brought them to the New World, specifically here.
GILES: You seem to know a lot about them.
WESLEY: I didn't get this job because of my looks.
BUFFY: I really, really believe that...

EPISODE CREDITS

Season Three, Episode 14

First aired: 02/09/99 (US) & 10/28/99 (UK)
written by: Douglas Petrie
directed by: Michael Lange
Main actors this scene:
wesley wyndam-pryce: Alexis Denisof
rupert giles: Anthony Stewart Head
buffy summers: Sarah Michelle Gellar

WHY SO COOL?

The Wesley we first met in *Buffy* and the Wesley we all came to love in *Angel* couldn't be more different. Be it his condescending manner or smug smile, this scene perfectly showcases just how irritating and patronizing a Watcher Wesley was. And boy, did we love him for it!

EPISODE TRIVIA

Originally, the Wesley character was going to be a bit like Michael J. Fox in the *Back to the Future* movies. But in the end, the writers decided to make Giles cooler and rebellious by making Wesley so straight-laced...

Compiled by Kate Anderson

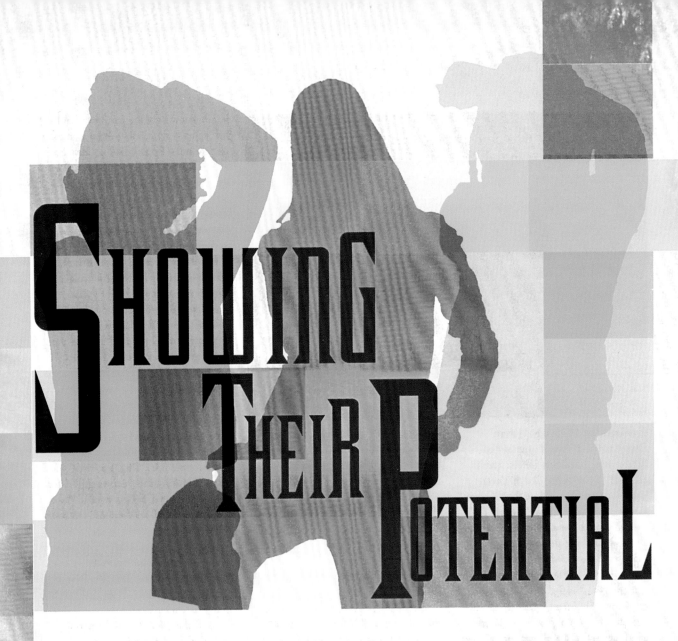

SHOWING THEIR POTENTIAL

SLAYER MYTHOLOGY WAS FULLY EXPLORED LAST YEAR AS THE
POTENTIALS HIT SUNNYDALE! WE MET UP WITH THREE OF THE GIRLS,
SARAH HAGAN (AMANDA), INDIGO (RONA), AND FELICIA DAY (VI),
TO CHAT ABOUT SEASON SEVEN, KICKING ASS, AND... KNITTING??!

BY TARA DILULLO

Sunnydale's population was on the rise during Season Seven of Buffy, and the new inhabitants weren't sporting fangs, horns or any other slimy appendages. Matter of fact, it was a crop of fresh-faced girls who made their way to the Hellmouth – all of them with the potential to be the next Slayer.

Whether they were fleeing The First Evil or being rounded up around the globe by Giles, these Potentials were being convened so they could get a crash course in fighting evil from the Chosen One herself, Buffy Summers.

While they may be young, Felicia Day, Sarah Hagan and Indigo were all

Hollywood veterans when they landed their parts on Buffy. Felicia has done many national commercials and television appearances; Indigo played a reccurring character on Boston Public, and Sarah was a regular on Freaks and Geeks. When they got their calls for Buffy, none of them were watching the

show with any frequency. "I wasn't a fervent fan but I would tune in from time to time," explains Felicia. Sarah adds with a shy laugh, "I didn't even know the show was still on the air when I went in to audition. I don't watch TV."

The women were called into separate auditions, which ended up being a unique experience for each one of them. Sarah was the first to go in for a part in Episode Four, "Help." While there, she ran into an old friend, who helped seal her fate. "I was going for the call-back and I saw Rebecca Kirshner [Buffy writer and former Freaks and Geeks scribe] there," Sarah explains. "I didn't know that she was working there as a writer. She asked me, 'What are you doing here?'

and I told her I was going in for the call-back for Amanda. She said, 'Amanda! I wrote that episode.'" Sarah was ultimately cast for the part, and she was called back to return as Amanda in "Potential." Sarah adds, "[Rebecca] is definitely the one who brought me back. They could have brought in a whole new person for that Potential role, but Rebecca ended up writing that episode too. I give her total credit."

Indigo originally auditioned for the role of a friend of Dawn's. She wasn't cast, but she came back again. "It's funny. The last time I auditioned, it was for Molly the English girl. I went in there with a cockney English accent and they liked it. A couple of days later, they

let me know I got the part but what they had actually done was written a different part for me – Rona. I had no idea. So, when they told me I got the part, I'm thinking, 'I'm the English girl.' I got a dialogue tape and practiced the accent all week." Indigo laughs, adding, "On Monday, when I got to work and we were running a rehearsal, I noticed one of the other actresses, Clara [Bryant, Molly] was using an English accent. I figured out on my own that I was a completely different character."

Felicia had a similar experience. She originally came in to read for Eve, the Southern Slayer killed by The First. "I was in the room with five blondes at the callback and I looked around and thought, 'Okay, I'm not getting this job,'" Felicia says with a laugh. "So, I went in, auditioned and then I left. Twenty minutes later, they called me back and said I got the role. 'Oh, I got Eve?' 'No, no you got this other recurring role, for Vi.' Furthermore, Felicia details, "In the original script, Vi was supposed to be an Asian girl who couldn't speak English [eventually Chao-Ahn]. So, they brought in another actress for that role." Laughing, she adds, "But, as a joke, I went to [writer] David Fury and told him I could do the accent."

Motivation for their characters and individual backgrounds was very much open for the actresses to explore. Indigo explains, "David Fury gave us total freedom. I remember a couple of times in between takes he would ask us what

POTENTIALS BODYCOUNT:
Annabelle
Chloe
Eve
Molly

POTENTIALS STILL BREATHING:
Amanda
Vi
Rona
Chao-Ahn
Caridad
Kennedy
Shannon

"WE ALL KNEW, EVENTUALLY, WE WOULD PROBABLY GET KILLED OFF, BUT NOBODY KNEW UNTIL WE GOT THE SCRIPT WHO IT WAS GOING TO BE. YOU WOULD FLIP TO THE BACK TO SEE WHO WAS DEAD."
– FELICIA DAY

we thought about our characters and what direction we wanted our characters to go in. I appreciated that. He actually gave me a little scoop," Indigo explains. "Rona actually derives from the word 'Ronin'. Ronin were ancient, nomadic Samurai and that's why, when Rona is first introduced, you don't know anything about her. She just gets off the bus. I liked that idea of not knowing where she was from and I kept that with me to keep the mystery going."

Sarah drew most of her inspiration from "Help", where Amanda was introduced. "[Amanda] came from a poor family. She is sort of dorky and goofy in her own way and shy too. She got picked on in school."

While each Potential had a distinct personality, behind the scenes, all the actresses shared at least one common experience: none of them were ever told by the producers how long their tenures would be on the show. "Every week, we would guess who was going to die that episode," Indigo says. "We all knew,

eventually, we would probably get killed off," Felicia adds, "but nobody knew until we got the script in the mail who it was going to be. The script would come and you would flip to the back to see who was dead."

Acclimating to an established cast and set is a common occurrence for guest actors and one that can be less than inviting depending on the environment. But that wasn't the case for the women at Buffy; to their surprise and pleasure it was the exact opposite. "It takes me a while to get used to different sets, but they've been amazing on Buffy and even though they are a family, they still reached out and welcomed us," Sarah Hagan says. They all point to one person in particular – Sarah Michelle Gellar. "I was a little intimidated, but the first scene I shot was the one where Buffy is bringing me into the house to introduce me to everyone. She made me feel so comfortable right away. She was very friendly and funny and I just eased into it," says Indigo. "I have so much respect for her. It's very

FELICIA DAY

Age: 24
Born: Alabama
Talents: Violinist, Ballet
First TV Gig: *Starburst* candy
Hobbies: RPG games
Next project: *Bring it On Again* – DVD in December

QUICK QUESTIONS
Which Potential could Vi easily take in a fight?
"Molly – because she was always in skirts."

Which Potential would kick Vi's butt?
"Kennedy – she has the devil in her when she fights."

Who's hotter: Spike or Xander?
"Spike. We were in an embrace for 4 hours."

Faith and Buffy in a fight – who wins?
"Buffy – she's quicker."

Ìnḋiġo

Age: 18
Born: Los Angeles, California
Family ties: Father is an actor
First Gig: *Armor Hot Dogs*
Next project: ABC series *10-8*, Sundays at 8pm

QUICK QUESTIONS

Which Potential could Rona easily take in a fight?
"Molly."

Which Potential would kick Rona's butt?
"A tie betweem Kennedy, Vi and Amanda."

Faith and Buffy in a fight – who wins?
"Buffy."

exhausting. There were days where we wouldn't get home until 3am. I admire her so much for doing it as long as she did."

The Potential actresses ended up becoming really tight with one another as friends over the episodes they shot together. "We just really liked each other. We all got hired around the same time and just got along great," says Felicia. Sarah Hagan was a little late to the group-bonding since she returned later in the season. "They had worked on the other episodes together before 'Potential', so they knew each other before I knew them. It took me a while to open up and hang with them. Once I did, everyone was so sweet. We would talk and knit."

Knit? Yes, it seems the secret Buffy set rituals don't involve expected blood-lettings or sacrifices but more like wool and knitting needles. "It was Alyson Hannigan's idea to start knitting," explains Felicia. "I made fun of her in the make-up trailer one day because she said she was going to start knitting. The next day, I decided I was going to start knitting because I really wanted to do it secretly." She adds laughing, "Sarah Michelle Gellar also knits. She said we should start knitting the stakes."

Watching the group clicking away between takes, Sarah Hagan adds, "It was really funny. When I saw them doing that, I was like, 'Okkayyy?' Then I decided to go home and learn myself. I went back to the set and they were all surprised." Felicia continues, "We would sit there and have a knitting circle. We made like 50 scarves. It was good to pass the time and we'd just talk and bond. Basically at the end of the show everyone

was in it, except for Indigo. She watched." Sheepishly, Indigo offers with a laugh, "I was the only one who wasn't [knitting]. I felt so bad. Every day, someone new was knitting and I felt like such a loser because I wasn't!"

Apart from her initial knitting problems, Sarah found that playing Amanda provided new acting trials. "It was really intense for me. I hadn't done anything like it before, like acting scared or having a vampire chase you. It was pretty creepy." She also found the sewer episodes, "Touched" and "End of Days", tough to get through, "just because the set was pretty crowded and hot and mildew-y. We had to stand around a lot while they changed the sets. We were all dirty and they were long days."

Indigo cites one particular scene as the most disturbing to get through. "The episode ['Get It Done'] where we find Chloe hanging in the bathroom, that was really hard. It looked very real and it was sad seeing her up there like that."

Then there was the fighting and stunt work, which though arduous ended up being a lot more fun than expected for the actresses. "It was the first time I had to fight," says Sarah. "Most of the time, I didn't use my stunt double. In 'Potential', I didn't use my stunt double at all. I got kicked in the head a couple times but I was okay. Everyone was pretty impressed."

Felicia was also new to the physical demands but she based the movements on her extensive dance background. "I've been dancing since I was nine so I approached it more like, 'Oh, this is like choreography.' I just had to be a little more aggressive with it. I found it to be very graceful. The stunt people on the show were so patient with us. They put

"SARAH MICHELLE GELLAR MADE ME FEEL SO COMFORTABLE RIGHT AWAY. SHE WAS VERY FRIENDLY AND FUNNY. I HAVE SO MUCH RESPECT FOR HER." – INDIGO

me on a wire for the last episode, which was challenging but really, really fun too." She adds with a giggle, "I knocked a couple of people in the teeth. Thank goodness they were okay – it was a wimpy kick."

Across the board, the women cite "Potential" as their favorite episode of the season. Sarah explains, "I had so much more to do in it than any other episode. I really liked the dialogue. I like the fighting but I'm more of a conversation person." Indigo adds, "That episode was really fun," while Felicia chimes in, "I got some great lines and there was the demon bar scene and Spike biting me. I felt like I really had fun with the character and the dynamic between all of us was well set up for the rest of the season."

Luckily, all three characters made it to the series finale, where they were also rewarded with the chance to be directed by the man himself, Joss Whedon. Felicia shares, "He is amazing. Talk about smart! Your brain has to work overtime with Joss. He is so energetic. After being on the show for so long, for him to come in and be so excited about shooting it, I really admired that. He was a great director and he always made time for everybody. It was a real privilege to be able to work with him." Similarly, Indigo says, "Joss is amazing. I really got to know who he was once I got to work with him. He really came up with something

incredible. It's very rare, especially in this industry, for women to be portrayed as being strong. This show pushed that and I respect him for that."

Felicia was also particularly humbled and appreciative of the part Vi played in the finale. "Just the fact that Vi was so wimpy, that Joss gave me that moment at the very end to get it together. I think we are all tormented with 'Why are we here?' and when that flash of power came through everyone, I feel like Vi really discovered what was in her and that she could do this. It was a wonderful moment as an actor to have that change before the show ended."

While the ending of the series was indeed sad and emotional for the actresses and the rest of the cast, they all remark on how thrilled they were just to be included. "I felt very blessed that I was even able to be part of something so amazing," Indigo says. "This show is definitely going to go down in history and I was part of it." Felicia adds, "What I loved about Buffy – it was such a perfect balance of drama and comedy. As an actor, you can really stretch yourself because you have to use both ends of the spectrum. And not only did I make some really great friends on the show, but I took away a lot in terms of confidence and range in my acting." She pauses and then adds with a laugh, "Plus, I have my own trading card; I can retire. If I get an action figure, I'm moving to Montana." ✢

SARAH HAGAN

Age: 19
Born: Austin, Texas
Family ties: Sister, Katie Hagan, is an actress
First Gig: Reindeer Elf in school play
Next project: Auditioning

QUICK QUESTIONS

Which Potential could Amanda easily take in a fight?
"Molly or Vi."

Which Potential could kick Amanda's butt?
"Kennedy."

Who's hotter: Spike or Xander?
"Spike."

Faith and Buffy in a fight – who wins?
"Buffy because [the writers] would make her win."

KENNED CENTER

INTERVIEW BY TARA DiLULLO

THINGS WERE LOOKING
BLEAK FOR WILLOW
AFTER THE TRAUMATIC
EVENTS OF SEASON SIX
— AND THEN KENNEDY
CAME ALONG TO HELP
MAKE THINGS A LITTLE
BETTER. ACTRESS
IYARI LIMON CHATS
ABOUT HER TIME ON
THE SHOW.

She was feisty and opinionated, definitely flirty and had no qualms about stirring things up from the moment she set foot in the Summers residence. Love her or hate her, no one can deny that Kennedy, the Slayer-in-training, made an immediate impression on the *Buffy* landscape with her very first appearance on the series in "Bring on the Night". The outspoken Potential not only stepped up to a leadership role amongst her peers but she also won the heart of Willow Rosenberg.

Happily, the actress who played her, Iyari Limon, wouldn't have it any other

way. Animated and lighting up a room with her ever-present smile, the petite, 24-year-old bundle of energy calls her time spent on *Buffy* "a blessing," which allowed her to grow as an actress in ways she could never have anticipated.

Iyari (pronounced E-ya-di) was born in Guadalajara, Mexico, but moved to California with her family at the age of one. Interested in acting at a young age, she began to pursue a career in her mid-teens. "I actually started around 15 but I got my first job at almost 16." Her first professional gig was a big one – playing a part on the NBC series, *E.R.* "It was cool. I only had a few words but I was

really nervous. It was very nerve-wracking on set," she laughs. "I got to work with George Clooney and Julianna [Margulies] and just being around them was cool. It opened my eyes to the whole process and made me want to do it more."

While she was resolute in her passion, Iyari's parents had serious reservations about their daughter's choice of career and they tried to steer her away from acting. "I've always been kind of a rebel and done what I wanted anyway, so it didn't really matter," she explains. "They saw that this is what I wanted and nothing was going to get in the

Y'S

Buffy 63

way, not even them. I love them but I was tired of living a life for them and trying to make them happy because I wouldn't be happy. I did go to college for a year or two but it just wasn't my thing. They see how serious I am and they are finally letting go of the fact that I may not become a doctor or a lawyer. My mother is a little more supportive but, all in all, they know I'm going to do my own thing. I'm very goal-oriented and I'm taking it serious. But they still try to push me to go to college and 'Get a real job'," she adds with mischievous smile.

She spent the last few years doing guest spots on TV shows including *The Brothers Garcia*, *Strong Medicine* and *The Mind of the Married Man*, but Iyari is the first to admit how challenging her chosen field can be. "It's very hard, actually. There have been periods where I don't work for a while and you go through these depression slumps. When that happens, I try to do something else productive. I'll take Shakespeare [classes] in London or I'll go learn French. I try to keep myself occupied because I have accepted the fact that I'm not in control of it all and I like to control everything," she laughs. "This has

taught me to let go of stuff. I thought, 'Oh, I'll make it by the time I'm 19!' No way. Five years went by and I was 19 and nothing. It started to get really scary and frustrating. I've seen a lot of people come and go but I don't think I have a choice. I'm going to do this until the day I die," she says with a smile.

She attributes her recent success to a change in attitude. "A couple of years ago, I finally learned to let go of everything and that's when things started to happen for me. All of a sudden these doors started opening and I was on these paths that I never knew I was going to be on," she says. "I did a Radio Disney tour last year and I was in London when I got the job. I happened to audition for it the day before [I left] because my boyfriend, at the time, was auditioning for it. I didn't give it a second thought and flew to London the next day. They got a hold of me a week later and flew me back from London after my Shakespeare class. I toured the United States and that showed me to be open and do whatever comes your way because you never know where it will go."

As fate would have it, that path led to Joss Whedon. Originally, Iyari was called in to audition for Joss' *Firefly*. "I had read for Kaylee quite a few times and that didn't happen. Then I read for a guest star [part] and that didn't happen. My agents and I got on a conference call with casting and they said, "Joss loves her and is going to hire her for something whether it be *Angel*, *Firefly* or *Buffy*." Encouraged, Iyari kept plugging away returning for auditions. "I just kept going and then finally I went in for Kennedy. I thought I probably wouldn't get it either. I was so antsy all day thinking, 'Did I do okay?'," she remembers. "I got the job the same day. I thought it was only one episode but I was ecstatic because I loved Kennedy and I was going to work for Joss."

assertive, the character was now more guarded about her role as a Potential Slayer. "She is new and doesn't know anyone so she is keeping her distance and being careful – not really trusting anyone completely," Iyari explains. "But slowly she starts to open up to these people and her vulnerability comes out to Willow."

Kennedy's connection to Willow morphed into an unexpected season-long arc for the actress to play – one that grew organically as the season proceeded. "It unfolded as it happened," she says. "Right before we shot the next episode, it was "Oh, you are in the next episode." I only knew one episode ahead all the way up to the end."

As the season progressed, Iyari was thrilled to find Kennedy becoming Willow's new love interest. Playing an overtly lesbian character is still taboo for some actors but Iyari was at ease with the challenges and excited to explore the relationship. The biggest issue, actually, was fan acceptance. The Willow and Tara relationship was much beloved by the lesbian community as well as the general fanbase, and there was much rumbling at the idea of a new love in Willow's life after the

Iyari stepped into the world of the Slayers flying blind since she didn't follow the show. "I had seen stuff from the first two seasons years ago but nothing recent." All she knew was what she got on the page from the writers and even then, the Kennedy she auditioned for ended up being far different from the young woman she eventually played. "In the scenes I auditioned for, she was a little more wry and very in your face. There was a scene between her and Willow in the bedroom and she was trying to push Willow's buttons. I thought it was just going to be these two scenes with this girl having fun with Willow, liking her and obviously flirting and trying to get to her. Then the [actual] episode was nothing like that," she giggles.

When she showed up for work, Kennedy had undergone a transformation. Still

death of Tara in Season Six. Iyari wasn't aware of the possible backlash when she started the role but was put through her show history paces by Alyson Hannigan.

"She is so cute," Iyari laughs as she relates what Alyson told her. "We were in the make-up room one day and she was like "Okay, I have to tell you the history. First Willow was in love with Xander and when Oz came in, people were pissed. But they grew to love him. So when Tara came in, [fans] said she had to be with Oz! But then they grew to adore Tara. So, I'm just telling you, people aren't going to be too fond of you in the beginning but they will grow to love you."

Asked if knowing that history ahead of time would have affected how she played Kennedy, Iyari pauses and answers thoughtfully, "I might have taken a different

LIMON ILLUMINATION

Some quick Iyari facts!

Iyari means "Strong Heart"

Iyari is only the second Latina to play a lesbian role on U.S. T.V.

Iyari speaks fluent Spanish

Iyari's favorite movie is *The NeverEnding Story*

Iyari on Eliza Dushku: "I love Eliza. She is a cool chick. She is very professional but a lot of fun."

Iyari on Joss Whedon: "I only got to work with him right at the end, but I just wanted to work with him more and more."

approach and I would have been more nervous, not that I wasn't already. But it was cool because Kennedy didn't know anything [about the history] so it worked. As Iyari was learning Willow's history, Kennedy was learning Willow's history so it was very pure."

Some fans were indeed vocal in their hostile reaction to Kennedy once the burgeoning relationship with Willow became more apparent. They accused the producers of

making Kennedy a replacement for Tara too soon after her death. Iyari sees it differently. "I don't see it as a replacement and people are always saying that. If [fans] really cared about Willow they would want her to be happy and if Tara is gone, she needs somebody to make her happy. I went and watched all of [Willow and Tara's] stuff and I loved Tara too." Furthermore, she keeps herself distanced from any of the negative feedback. "I don't hear too much negative and whatever negative is out there, I don't look into it. I've had people ask if I have heard about all the stuff online and the Tara-shippers and I stay away from it."

Mid-season the producers gave Iyari a unique opportunity with the episode "The Killer in Me", which explored Kennedy and Willow's new relationship. It also gave Iyari an entire episode in which to shine. "I loved it," she gushes. "But [initially] nobody told me that I was even in the episode!" She started to put it together when Sarah Michelle Gellar jokingly made a comment to her about the differences she would experience in kissing Alyson versus Adam [Busch]. "I was like 'What are you talking about?' So I figured I was in the next [episode] and when I saw it I was like, 'Wow!'" She considers that episode her favorite of the season, followed closely by "Touched", because of the time given to developing her character. "I feel very lucky that they wrote so much for her. I felt I was able to show who Kennedy was underneath." Her favorite scene in particular was the intimate bar scene with Willow. "I really sunk into her shoes there. I was trying to get to [Willow], showing her who I am and trying to build this connection with her. It's so nice having been able to show

Kennedy and Willow connect like that."

Aside from the romance, Iyari gleefully cites the physical battles and stunt work as a Potential-turned-Slayer as her other favorite part of the gig. "I love it! I love getting dirty and not wearing make-up and getting all bloody and grubby and fighting. I thrive on it," she enthuses. "A lot of the stunt doubles would say to me, 'You are really good at it'. For them to tell me that, when that's their profession is great. They told me I should do action films. The more I do it, I get a high and I want to do it again. I'm like, 'No, one more take! Come on, I can do it better!'"

That enthusiasm led to some aches and pains as well. "The [scenes] with me getting punched in the face was all me. The next morning, I woke up and I couldn't move my neck. I was trying to figure out why I couldn't and then I realized it was from taking all those

hits. But then I saw it all put together and it looked so good and it was all worth it," she laughs. "Anytime I can do my own stuff, I do."

Having survived the series finale, Kennedy walked into the future with Willow as a full-fledged Slayer and into television history along with the rest of the cast and crew. A poignant fact not lost on Iyari. "Sometimes when I really thought about it, it was overwhelming. All in all, I felt very thankful to be part of a seven-year legacy and to be in the end of it was like, 'Wow.' At the end I went up to Joss and said, 'Thank you for letting me be part of this!'"

Reflecting on Kennedy, Iyari offers that, "I find a lot of Kennedy in Iyari and a lot of Iyari in Kennedy. I admire her strength and her courage. Her willingness to put herself out

> "I FIND A LOT OF KENNEDY IN IYARI AND A LOT OF IYARI IN KENNEDY. I ADMIRE HER STRENGTH AND HER COURAGE. HER WILLINGNESS TO PUT HERSELF OUT THERE, LIKE THIS IS HER JOB AND SHE TAKES IT SERIOUSLY."

there, like this is her job and she takes it seriously." All attributes that ring eerily similar to a certain young actress forging her own path in Hollywood. She beams at the comparison and adds positively, "I don't know where I will be two months from now but that is awesome! I'm just going with the flow and wherever life takes me. I love my career." ✝

The Slayers

BEFORE & AFTER

WILLOW ROSENBERG

played by Alyson Hannigan

FORMERLY...

Willow: "What could a demon possibly want from me?"
Xander: "What's the square root of 841?"
Willow: "29. Oh, yeah." (**"Puppet Show"**)

Study Skills: Willow's popularity with most people at school rests entirely on her abilities as homework coach for the dorky, the jocky, and the new-school challenged. Her reputation as a total academic nerd is so well-established that Buffy learns of it on her very first day.

Boyfriends: Willow admits she's completely incoherent when she's around boys. It takes a nice guy like Oz to see Willow's romantic potential. Being smart, quirky and quiet, like her, he's the perfect choice for her first big romance.

Byte Me: Willow's the computer queen of Sunnydale High, so good that Jenny Calendar drafts her as a teaching assistant. Her cyberspace skills come in handy with Scooby stuff, too, like locating police records and sewer tunnels.

Dress Stop: Willow wears the most un-cool clothes in Sunnydale High. She admits her mom picks them out, and doesn't even mind Cordelia snarking that Willow has "seen the softer side of Sears." Though her hooker Halloween costume is hot enough to make Oz look twice, Willow thinks it's not her style.

Naïveté, Your Name is Willow: She used to play Doctor with Xander – using real medical equipment. She only figures it out when Xander confesses he never had the heart to tell her what "playing Doctor" really means. And when she meets her vampire alter ego face to face, she notices that vamp Willow seems "kinda gay"...

Miss Congeniality: Nobody's nicer than Willow, who doesn't seem to have a mean bone in her body. Whenever she happens to hurt someone's feelings, especially someone like Oz, whom she cares about, she's practically speechless with genuine distress.

Spellbound: Willow's exposure to Giles's magic books starts her tinkering with spells and witchcraft. At first, she can't do anything more spectacular than float a pencil, but Tara eventually helps her tap into her remarkable witchy powers.

CURRENTLY...

"Afraid. Yeah. They all are. The coven is – they're the most amazing women I've ever met. But there's this look that they get. Like I'm gonna turn them all into bangers and mash or something. Which I'm not even really sure what that is." (**"Lessons"**)

Girlfriends: After Willow meets Tara, she discovers that she's a lesbian, though when Oz shows up, it seems she still likes him a bit. However, all her lust goes toward the girls, with Kennedy eventually taking Tara's place. Funny that she never seems to notice how hot Buffy is.

Byte Me: Willow's still a computer whiz who can find any data or hack into any system on line, as she proves when she's going cold turkey on magic. But once she's got her magic under control, computer power isn't nearly as effective as Willow power.

Dress Shop: After she graduates from high school, Willow's wardrobe gradually transforms to show off her looks with stylish, witchy clothes that look so good we hardly ever notice them. She didn't learn to dress like this from her mom! It must be magic.

Naïveté, Your Name is Willow: Even being the world's most powerful witch and going completely to the dark side can't entirely cure some things. When Fred gets excited over Willow's arcane knowledge and suggests they should spend time together, Willow assumes that the very straight Fred is hitting on her. Sometimes a spade is just a spade.

Miss Uncongeniality: The sweet little girl who could hardly hurt a rat has been seen doing unspeakably terrible things, like flaying Warren alive, and trying to end the whole world. It takes stuff as terrible as this to wake up the niceness in Willow, and scare her into retreating from the destructive power of her magic.

Spellbound: Tara unlocked Willow's power, and losing Tara unleashes it, in cataclysmic ways. After her trip to the dark side, Willow's afraid to go near any kind of power, for fear that she'll be corrupted again. "I can't do so much as a locator spell without getting dark roots," she says. She needs all her training, plus the faith of her friends, especially Giles, Buffy and Kennedy, to tap into the cosmic power of the Scythe, change the Slayers' world forever, and incidentally, discover that her magical power can be "nifty." ✚

By K. Stoddard Hayes

XANDER HARRIS

played by nicholas brendon

FORMERLY...

"I laugh in the face of danger. Then I hide until it goes away." ("**The Witch**")

Average Joe: From the start, Xander is the only "normal" kid in the Scooby Gang, with no supernatural or witchy powers, no arcane knowledge, not even any whiz-kid computer skills. But he's always there at the critical moment, to be a demon punching-bag, provide some Slayer-reviving CPR, or make an inappropriate wisecrack...

School Hard: Xander's school problems add up to a lot more than just "the math" or his basement SAT scores. He has a knack for getting into all kinds of Hellmouth High type trouble, like becoming prey for a carnivorous substitute teacher or turning into a human hyena on a school trip.

Living Space: To avoid the misery of his parents' family life, Xander makes his home in a tidy little efficiency in his parents' basement. Okay, not so tidy. It's damp, gloomy and full of plumbing, and he hates it!

Love is Hell: The original high school dork who can't get a date, Xander gets a crush on Buffy the very first time he sees her. Since Buffy's oblivious to him, he gets a hot case of broom closet lust for the girl he loves to hate, Cordelia.

Best Friends: Xander has been Willow's best friend since they were in diapers. She's so close, he can't see she's got a crush on him, even when she's got ice cream on her nose. When he finally discovers she could be more than a friend, their brief relationship completely messes up four lives – Willow, Oz, Xander and Cordelia.

Green-eyed Xander: Xander can't stand vampires, especially the good ones. Sure, Angelus will give him plenty of good reasons for hating Angel, but let's not kid ourselves. His hostility really begins the moment he discovers the vamp with a soul is dating Buffy, the girl of his dreams.

Eye See: Being a hormonally active teen, what Xander mostly sees is how other people look – whether it's the new substitute teacher wearing a very nice chest – er, dress! – or that Buffy's mysterious friend Angel is much hotter-looking than his would-be rival, Xander.

CURRENTLY...

Xander: "I got hurt, but I'm not done, I can still fight... I just always thought that I would be there with you for the end... I should be at your side. That's all I'm saying."
Buffy: "You will be. You're my strength, Xander. You're the reason I made it this far. I trust you with my life." ("**End of Days**")

GI Joe: Still no supernatural powers. But Xander has accumulated plenty of monster-fighting experience – and he's really good at repairing the broken furniture after a big fight.

Hard Hat: While most of his friends go to college, Xander goes into construction work, where he proves his smarts in non-brainy ways by becoming a successful construction boss and the only Scooby to actually have a "normal" career.

Living Space: With the ego and money boost from his promotion, Xander moves into a sunny upstairs apartment with plenty of room to dance, bicker and fight off the odd demon. We're sure he'll find something equally lovely outside the boundaries of the crater formerly known as Sunnydale.

Love is Hell: When Xander tells Buffy she's messing up her relationship with Riley, he looks like the one Scooby who's really got this love thing figured out. Then he leaves Anya at the altar, and his love life goes back into the toilet. He can't help caring about Anya, but he's hurt her too deeply to mend the breach in the time they have left.

Best Friends: Even the end of the world can't stop Xander from being Willow's friend. When he decides the best thing to do is spend the big day with his best friend, his love proves deep enough to heal all the hurt she's feeling and bring her back from darkness.

Green-eyed Xander: A vamp with a chip is just as bad as a vamp with a soul. Spike drove Xander crazy by living in his basement for weeks, and finished the job by falling into Anya's arms.

Eye See: Xander may have only one eye left to see things, thanks to Caleb, but he's still the person Buffy trusts with the safety of Dawn, her most precious responsibility. And he still sees to the heart of matters more clearly with one eye than most do with two. ✚

By K. Stoddard Hayes

RUPERT GILES

played by anthony stewart head

FORMERLY...

Giles: "I must consult my books."
Xander (to Willow): "Eight minutes and 33 seconds. Pay up!" (to Giles) "I called 10 minutes before you had to consult your books about something." ("**When She Was Bad**")

The Quiet Man: Giles appears to most people as a tweedy fuddy-duddy, old before his time; a man whose best effort at raising a fuss is to tut and stammer and wipe his glasses. What a surprise to learn that his old friends knew him as "Ripper" – and not because he used to rip up papers.

Working Papers: Once a curator at the British Museum, Giles gets himself a post as librarian at Sunnydale High, so that he can keep a close Watcher eye on the newest student, the Slayer. He ought to be an excellent librarian – although he seems to spend most of his time training Buffy and researching demons, and very little time helping students with schoolwork.

Watch Over Me: Giles quickly develops a strong emotional attachment to his young Slayer. When Buffy freaks out at the prophecy that the Master will kill her, Giles resolves that he is not going to watch her die, and prepares to do battle with the Master himself.

Bad Council: Nominally a faithful follower of the Watchers Council, Giles finds their actions and their authority intolerable when they terrorize Buffy and endanger her mother with their coming of age ritual. Giles' emotional involvement leads to the Council firing him, and ordering him to stay away from Buffy and her new Watcher. Like that's gonna happen!

Generation Gap: Much as he cares about Buffy and her friends, Giles finds them eternally perplexing as well. Their clothes, their conversation, the music they listen to, and their interest in "cult" activities like cheerleading and going to the mall, lead him to conclude that if saving the world depends on them, then the world is probably doomed.

Temporal Displacement: Giles is actually a lot more comfortable with the distant past than he is with the present. He hates computers, and Jenny Calendar tells him he should occasionally read something published later than 1066.

CURRENTLY...

Willow: "Is there anything you don't know everything about?"
Giles: "Synchronized swimming. Complete mystery to me." "**Lessons**"

The Quiet Man: Giles may still occasionally tut and stammer, but we know now that his quiet manner hides a ruthless fighter who can kick butt with the best, endure horrific torture, call down major magic, and even conspire to kill off Spike when he thinks Buffy's too soft to get rid of The First's secret weapon.

Working Papers: Fired as Buffy's Watcher, Giles takes over The Magic Box, which he thinks might be better than running a library, because at least people pay for things they never return. The shop gives him a good place to train the Slayer, and plenty of access to arcane goods and books. It also means he has to endure having Anya as an assistant, and watch his store get trashed every time some Big Bad comes looking for one of the Scoobies.

Watch Over Me: Giles will always care for Buffy, but when he sees how she depends on his care after her resurrection, he knows that he has to leave her and go back to England, so that she will learn to survive on her own.

Bad Council: Though Giles was re-instated, retroactively, as Buffy's Watcher, his relations with the Council haven't changed. He has even less use for them than they for him. And when The First shows its power, Giles cuts through all the Council's infuriating bureaucracy by stealing critical texts about The First, so that they will reach the person who needs them most – the Slayer.

Generation Gap: Some things will never change. Moments before they go into the Hellmouth to do final battle with The First's army, the Scoobies plan a post-apocalypse trip to the mall. Giles listens with disbelief, and the inevitable feeling that he's become invisible. As he did seven years ago in "The Harvest", he observes with quiet chagrin, "The earth is definitely doomed!"

Temporal Placement: Giles may be out of date in some ways, but his knowledge of supernatural history has saved the Scoobies' butts on many occasions. And there's a lot to be said for staying in touch with ancient forces, like the coven that gives him the power to defeat Willow. ✝

By K. Stoddard Hayes

SPIKE

played by james marsters

FORMERLY...

"You know what I find works real good with Slayers? Killing them. Yeah, I've done a couple of Slayers in my time. I don't like to brag... Who am I kidding? I love to brag!" ("**School Hard**")

Family Man: The former poet spends most of his vamp life with his vamp family: his great grandsire Darla, his grandsire Angelus, and his sire and lover, Drusilla. Together the four make two hellish couples – proving that Freud invented the term "Oedipus complex" just to describe vampires.

Tomb, Sweet Tomb: Spike shacks up with Drusilla in a cozy underground lair, decorated with Dru's lacy porcelain dolls, and the occasional fresh human snack. He later trades this for a crypt done up in Harmony's favorite style, early satin schlock.

Keeping Score: Spike has killed two Slayers in his time; a Slayer in China 100 years ago, and Robin's mother Nikki. He even makes a science of Slayer-killing, setting up Buffy for a fight with another vamp so he can study her style before taking her on himself. He tells Buffy that when she gets more interested in death than in life, he'll be there to take her, too.

Doing the Slayer: Spike comes to Sunnydale just to add Buffy to his trophy collection. Over the years, all his plans to kill her go awry, starting with his discovery that this Slayer has plenty of friends and family, including an axe-wielding mom; and ending with a high tech chip implant that prevents him from hurting anything human.

True Lover: Spike will do anything for Drusilla. He starts by trying to bleed Angel dry to restore Dru's strength. When Angelus releases Acathla and triggers what looks like the end of the world, Spike sides with Buffy to save Drusilla. And when Dru dumps him for his betrayal, he figures the best way to get her back is to show her how bad he can be.

Letting in the Sunlight: Spike gets tired of the bossy, bratty Anointed One ("Annoying One" as Spike calls him), and hoists him into a sunbeam for a little dusting – thus claiming for himself the position of Biggest Bad in town.

CURRENTLY...

"Thanks, you cured me after all. I got my own free will now. I'm not under The First or anyone else's influences now. I just wanted you to know that – before I kill you." (**To Principal Wood, "Lies My Parents Told Me"**)

Family Man: Before he was a vampire, Spike was the doting son of a loving mother – until he made the mistake of turning his mother into a vamp. Vamp mom's openly-expressed contempt for him is a wound he carries secretly for a long, long time, until he ultimately realizes the contempt came from the demon in her, not the mother he loved.

Tomb, Sweet Tomb: Spike moves into an austere but nicely private crypt, where he can be alone for secret trysts with Buffy or the Buffybot, and get good TV reception for his favorite soaps.

Keeping Score: The old Spike would have taken great pleasure in killing a son who came after him to avenge the killing of a mother. When Robin goads Spike into vamping out so he can kill the monster that robbed him of his mother, Spike beats him nearly senseless and bites him – but lets him live. He tells Buffy that he "gave him a pass" because he killed Robin's mother – and even more, perhaps, because Robin helped him rediscover his own mother's love.

Doing the Slayer: When Spike falls for Buffy, he's happy at first just to share sack time with her. After a while, her hatred for him and for herself gets to him, and he resolves to make himself worthy of her love. His trial to win back his soul makes him more than a little crazy for a while, but he ends up being among the sanest of the Scoobies. Who'd have thought the happiest night of his life would be spent just watching Buffy sleep in his arms?

True Champion: When Angel brings Buffy a powerful amulet for the battle against The First, Spike immediately claims it as his own, because he has a soul and superhuman powers. Buffy observes that only a champion may wear it – and hands it to her blond champion.

Letting in the Sunlight: Wearing the amulet, Spike becomes a channel to bring the all-consuming power of the sun into the deeps of the earth. He radiates brilliant beams of light that dust every Ubervamp in the Hellmouth, and consume him in fire and glory as well. ✦

By K. Stoddard Hayes

BEFORE & AFTER

DAWN

played by michelle trachtenberg

"She still thinks I'm Little Miss Nobody. Just her dumb little sister. Boy, is she in for a surprise!" ("**Real Me**")

FORMERLY...

Oh, Grow Up! Dawn doesn't want to be treated as a brat kid sister, she wants to be treated as an adult, or at least Buffy's equal. She thinks Buffy's her mother's favorite, just because she has Slayer powers.

Dumb Teenage Stuff: Dawn keeps a diary full of complaints about her sister, gets a crush on her sister's best friend Xander, and complains about her mother and sister both thinking she needs a babysitter. She also gets captured by Harmony as Slayer bait, and hunted by a giant psychic snake who's looking for the Key.

Who Am I? It's the question that obsesses every teenager in search of herself. Dawn is freaked to discover that she's not a little girl, nor even human, but a mystical Key hidden in the form of Buffy's sister.

Family Dies: As much as she wants to be a grown-up, Dawn's not yet ready to stop being someone's child. Joyce's death rocks her world so much that she performs a dark spell to bring her back from the grave.

CURRENTLY...

Oh, Grow Up! Dawn won't let anyone treat her as a kid sister anymore, not even to protect her. When Buffy has Xander kidnap Dawn and take her safely away from the war with The First Evil, Dawn zaps Xander, un-kidnaps herself, and gives Buffy a swift kick as payback.

Dumb Teenage Stuff: Still feeling the deaths of Buffy and Joyce, Dawn tries to get attention from the Scoobies by doing some normal troubled kid stuff, like shoplifting, and some not-so-normal stuff, like unwittingly creating a spell to hold everyone in the house with her.

Who Am I? Dawn's excited to learn that she may be a Potential Slayer – now she'll really be able to share Buffy's life. Of course, there's a down side, since The First Evil is trying to kill all the Potentials…

Family Ties: Dawn may be old enough to stand beside Buffy as an equal, but that doesn't mean she wants to be alone. When the last bus leaves Sunnydale without her sister, Dawn watches out the back window to make sure that Buffy has escaped the apocalyse, and welcomes her back with the world's best sister hug. ✚

By K. Stoddard Hayes

FAITH

played by eliza dushku

"It didn't have to be this way, but you made your choice. I know you had a tough life, I know that some people think you had a lotta bad breaks. Well, boo hoo! Poor you! You had a lot more in your life than some people. You had friends like Buffy. Now you have no one. You were a Slayer, and now you're no one. You're just a big, selfish, worthless waste." (**Willow to Faith, "Choices"**)

FORMERLY...

Rogue Slayer: Faith is the wild child of Slayerdom, convinced that the life of the Slayer is simple: take what you want, when you want it, because your power makes you superior. Her tough outside is armor for a girl who's never gotten over seeing her Watcher brutally murdered, and who hurts others to hide from the hurt inside.

Party Animal: Faith loves to have a good time, whether she's beating vampire butt, or partying at the Bronze. She'll happily take a tumble with any hot guy – whether or not he's someone else's boyfriend, like Xander or Riley.

Trust Me: After seeing her Watcher murdered, Faith refuses to trust anyone except herself. And that gets her nowhere except in a cage or in a coma.

CURRENTLY...

Reformed Slayer: An Angel-style redemption and two years in prison turn Faith into a strong, centered and fearless woman who knows the difference between right and wrong. But a little bit of that frightened girl is still inside. When it's time to take on the leadership of the Potentials, she wonders how Buffy managed.

Party Animal: Faith still loves a good time, like partying at the Bronze, or beating on a bunch of cops-gone-Hellmouth. And she still loves to take a tumble with a hot guy like Robin Wood – but maybe she'll make sure he's no one else's boyfriend this time.

Trust Me: Working as part of a team means Faith has to rely on others, and be reliable herself. And this time, she's got it down; she comes through for Angel and she comes through for Buffy. ✤

By K. Stoddard Hayes

BEFORE & AFTER — ANYA

played by emma caulfield

FORMERLY...

"For a thousand years I wielded the powers of the Wish. I brought ruin to the heads of unfaithful men. I brought forth destruction and chaos for the pleasure of the lower beings. I was feared and worshipped across the mortal globe. And now I'm stuck at Sunnydale High. Mortal. Child. And I'm flunking math... Do you have any idea how boring twelfth graders are?" ("**Doppelgangland**")

Demon to Human: Anyanka's vengeance magic is strong enough to alter the world when Cordelia wishes Buffy had never come to Sunnydale. However, Giles destroys her amulet to break her spell. One smash, and she's an ordinary human girl, with no power to change anything except her clothes.

Material Girl: After being an immortal demon for 1000 years, becoming an ordinary mortal who will grow old and die is pretty scary. Anya compensates by going after the perks of mortal life – especially money, the best hedge against old age.

Mind Your Manners: Demons don't have any. So Anya, as a human, has to learn everything about how to behave – and especially about how to keep her mouth shut, instead of always saying the first thoughtless, tactless or downright rude thing that comes into her head, whether that's pointing out that someone else is selfish because they won't let her have her way, or describing her sex life with Xander to the entire Scooby Gang.

Free Love: Despite her love of money and other goods, Anya thinks that sex is the best thing about being human. Her obsession hits a high when Xander is split in two by a demon spell, and Anya wants to take both boys home so she can have sex with them both. "It's not as if it would be cheating," she pouts.

Unlikely Pairing: Anya seems a very unlikely choice for Xander – though it's possible her famous tact reminds him a bit of Cordy! What Anya sees in Xander at first is obvious, especially when she makes it crystal clear by ordering him to have sex with her so she can get over him. Since his betrayal of Cordelia is the cause of Anyanka's fall, maybe he's the perfect partner for a former vengeance demon, after all.

Bunnies: She hates them – fluffy, floppy, wiggly noses. The scariest Halloween costume in the world is a giant bunny suit.

CURRENTLY...

"I just realized how amazingly screwed up [humans] are. I mean really, really screwed up in a monumental fashion... And yet here's the thing. When it's something that really matters, they fight. They're lame morons for fighting, but they do. They never – never quit. So I guess I will keep fighting too." ("**End of Days**")

Human to Demon: When Anya gets her demon powers back, she becomes a very bad girl, causing all kinds of nasty, crawly chaos in her rage to get vengeance on Xander, or any other man who's unlucky enough to cross her path. Lucky for Xander she can't get any of his friends to wish something bad would happen to him.

Material Girl: Working for Giles at The Magic Box, Anya finds her true calling in taking care of the cash register, counting money, and collecting money from customers (and then telling them to leave). She comes into her own when Giles returns to England, leaving her in charge of the shop – which she probably runs better than he did.

Mind Your Manners: Anya has finally learned not to say the first thing that comes into her head about her sex life or her opinion of someone. But she still has her inimitable gift for verbally flattening people when necessary, especially when she tells Buffy that she has no right to her leadership, because her Slayer talents were not earned, just handed to her.

Free Love: Still burning from Xander's abandonment at their wedding, Anya takes a tumble with Spike, which does not improve the Xander situation in the least. But somehow, Anya and Xander still can't keep their hands off each other. They keep getting back in the sack, to have a farewell encounter.

Unlikely Pairing: Anya and Andrew. Did anyone see that coming? All you have to do is watch them teaming up to give a nerdy briefing to the Potentials, or having a wheelchair fight, to know that they're a perfect match in self-centered obliviousness, slowly struggling toward maturity.

Bunnies: Some things never change. Bunnies are still her biggest nightmare. But they have their uses. When Andrew mentions bunnies, Anya's pre-battle jitters disappear, as she thinks about chopping bunnies to bits. ✝

By K. Stoddard Hayes

BEFORE & AFTER

ANGEL

played by David Boreanaz

Buffy: "Angel? I can just see him in a relationship. 'Hi, honey, you're in grave danger. I'll see you next month.'"
Willow: "He's not around much, it's true."
Buffy: "When he is around, it's like the lights dim everywhere else." ("Angel")

FORMERLY...

Soul Man: After living an aimless century, Angel learns he is to help the Slayer. One look at Buffy, and he's totally committed to the job.

Dear Boy: Angel lived for so long as Darla's lover that even with a soul and a conscience, he's still a little under her spell. He can barely bring himself to stake her, even when her back is turned.

Touched by an Angelus: Angel lives every day in guilt for Angelus' crimes, and fear that Angelus might come back again. To end that misery, he's ready to dust himself in a winter sunrise – but the Powers That Be send a miraculous snowfall to save the life of their champion.

True Happiness: Angel tries to keep his distance from Buffy because he's afraid a romance between a vampire and the Slayer would never work out. One night in her arms proves that he's horribly right.

CURRENTLY...

Soul Man: A prophecy promises that the vampire with a soul will become human again. Now Angel just has to keep his soul, and his integrity, as the new boss of the largest and nastiest supernatural corporate office in LA.

Dear Boy: When Darla returns as a human, Angel will do anything to save her, and anything to stop her from turning vamp again. When she brings his child into the world, he protects her until his love, and his child's soul, finally bring Darla's salvation and closure for Angel.

Touched by an Angelus: Angel hates Angelus and respects his power, but he's no longer terrified of him. When he needs Angelus to defeat The Beast, he summons his evil alter-ego, whips his butt in an out-of-body encounter, then binds him back into limbo – with help from Faith and Willow. Is this the end of the curse?

True Happiness: Angel broke up with Buffy because of the 'perfect happiness' curse, and he missed his chance with Cordelia. When Buffy tells him she may not be ready for someone in her life for a long time, he says, "I'm not getting any older." He can wait. ✚

By K. Stoddard Hayes

CORDELIA— CHASE

played by charisma carpenter

Giles: "Why should someone want to harm Cordelia?"
Willow: "Maybe because they met her?" ("**The Witch**")

FORMERLY...

Queen and Goddess: Cordelia rules Sunnydale High – deciding who's hot, who's nerdy, and who's a hopeless fashion dinosaur. She carries off her tyranny with the absolute conviction of her divine right to be social queen. Well, at least until she falls in with a certain uncool Vampire Slayer and learns the world is full of critters who are a lot scarier than she is.

Money's No Object: And why should it be? Cordelia's family is the wealthiest in Sunnydale – until the IRS catches up with her parents. Then she has to work in a dress store to afford a prom dress worthy of her.

Fashion Goddess: No one knows clothes better than Cordelia; a mall full of high end fashion stores is her paradise, and she's got more shoes than Imelda Marcos.

For Love and Money: The Queen of Sunnydale High insists on the best when it comes to boyfriends – so why does she keep jumping in closets with uncool poor boy Xander?

CURRENTLY...

Queen, Goddess, Higher Being: Cordelia's power to win friends and influence people in high school is nothing to the power of a goddess or a Higher Being, translated to a different plane of existence.

Money's No Object: After countless supernatural visions of suffering and years of fighting against the darkness, Cordelia has learned to value much more than material goods. Well, except for little things like Angel buying her forgiveness with a shopping spree...

Fashion Goddess: Cordy can still go toe-to-toe with Lilah on who's more hip in essentials like shoes. But if her personal taste hasn't slipped under the influence of pregnancy, what's that black lacy pseudo-Goth outfit she's wearing when she makes her big announcement to Angel and the gang?

For Love and Sonny: Becoming a Higher Being messes up Cordy's chance for love with Angel. Coming back from the Higher Plane messes up Cordy. She jumps in bed with the kid who was her surrogate son only a few months before: Connor.. ✦

By K. Stoddard Hayes

BEFORE AFTER

RILEY — FINN

played by marc blucas

"Buffy's like nobody else in the world. Half of me is just on fire, going crazy if I'm not touching her. The other half is so still and peaceful, just perfectly content, just knows, this is the one. But she doesn't love me." (**"The Replacement"**)

FORMERLY...

Schoolboy Soldier: Professor Walsh's teaching assistant is also her favorite soldier boy, a commando in The Initiative.

Sparring Partners: Riley's immediately drawn to Buffy, and when he finds out she's the Slayer, things really heat up.

CURRENTLY...

Once a Soldier... When the Initiative starts experimenting on Oz, Riley goes AWOL and helps the Scoobies. When the military calls on him again, he rejoins them, leaving Buffy behind.

Sparring Partners: Riley always knew Buffy hadn't truly let him into her heart. Now he's busting demons with his beautiful, kickass wife. She may not be a Slayer, but at least she's all his.

OZ

played by seth green

"Well, I like you. You're nice and you're funny. And you don't smoke. Yeah, okay, werewolf, but that's not all the time. I mean, three days out of the month I'm not much fun to be around either." (**Willow to Oz, "Phases"**)

FORMERLY...

Chillin' Dude: Oz is so laidback that he takes everything in his stride, including failing to graduate, and discovering that Sunnydale is heavily populated with vampires and demons. A few things excite him: playing the guitar, animal crackers, and Willow – especially in her hot Halloween costume.

Werewolf Unaware: Oz never knew why he always seemed to sleep through a full moon – until his friends discover that he's not sleeping under the moon, he's howling at it.

CURRENTLY...

Chill Out, Dude: After many months of struggle to control his wolfish days, Oz meets a girl werewolf who wants him to seize the night and explore the joys of wolfishness. Romping with her proves too much excitement for him and for Willow.

Werewolf Aware: Oz hits the road, going as far as Tibet to learn meditation and other spiritual mojo that will help him keep his hairy side in check. This works fine until he sniffs out the discovery that Willow's in a relationship with Tara.

TARA MACLAY

played by Amber Benson

"I lived my life in shadow, never the sun on my face. It didn't seem so sad, though. I figured that was my place. Now I'm bathed in light… It's magic I can tell, how you set me free, brought me out so easily. I'm under your spell, nothing I can do, you just took my soul with you…" (**"Once More, With Feeling"**)

FORMERLY…

True Witch: When Willow goes looking for real witchcraft, she finds Tara – or Tara finds her. The quiet one is an adept who recognizes Willow's potential and begins teaching her the ways of witchcraft.

Unhappy Family: Tara believes she's destined to become a demon and live in subjection to the men of the family. Then Buffy declares that Tara's one of her own, and Spike gets a headache to prove that she's no demon.

CURRENTLY…

True Witch: Willow may be more powerful, but Tara knows the ways of magic far better, and does her best to keep Willow on the straight path. Willow's magic power trip makes Tara break off their relationship.

Happy Family: Once an outsider, Tara is now so much part of the Scooby Gang that she lives in Buffy's house with Willow, helps to mother Dawn, and even gets mistaken by Glory for the Key in Buffy's care.

JOYCE SUMMERS

played by Kristine Sutherland

"Principal Snyder said you were a troublemaker… and I could care less. I have a daughter who can take care of herself, who's brave and resourceful and thinks of others in a crisis. No matter who you hang out with or what dumb teenage stuff you think you need to do, I'm going to sleep better knowing all that." (**"School Hard"**)

FORMERLY…

Anxious Mom: Joyce will do anything to protect Buffy from flunking out of school, and from becoming a juvenile delinquent.

A Life of Her Own: Sometimes Joyce does stuff that reminds her daughter she's more than a mom. Stuff like dating an abusive robot boyfriend, or reverting to teenager and having sex on the hood of a car – with Giles.

CURRENTLY…

Anxious Mom Times Two: With a brain tumor and a new mystical younger daughter, Joyce doesn't worry any more about whether Buffy is a juvenile delinquent or the Slayer; she just worries about whether Buffy can grow up to fill her shoes and take care of Dawn

A Death of Her Own: Joyce develops a brain tumor, and goes on a lonely journey that not even Buffy, can share with her. Her death takes apart the Scoobies' safe haven in the non-supernatural world. ✚

By K. Stoddard Hayes

By Paul Simpson

REVENGING ANGEL

Emma Caulfield's been a busy lady since she finished *Buffy the Vampire Slayer*. Not only has she been producing and starring in her own film, *Bandwagon*, she's also been attending conventions and even found time to guest-star in an episode of the drama show, *Monk*. *Buffy Magazine* talks to the popular actress to find out about life after *Buffy*, her hopes for the future, her feelings on Anya's gruesome death, and dancing in her underwear…

Emma Caulfield has obviously been having a great deal of fun. For two days she has been entertaining the fans at the Starfury Fusion event in the UK, working alongside (and quite often scoring points off of) her on-screen lover Nicholas Brendon, as well as going out onstage on her own and being extremely open and honest about her feelings about working on *Buffy the Vampire Slayer*. She's so dedicated to giving the fans the maximum pleasure that she decides not to go back to the hotel a little further out of town where the guests are staying at lunchtime on the final day, but instead remains at the convention so that everyone can have a chance at getting the autograph that they've been waiting so patiently for. It even means that she almost misses a chance at having some lunch, although the eagle-eyed staff of the convention quickly ensure that something is ordered for her as she sits to chat with *Buffy Magazine*.

It doesn't seem that long ago that she last graced our pages, but that was to talk more about her new movie, *Bandwagon*. Still, she's more than happy to cast her mind back to the Santa Monica stages where *Buffy* was filmed. "You know, I don't think I knew that I could be funny," she comments wistfully. "That really was a gift."

Given how much of the series' humor has derived from the centuries-old vengeance demon's slightly askew view of the late 20th and early 21st Century, it's something of a surprise to hear Emma say that. "I always knew that comedy would be the hardest thing that I would attempt to do, and it really is," she explains. "It's incredibly difficult. It's so challenging to find the right timing, and the right balance between being believable and being ridiculous."

There's probably not a *Buffy* fan out there who wouldn't agree that Emma was able to find that fine line. "Anya was that just in the character herself, so to be able to play that for almost five years was a gift," Emma says. "I was really lucky, it spoiled me, actually. I love doing comedy, and so much out there just pales in comparison to the writing that I was able to enjoy, and do, and perform, while I was on *Buffy*."

That's something that's been said by so many of the cast. "There was such a high standard of excellence on that show," Emma agrees. "I'm just grateful that I was able to be a part of that for as much as I was."

With certain acting parts, an actor can bring something of their own personality to the role. Since Emma hasn't ever been a scary vengeance demon (or at least, not that she can recall), all she could bring were some of Anya's attitudes. "I'm trying to curb this, and be

better with it, but I have had a tendency in my life to be kind of tactless," Emma admits. "In the sense that I can be brutally honest when it's inappropriate to be so, and that can come off as really rude and uncaring."

Certainly, there were times when the Scooby Gang wondered where Anya was coming from, and Emma has had the same experience. "I always have the best of intentions," she maintains, "like Anya does. I don't think she set out to make anybody angry or upset, but she probably did. That's really probably the only element of myself in her. The rest of her is just the creation of great writers."

Emma never felt the urge to press the writers to take Anya in any particular direction. "I never really had to ask for anything to be added," she says. "They wrote her so well, and the evolution of that character was so beautiful and so intricate that I never really had to want for anything. I got to do everything, I really did, and I was very blessed.

"I felt really comfortable with her the moment I read the character," she continues. "I just got her straight away. I don't know why, but I just got her. And then I was just fortunate that they liked me enough to keep bringing me back."

That instant understanding of a character is not something that's

{ "[Anya's death] was so abrupt and so sad. But I think that it made the whole journey that much more poignant that she did die that way. She didn't get a big maudlin send-off, it was just quick and to the point – very Anya in that respect." }

Photo: Albert Ortega

happened regularly to Emma during her acting career. "You know what? It happens very rarely," she notes, "but when it does, it usually ends up being this great experience. You read a lot of different things, and you think, 'Okay, I can do this, maybe I can do that... I can push myself to do that', but it's really rare when you hear the character in your head and go 'Okay, yeah, I got her'."

In fact, Emma feels that she knew the character so well she could probably predict what Anya would do in any given situation. "But there was really very little guess-work to do with Anya because she was just so well written," she adds. "It makes a huge difference when the writers give you a lot to work with. It takes out a lot of the labor."

Emma admits that the arrival of the romance between Xander Harris and Anya came as much of a shock to her as it did, initially at least, to the audience. "I think they tried it out to see if Nick and I had any chemistry, and we did," she recalls. "It just naturally progressed. Working with Nick was great. He's so funny and so sweet. He was a great partner to have for the years I was there."

For many fans, the musical episode, "Once More, With Feeling," was one of the high spots of the show's later seasons, and in particular, the wonderful duet between Xander and Anya, complete with dance routines and razor sharp repartee. "I had a great time doing that," she says with a large grin. "Luckily I had done a lot of musical theater in high school, so I was rusty, but it was a lot of fun to tap back into that side of myself which had been put on a shelf for a while."

Of all the routines she had within that episode, the one she found most challenging was "dancing in heels on the carpet. That was very difficult," she explains, "because in all of the rehearsals that we had, I never had the heels, and we always danced on a hardwood floor. That was a sudden switch... and in my underwear too, which was fun. It's just a charming song – it's such a throwback to the old Busby Berkeley style of musicals."

Emma is in awe of Buffy creator Joss Whedon's talents. "I don't think there's anything he can't do... he's so talented," she notes. "He was hugely influenced by Stephen Sondheim for that number."

When Emma auditioned for the part of Anya, she wasn't given a whole script, just some 'sides' – pages with the relevant scenes on

them from the episode. "I went in and met Joss, and I think it came down to 'Can you start work tomorrow?'" she recalls. "It was a nice entry back into the business, because I had taken such a long time off."

But now, after the excellent writing that she worked with on the show, Emma is fussy about what she does, and has certain criteria when she looks at a script. "Probably the most important thing I think is, 'Can I have fun doing it?'" she says. "The fun factor has to be pretty high at this point in time because Anya was so much fun. Like I said earlier, it's hard to find something good. There are so many great writers out there, but it seems so odd that so many of the projects that are given the green light just aren't that original. It's unfortunate. It's tricky – but there is good work out there, and there are good scripts. It's a very competitive business, and everybody has their time. If you lose 10 jobs, you wind

up getting the 11th, and at this point, it's kind of a game of odds." It's perhaps a little surprising then, given how pleased she was with the writing on the show, that Emma had already made up her mind that Season Seven of Buffy would be her last, even before Mutant Enemy announced that the series would draw to a close that year. "My contract was up anyway," she says pragmatically, "so it was just time. I feel like that. If you set out do something, and then your job's done, then your job is done, and there's a reason for it. I would have stayed longer had my contract dictated me to do so, but it was just time. I'd done everything I could with Anya, and it was just nice to go out on top before things started to become redundant. I think that Anya's journey had been complete at that point, and to take her on after that... I don't know if it would have worked or not."

{ "I'd done everything I could with Anya, and it was just nice to go out on top before things started to become redundant. I think that Anya's journey had been complete at that point." }

Emma was aware that Anya was destined to die in the season finale long before she read it in the script for "Chosen." "I knew that upset a lot of people," she adds, "but I think it was very poetic for her to have died. I liked that she died doing good, she kind of really had come into her own."

She agrees that one of the Scooby Gang needed to die to make the point that this was a major battle, and Anya's death hammered the point home. "I liked how they did it," she says. "It was so abrupt and so sad. But I think that it made the whole journey that much more poignant that she did die that way. She didn't get a big maudlin send-off, it was just quick and to the point – very Anya in that respect."

After five years of constant work on Buffy, and the hours that are required to make a television series for 39 weeks of the year, Emma isn't particularly looking for another role in a long-running series. "I haven't really been wanting to – at least not an hour-long show," she says. "If there was a

great half-hour show, that could be fun. I'd like to get back in front of a live audience for a comedy, and tap into my theater days. That could be a lot of fun, but I've had a really good time going behind the camera. Although I was in Bandwagon, I was also a producer on it, and helped to create it. I've been writing as well, so just going around that side of the business has been that much more interesting. You have far more control when you're on that side of the camera, as opposed to being an actor. There are very few actors who have a say in how anything goes down, and it's unfortunate."

She'd also love an opportunity to go back to the theater. "I don't know when – but at some point," she says. "Maybe look for a good musical comedy – that would be fun. Maybe a Neil Simon play, or some sort of absurd comedy."

Emma's food arrives, and she brings the interview to a close with a smile. "I was just so lucky," she says. "I had a great time on Buffy. I had an amazing character to play; she was just ridiculous, fun, and smart!" ✦

CAULFIELD'S CREDITS

If you're an Anya fan, why not check out some of Emma's other projects?

Film Credits

Bandwagon (2004) – as herself

I Want to Marry Ryan Banks (2004) – Charlie

Darkness Falls (2003) – Caitlin Greene

TV Credits

Monk (2004), Meredith Preminger in "Mr. Monk and the Girl Who Cried Wolf"

Buffy the Vampire Slayer (1999-2003), Anya

General Hospital (1996-1997), Lorraine Miller

Beverly Hills, 90210 (1995-1996), Susan Keats

Silk Stalkings (1997), Kate Donner in "Guilt By Association"

Weird Science (1995), Phoebe Hale in "What Genie?"

Saved by the Bell: The New Class (1994) Nurse Brady in "Blood Money"

Burke's Law (1994), Beth in "Who Killed the Beauty Queen?"

SHE

CHARISMA CARPENTER SETS

THE RECORD STRAIGHT ON

HER LA STORY, A CLOSE

CALL ON THE SET AND

WHAT'S IN A NAME

S GOT

HARISMA

By MIKE STOKES

William Shakespeare once wrote, "That which we call a rose by any other name would smell as sweet." Exactly why he chose to talk like that, nobody really knows. But after all these years, he still has a point. It's doubtful that the inspiration behind his observation came from watching a medieval prom queen yucking it up with her vampire-slaying friends at the old Globe Theatre centuries ago. Yet if he'd lived long enough to meet Charisma Carpenter, he'd probably look like Yoda – but he'd also be secure in the knowledge that he was right.

Based on her acting career, Carpenter could just as easily have been named Lucky or Charmed (though not Lucky Charms, because that would sound ridiculous). Shortly after moving to Los Angeles and taking the plunge into acting, she landed a starring role on the prime-time US soap opera Malibu Shores, playing snobbish high schooler Ashley Greene. While it wasn't long before Malibu Shores eroded, Carpenter had already landed another role on a new series called Buffy the Vampire Slayer. Fearful of becoming type-cast, she was admittedly reluctant to audition for the role of another snobbish high schooler – especially for a new show with a strange title on an unproven network. But when she found out the series was created by a young hot-shot Hollywood scribe by the name of Joss Whedon, she decided to give it a go.

CORDELIA CARPENTER

Cordelia

Well into her third season as Cordelia Chase at the time of the interview, it'd be easy to say that the rest is history, but Carpenter's story (as well as Cordelia's) is actually just beginning. No longer the quirky new kids, *Buffy* has established a strong TV following. Suddenly Carpenter finds herself leading the way for her friend and fellow *Malibu Shores* alumnus Keri Russell, who stars in the title role of *Felicity*, a new drama previously shown after *Buffy* on US TV.

Much to her delight, the success of *Buffy the Vampire Slayer* has coincided with the evolution and expansion of the character she plays, making Cordelia a much more complex character than the snooty head-cheerleader archetype that has long become a standard in high school-based shows.

On paper, it'd be easy to blur the lines between the actress and her role. In reality, they are simply both strong-willed women who say what's on their minds. The big difference is that while Cordelia has been known to say things before her mind can actually process what she's saying, Carpenter is a little more thoughtful, a little more genuine and surprisingly open.

So what's in a name? Honest or articulate, funny or sharp – any of these attributes would be a suitable name for Carpenter. Still, none would have the same ring or be as fitting as Charisma. On that, even Shakespeare would have to agree.

BUFFY THE MAGAZINE: HOW DID YOUR PARENTS DECIDE ON THE NAME CHARISMA?
CHARISMA CARPENTER: They decided to curse me and give me a really hard time and make my life as miserable as possible. My name was undecided – for three days, I was nameless. They were bickering over it, and my grandma brought them this Avon perfume bottle [called Charisma], and my mom thought the perfume was horrible but she loved the name. Hence, my curse. (laughs)

BTM: WERE SIBLINGS ALSO CURSED?
CC: No, they're very normal – Michael, Troy and John Kenneth.

> I DO HAVE A TENDENCY TO KINDA BLURT SOMETHING OUT AND THEN GO, "HMM...SHOULD I HAVE SAID THAT?"

BTM: YOUR PARENTS MUST HAVE HAD A GOOD FEELING ABOUT YOU, BECAUSE THAT'S REALLY GOING OUT ON A LIMB. THEY COULD HAVE NAMED YOU HAZEL AND TAKEN THE PRESSURE OFF.
CC: Yeah. I grew out of the 'I hate myself' phase when I was thirteen and decided I could deal with Charisma.

BTM: ARE YOU RELATED TO THE CARPENTERS SINGING DUO?
CC: No. (laughs)

BTM: HOW ABOUT JOHN CARPENTER, THE DIRECTOR?
CC: No.

BTM: HAVE YOU EVER BUILT ANYTHING?
CC: That's a very clever question. I appreciate that.

BTM: IF YOU THROW A HUNDRED AT THE WALL, ONE'S BOUND TO STICK.
CC: I tried with cards to build a house once. Does that count?

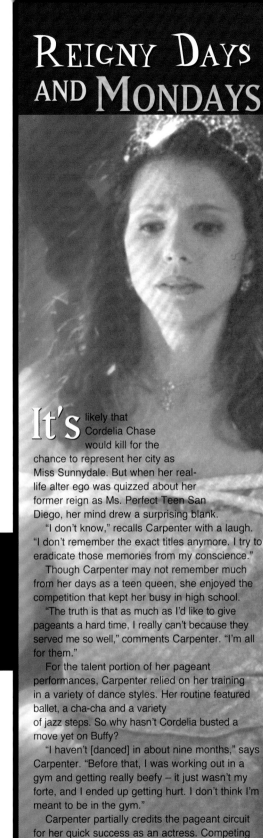

REIGNY DAYS AND MONDAYS

It's likely that Cordelia Chase would kill for the chance to represent her city as Miss Sunnydale. But when her real-life alter ego was quizzed about her former reign as Ms. Perfect Teen San Diego, her mind drew a surprising blank.

"I don't know," recalls Carpenter with a laugh. "I don't remember the exact titles anymore. I try to eradicate those memories from my conscience."

Though Carpenter may not remember much from her days as a teen queen, she enjoyed the competition that kept her busy in high school.

"The truth is that as much as I'd like to give pageants a hard time, I really can't because they served me so well," comments Carpenter. "I'm all for them."

For the talent portion of her pageant performances, Carpenter relied on her training in a variety of dance styles. Her routine featured ballet, a cha-cha and a variety of jazz steps. So why hasn't Cordelia busted a move yet on Buffy?

"I haven't [danced] in about nine months," says Carpenter. "Before that, I was working out in a gym and getting really beefy – it just wasn't my forte, and I ended up getting hurt. I don't think I'm meant to be in the gym."

Carpenter partially credits the pageant circuit for her quick success as an actress. Competing prepared her for the competitive nature of the business and has helped her stay cool under pressure.

"The whole system, whether you won or lost, is just subjective opinion," she says. "It's just a very few people deciding that you're 'it.' I tend to not take it too seriously because of that. But it was good, and it served me in the regard of competition and getting familiar with that concept. It was a really great thing."

Cordelia's Finest Hours

Welcome to the Hellmouth, season 1, episode 1
Intrigued by tales of the Los Angeles shopping scene, Cordelia is the first to welcome Buffy Summers to Sunnydale. When she learns there's more to the new girl than meets the eye – and nearly gets staked – she is also the first to turn on her.

Witch, season 1, episode 3
As a witch casts spells on the cheerleading squad, a teacher's death spurs a prime example of Cordie's compassion: "I'm not saying that we should kill a teacher every day just so I can lose weight, but when tragedy strikes, we have to look on the bright side." Enough said. Cordelia's all heart.

Nightmares, season 1, episode 10
As everyone's worst fears become reality, Cordelia can't help dressing like a nerd, joining the chess club or having a bad hair day.

Invisible Girl, season 1, episode 11
Cordie seems jinxed as those close to her become targets for a ghost with a grudge. This episode is also the first time Cordelia shows signs of being human when she offers heartfelt gratitude to Buffy, but peer pressure quickly reclaims her.

When She was Bad, season 2, episode 1
Cordelia confronts Buffy about her nasty 'tude and officially joins "the Scooby gang" when she's attacked by vampires and learns the secret.

Some Assembly Required, season 2, episode 2
While cheering at a football game, Cordelia is abducted by a young Frankenstein who has designs on amputating her head and attaching it to a patchwork body for a life of zombie love. When the ordeal is over, Cordelia goes right back to cheerleading.

Reptile Boy, season 2, episode 5
Cordelia's quest for permanent prosperity continues as she convinces Buffy to accompany her to a frat party, where they awaken shackled in the basement as sacrifices to the reptile monster Machida.

What's My Line (part two), season 2, episode 10
Hiding from a man made of worms, Cordelia and Xander forever change the course of history when they put aside their hatred and share their first kiss.

Innocence, season 2, episode 14
Under pressure from her cool friends, Cordelia dumps Xander on Valentine's Day. He then becomes every woman's object of desire – except Cordelia.

Band Candy, season 3, episode 6
Is it the beginning of the end for Cordie and Xander? Cordelia keeps Willow and Xander on edge while considering an age limit on lycra pants.

BTM: Nope.
CC: I've refinished furniture before.

BTM: That counts – that's a carpenter-like skill.
CC: [Silent satisfaction]

BTM: Is it coincidence that you share the same initials as Cordelia Chase?
CC: Ooooh – you'd have to ask Joss. But his wife did tell me that he was like, "God – her name had to be Charisma! How am I gonna top that?" Then he came up with Cordelia. Actually, his wife helped him with it because she went to college with this person named Cordelia. Now I'm Cordelia. Chase – I don't know where that came from, but I like it.

BTM: How much of Cordelia's personality is in you?
CC: I don't know how much is in me, but I think there must be some dwelling in there for me to be able to perform it. I don't know. I think I have a tendency to speak the truth. No matter how people might prefer it to be sugarcoated, I do have a tendency to just kinda blurt something out and then go, "Hmm... should I have said that?" (laughs) I think that's the only difference between us – in me there's a conscience going "I'm sorry" and Cordelia would just be like, "There ya have it. Deal with it."

BTM: Would the two of you have been friends in high school?
CC: I think she's becoming a little more complicated. The scary thing about Cordelia is that she's like a Jekyll and Hyde; she can be really heroic and charming, and then she can be really nasty. I'm more compelled to be drawn in by that, so I probably would have been friends with her. Maybe I could have pointed those flaws out to her and done some work on her like, "Do you have to be such a s— all the time?" (laughs) I might have, I don't know. Maybe I would have flung her around a little bit.

BTM: Are you glad that Cordelia's attitude has mellowed a little bit?
CC: We were actually just talking about that. I love it because she gets more screen time. (laughs)

BTM: How do you like getting recognised when you go out?
CC: I'm really happy for it. I'm glad people aren't scared off by my obnoxious behaviour on the show.

BTM: Was it fun for you to meet fans at the San Diego Comic Convention in August 1998.
CC: I was really impressed with the appreciation for Joss. Usually in a TV show, no one really cares or knows personal details about the writer and the creator. I guess when it's a quality show, people want to know the genius behind it, and I thought that was the ultimate compliment to our show – they were very intrigued by him – picking his brain, and wanting to know more about the future and how he gets his ideas and was he married. (laughs) I thought that was just a really impressive thing. Go Joss!

BTM: Are you a good driver?
CC: (laughs) Yeah. I used to be an even better one back when I drove a little car; it could weave in and out of traffic. Now I have a big truck, so I tend to forget the size of the car – now it's like, "I'm comin' over! Make room!" (laughs) My boyfriend either drives like a grandpa or he'll ride people's butts. He was like, "I can't believe how much you talk about my driving; you're not that good." But I think I am. I don't freak out; if there's an accident about to happen, I think I'm agile enough to think clearly and avoid it.

BTM: When did you start acting?
CC: I moved here in '92 – the day of the riots – and I began acting in '93. I started acting class in '93, and I actually got an agent a year after that, in '94, so I've been acting for about three or four years now.

BTM: Wait a minute. You moved to LA the day of the riots? What kept you from turning around and going back home?
CC: I was so in love and so naive, there was no turning back. My father called me and said, "Get outta there!" I told him that even if I wanted to, I couldn't – it was Kuwait. I stood on the top of my building and did a 360 turn, and there were fires everywhere. It was reminiscent of what I had seen on CNN about Kuwait. You couldn't get out, because the smoke was so thick that you couldn't take off; the airport was closed. There were two people on the freeway that night – there was a curfew on how late you could leave town, and no one was supposed to be out, but they were breaking curfew – there was a television camera on these two cars via

CHARISMA
Cordelia
AS CORDELIA

helicopter, and they ended up crashing into each other. They were the only two people on the freeway and they crashed – I thought that was sorta funny.

BTM: YOU'VE FOUND A LOT OF SUCCESS IN A SHORT TIME.
CC: Yeah, it came really fast and really early on, which I'm so grateful for. God didn't make me starve too long. There's no telling, though – He might catch up with me later. (laughs)

BTM: DESCRIBE THE SCENE WHEN YOU GOT THE PART ON *BUFFY*.
CC: It's a cute story. I was on *Malibu Shores* at the time. It was around five or six o'clock, it was raining and we were running late, so I didn't know if I was going to make the screen test. I ran over to wardrobe and borrowed a cute outfit, because I didn't have time to go home, and I asked transportation the best route to Burbank, because traffic was going to be bad, and I was coming from really far away. I ended up taking a big fat unnecessary circle and wound up downtown sitting on pins and needles in traffic. Then I get this 9-1-1 page from my agent, so I pull over at a 7-Eleven and answer the page, and she's like, "They're gonna leave – you have to get there." I'm telling her that they *better* wait, because I just sat through an hour and a half of the gnarliest traffic of my life. [I said to] order pizza or something, because they're gonna meet me *tonight*.

BTM: IT TURNED OUT ALRIGHT.
CC: I went in and they were all very excited and antsy to meet me. I read and they were laughing in all the right places, so I got the part. I was very happy.

> I'M GLAD PEOPLE AREN'T SCARED BY MY OBNOXIOUS BEHAVIOUR ON THE SHOW.

BTM: WHAT DID *MALIBU SHORES* THINK WHEN YOU LEFT TO AUDITION FOR A DIFFERENT SHOW?
CC: I think they thought I was smart (laughs), because *Malibu Shores* was getting cancelled.

BTM: YOU ALREADY KNEW THAT?
CC: No, my agent did, and I was very happy for that, but I almost didn't audition [for *Buffy*], because my *Malibu Shores* character, Ashley, and Cordelia were too much alike. I was concerned about being typecast, and it was on the WB, which at the time, I wasn't sure was a good thing. My [former] agent kept telling me all these negative things about it, almost talking me out of it. Then I get a call from her mentor telling me who all these people are. It was a completely different take on things. I just thank God that I listened to her.

BTM: HAVE YOU BEEN GETTING ASKED TO READ FOR A LOT OF MOVIES SINCE *BUFFY* TOOK OFF?
CC: Yeah, but they're usually Cordelia-oriented, so I stay away.
BTM: IS THAT FRUSTRATING?
CC: Yes. Maybe that'll cost me a movie career, who knows. My old agent and manager were always hounding me about that – I have new ones now. We didn't have the same vision, so I had to adjust and find someone who was on the same page as me.

BTM: THEY WANTED YOU TO KEEP DOING THE SAME KIND OF ROLES?
CC: They were like, "Just do a movie, just do a movie," and I don't need to do a movie that bad. I'd rather do something small, find a bit part in a great movie or something Sundance. Something meaningful and truthful and a departure from what I'm doing now, because I have a whole year to do that.

BTM: SO YOU'RE WILLING TO WAIT FOR SOMETHING YOU REALLY LIKE BEFORE HITTING THE BIG SCREEN?
CC: Yeah. I'm not in a hurry yet. Right now, I'm able to keep the wolves at bay.

BTM: AS AN ACTOR, DO YOU FEEL ANY COMPETITION WITH THE REST OF THE CAST AS MORE AND MORE MOVIE PARTS KEEP COMING THEIR WAY?
CC: Wouldn't *that* be juicy! If I said, "Yeah, it really *pisses me off*" and just went all Sam Kinison on you? Not at all. I think it's terrific and it brings more viewers to the show. The more viewers we have, the longer the show stays on and the longer I have a job.

BTM: DO YOU HAVE A FAVOURITE CORDELIA LINE OF DIALOGUE?
CC: There's one where Giles goes, "Do you have any tact?" because I said something

CHARISMA CARPENTER

Vital Signs

BIRTHDAY
23 July in Las Vegas, Nevada

FOOD
"Anything Mexican – breakfast, lunch and dinner."

TV SHOW
Buffy the Vampire Slayer, Felicity

MOVIES
Wings of the Dove

SONG
The Rolling Stones' "Sympathy for the Devil"

COLOUR
Yellow

BOOK
The Notebook by Nicholas Sparks

SPORT
Rock-climbing

FAVOURITE

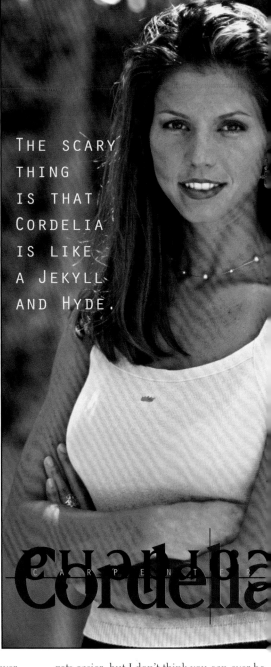

THE SCARY THING IS THAT CORDELIA IS LIKE A JEKYLL AND HYDE.

Cordelia

---

quick to point out what's wrong with everyone else, but I'm also able to talk about what's wrong with me.

BTM: IS IT ALSO TRUE THAT YOU'RE KIND OF A THRILL- SEEKER? YOU SKYDIVE?
CC: Yeah.

BTM: HOW DOES JOSS WHEDON FEEL ABOUT THAT?
CC: Well, I don't do it while I'm on the show. I did go rock-climbing, but I haven't heard anything from him about it. I did want to get a motorcycle; Alyson [Hannigan] and I wanted to go together and get motorcycle licences so that we could drive one, but in all reality, it's not the smartest thing. Traffic is so bad, and it's not so much you as a driver or how skilled you are, but how lame other people are. I'm not interested in cracking my melon.

BTM: IT CAN BE A DANGEROUS WORLD OUT THERE.
CC: I had an accident on the set where I basically broke my fall on the bridge of my nose on a dresser. I had this really small thing to do, and I ended up tripping over these antlers and falling on my face into this dresser. I got a black eye, and they didn't know if I had broken my nose. It was a really great reality check; life is fragile, and if I mess up my face, I'm not gonna have a job. So I think I'm gonna hold off on the whole motorcycle thing. Then if I have children, I'm really gonna hold off on the motorcycle thing. I think that whole dream may never come to fruition.

BTM: WHEN YOU AND NICHOLAS BRENDON DO HAVE ROMANTIC SCENES, HOW DO YOU DEAL WITH THE TENSION?
CC: He's a bigger nervous wreck than I am. That's been my experience. But then after a couple takes, we relax. As the years go on it

really rude to Buffy when she was at the hospital. It was in the fifth episode of the second season called "Killed by Death." And I said, "Tact means just not saying true stuff," or something like that. I thought that was really funny because she's not going to sacrifice the truth to sugarcoat it or be politically correct.

BTM: DO YOU GET TIRED OF POLITICAL CORRECTNESS?
CC: I think there's room for it. There are moments when you need it, but it would be nice if people were more truthful in general. Say you give some guy your phone number, but have remorse about it later. It'd be great if you could just tell him that it's not anything personal – I don't even know you well enough for it to be personal – but I'm not in that space right now. Instead, we just talk and later groan about it, or if he calls again, you're like, "I'm not home." That's just a random example of where it would be so much better to just be honest. If people were honest with themselves, there'd be so much more peace in the world. You'd just acknowledge that you're a basket case and need help. Maybe that's being really

gets easier, but I don't think you can ever be 100 per cent comfortable kissing someone you're not intimate with or that you don't feel that way about. It is kinda awkward, but then you warm up to it.

BTM: DOES YOUR BOYFRIEND EVER GET JEALOUS OF XANDER?
CC: No, no. Not yet. [laughs] I haven't experienced that.

BTM: IN REAL LIFE, WOULD YOU FALL FOR A GUY LIKE XANDER?
CC: Probably. Nicky [Brendon] is very good looking, and he's very witty and fun to be around. And he's heroic.

BTM: HE IS HEROIC.
CC: Every woman wants a hero. ✢

EPISODE SPOTLIGHT

"Bewitched, Bothered," and Bewildered

First US airdate 10/02/98

First UK airdate 11/07/98

SEASON 2
EPISODES 16

Synopsis

It's Valentine's Day, and Cordelia decides to break up with Xander because she's a laughing stock to her so-called friends. To make matters worse for poor Xander, the whole school seems to know she's dumped him.

Xander blackmails Amy into casting a love spell on Cordelia. But the spell backfires – instead of making Cordelia fall head over heels in love with Xander, everyone *but* Cordy wants to jump the X-man's bones! You name 'em, they have the hots for him: Willow, Amy, Jenny, Drusilla – even Buffy (until she's turned into a rat). Things go from bad to worse when an angry mob of girls battle each other for his affections – even Buffy's mum gets in on the act!

Thankfully, Giles and Amy are able to reverse the spell and Cordelia eventually realises how superficial she's been. She decides she'll date whoever she wants to – no matter how lame they are!

Trivia

- The song playing as Xander walks through the hall in slow mo is 'Got the Love' by the Average White Band, from their 1974 Atlantic Records album *AWB*.
- In the UK, "Bewitched, Bothered, and Bewildered" was the last episode to air on Sky One for more than a year. Sky pulled the series from its 8pm Saturday slot, claiming it had low viewing figures. Ironically, the show they replaced it with – *Third Rock from the Sun* – drew far worse ratings.

Guest Star Info

Regular *Buffy* guest Seth Gesshel Green, who has a minor role in this episode, decided he wanted to become an actor at the tender age of six, after performing in a summer camp production of *Hello, Dolly!* Seth actually appeared in the original 1992 *Buffy the Vampire Slayer* movie, only to have his scenes end up on the cutting room floor. He will reprise his role as Scott Evil in the third *Austin Powers* movie, *Goldmember*, due for release in July. Seth recently appeared in *America's Sweethearts* and *Rat Race*, and future projects include *Knockaround Guys* (with Vin Diesel), and *Party Monster* (with Macaulay Culkin). He is currently starring in Fox's new hit comedy series *Greg the Bunny*.

Memorable Dialogue

Cordelia (to Harmony): "You're a sheep. All you ever do is what everyone else does, just so you can say you did it first. And here I am, scrambling for your approval, when I'm way cooler than you are, 'cause I'm not a sheep. I do what I wanna do, and I wear what I wanna wear. And you know what? I'll date whoever the hell I wanna date. No matter how lame he is."

Statistics

No. of times Buffy gets to kick ass: 2

No. of deaths: 2
(1 vamp, 1 human)

No. of scary sights: 1
(Joyce coming on to Xander!)

No. of tear-jerking moments: 2 (Giles and Jenny's awkward conversation; Cordy breaking up with Xander!)

EPISODE CREDITS

Written by Marti Noxon   **Directed** by James A. Contner

Buffy Summers	Sarah Michelle Gellar	Oz	Seth Green
Xander Harris	Nicholas Brendon	Joyce Summers	Kristine Sutherland
Willow Rosenberg	Alyson Hannigan	Spike	James Marsters
Cordelia Chase	Charisma Carpenter	Dru	Juliet Landau
Rupert Giles	Anthony Stewart Head	Harmony	Mercedes McNab
Angel	David Boreanaz	Amy	Elizabeth Anne Allen

Compiled by Kate Anderson

A M B E R

BIDDING A FOND FAREWELL TO HER TIME AS TARA IN *BUFFY THE VAMPIRE SLAYER*, AMBER BENSON MUSES ON HER ALTER EGO'S LIFE, LOVES, DEATH – AND WHAT'S NEXT.

GOODBYE To you

BY ABBIE BERGSTEIN

Tara Maclay may be the most mourned character ever to depart from Buffy the Vampire Slayer. Over the course of three seasons, we watched her grow from a painfully shy college student into a compassionate, firm-minded woman whose good judgment made her the chief voice of reason among the Scoobies in Season Six – and whose innate gentleness didn't stop her from axing a demon when her beloved Willow was in danger. Tara's life was cut short not by monsters or magic, but by a bullet intended for Buffy, fired by a man who didn't even know Tara was there.

BUFFY MAGAZINE: YOU PLAYED TARA FOR THREE YEARS ON *BUFFY*. HOW MUCH DID YOU ENJOY PLAYING THE CHARACTER, AND DID YOU FEEL YOU GOT TO KNOW HER PRETTY WELL OVER THAT TIME?

AMBER BENSON: I really love Tara – I have an affinity for her. She was very reticent and insecure in the beginning. I think by the end she was much more comfortable with who she was and a much more happy person. Until this season, she was always over-ridden, she never really pushed the issue. I wanted to shake her and say, 'Stand up for what you believe! Don't get walked over!' But that's how some people are, and there's nothing wrong with that. It's hard to assert yourself, especially with very aggressive people around you like the Scoobies, who fight monsters for a living. Toward the end of this season, she really did stand up – she put that coffee mug down and spilled that coffee everywhere, telling Willow not to use her magic anymore! She definitely thought things through. She became the Giles when Giles left.

B E N S O N

TARA SEEMED TO GET MORE LOVE SCENES THAN GILES DID, ESPECIALLY THIS SEASON...

There'd been hints that we were going to have some sort of love scene [in "Seeing Red"], but I didn't really understand what the extent of that was going to be until I went in for a wardrobe fitting and Cynthia, the wardrobe supervisor, said, 'Now, what kind of modesty clothing [flesh-toned garb to simulate nudity] do you want?' I hadn't read Steve DeKnight's script yet, and I was just like, 'What are you talking about? Modest – I'm not modest – I want fully clothed!' We [Amber and Alyson] both had band tops. I had boxer shorts and she had biker shorts. We were in bed with the stupid satin sheet. I'd never experienced satin sheets before. I'd pull the sheet up, and two seconds later, she's pulling on it, and it goes down, and I'm pulling it up – it's

She was very good about it. She wants to be a stuntwoman. I'm the biggest klutz on the set. Remember Emma in that wedding dress? I got that dress off of her at least four times, because I'd be following her and I'd step on the dress and she'd be pulling it back up. But she looked gorgeous in that dress.

WHEN DID YOU FIND OUT THAT TARA WAS GOING TO DIE?

I knew at the beginning of Season Five that Willow was going to go bad and that I was going to be the impetus for that, but I wasn't 100 percent certain about the dying until the very end of last season. I mean, I wasn't at all surprised when Joss finally told me when we were shooting the season finale for last year. He was all excited about it. In fact, I even knew I was going to be in the main credits just for the one episode ["Seeing Red"]. Joss was

IT ALL HAPPENED SO FAST IN "SEEING RED" – DO YOU THINK TARA EVEN KNEW SHE'D BEEN SHOT?

We never really talked about it. I'm assuming she realized, as we all do when we die, that we're dying. I hope – I mean, maybe we don't all realize, maybe we just die, we don't even have the consciousness of the act.

WHAT WAS IT LIKE FILMING THAT FATAL SCENE?

I've never played a character that dies before. It was quite enlightening – now I know how to die properly. You didn't ever see me *get* shot. You saw the blood splatter on Willow first, and then you come to me and you see the bullet hole. It was just put on my costume. They had trouble because the fake blood was so thin. It didn't have body to it; it was just

> { "I KNEW AT THE BEGINNING OF SEASON FIVE THAT WILLOW WAS GOING TO GO BAD AND THAT I WAS GOING TO BE THE IMPETUS FOR THAT, BUT I WASN'T 100 PERCENT CERTAIN ABOUT THE DYING UNTIL THE VERY END OF LAST SEASON." }

so slick that it won't stay where you put it. It slides. So I'm like this." [Amber mimes holding the sheet to her chest for dear life.]

WHAT ABOUT THE STAGING?

It was very low-key. Basically, they told me not to touch Alyson so much, because if Tara's in bed with this girl that she's in love with, of course, you're going to be touching. But apparently I was overzealously running my hand up and down her arm. Alyson didn't care, but the censors were going to care.

SPEAKING OF PHYSICAL ACTION, WHAT ABOUT FALLING ON THE STAIRS IN "NORMAL AGAIN"?

That's all the stunt double – although I did [really] trip going down the stairs, a non-planned fall [Laughs]. Jamie, Alyson's stand-in, actually went to fall.

like, 'I want to put you in the credits,' and I'm like, 'That's so evil! How can you do that to the fans?'

As much as I hate the fact that she died, I think that it was needed. I know they were really worried about making people unhappy, but it was the only way to take Willow to another level. It furthered the plot and made it possible for Willow to go bad. This was the only thing that could have pushed her over the edge. I was all for me being maimed and coming back, but it wouldn't have been enough. I feel as upset about it as the fans do. I know it was necessary, but still, 'No, don't kill her, I love her! She's part of me!' I thought I was going to be dead in the 16th episode. They just kept pushing it back, so I didn't know when I was going to be dying, because they switched around episodes.

watery. It would hit Willow's shirt, and the shirt would just suck the whole thing up. It would be like a big stain. So they had to basically Scotch-Guard her shirt and figure out how to get it one way and make it stay that way. Alyson had to have that done a bunch of times. It was really intense.

DID YOU ENJOY PLAYING OPPOSITE ADAM BUSCH, WHO PLAYED WARREN, TARA'S MURDERER?

I only had one little scene with him in "Life Serial", when he planted the bug on Buffy. But I got to spend time with the guys [Adam Busch, Danny Strong and Tom Lenk] off-screen because a lot of times, we had two units at the same time – we'd be doing the boys in their lair and then we'd be doing the Scooby stuff. I love Danny and Tom and Adam. They're so sweet, I was totally bummed I didn't get to work with them.

WHAT WAS IT LIKE PLAYING DEAD?

It was actually really tough, because a good friend of mine passed away from cancer at the end of last year – Marti Noxon's assistant, J.D. Peralta, a wonderful, incredible human being. We were all really close to her at work and having to play dead in the same place where I spent a lot of time with this person was really unsettling. It just brought back a lot of memories. And then I had my cake afterwards. I was dead the last episode, so when they brought me the cake to say thank you for Tara, and it says, 'Tara' and it has a headstone and it says, 'Rest in Peace,' I was in tears. Everybody was crying, because it was so sad.

WHAT WAS THE FAN REACTION LIKE?

After the episode where Tara was killed, my friend Richard went on line and checked it out. People got really upset, writing, 'They killed the gay character, just because she was gay.' I think people were worried about that. I truly, 100 percent believe that was *not* the case, that was *not* the intention. If you look back on the progression of Tara and Willow's relationship, it was about two people who were in love, regardless of gender. And I think the death was treated the same way. If I'd been a guy, if I'd been Oz, it would have been the same thing.

A friend of mine on the show said, 'Do you want to go to this bar?' I said, 'Sure.' So my mom and I go to this lesbian bar with my friend and this girl comes running over: 'I think it's horrible! I can't believe they killed your character!'

I did a comic book signing in Santa Barbara. My mom came with me and was talking to this girl, who said, 'I

hope that Amber does more signings and conventions, because otherwise, I'll never see her again. It makes my life better to watch her on TV and I don't have that anymore, so make her go to more signings, so I can at least see her!' It really made me feel good that Tara had the impact that she had. Until people come over and say, 'Hey, you had an impact,' you don't know.

I've really enjoyed the relationship I've had with the fans. They've been so cool and supportive of what I do. Most of the fans online are really cool. We have some amazing fans. Look what they do with the Posting Board Party every year. They raise money for the Make A Wish Foundation.

IS THERE ANY POSSIBILITY THAT TARA MAY COME BACK?

I don't have a contract for next season. I don't know what's going to happen. So we'll see.

IN JUNE YOU WERE IN A PLAY, ALGOR MORTIS, AS PART OF THE BLANK THEATER COMPANY'S YOUNG PLAYWRIGHTS SERIES AT THE HUDSON THEATER IN HOLLYWOOD. WHAT ELSE ARE YOU WORKING ON AT THE MOMENT?

I'm finishing up post-production on Chance [the independent film Amber wrote/produced/directed/stars in, co-starring James Marsters and Andy Hallett]. People that have seen the rough cut really like it. It was an amazing experience – best time of my life, to tell you the God's honest truth. I love filmmaking – I think I can make an even better film next time.

WHAT DO YOU THINK YOU'VE LEARNED, BOTH AS A FILMMAKER AND AS AN ACTRESS WORKING ON BUFFY?

You need to be aware of what's going on, so I've learned a lot in that respect, just from the Buffy crew. The crew is fantastic and they are so excited to be asked about what they do. I think

any actor who doesn't utilize the vast knowledge surrounding them on the set is insane. Sarah's amazing, because she knows where her light is, she'll stop right where the light is because she feels it on her face; she always knows where the camera is. I'm an oblivious actor. I act. I get lost in what I'm doing. I've learned a lot from watching Sarah.

HAS WORKING ON BUFFY BEEN DIFFERENT FOR YOU THAN OTHER ACTING JOBS?

I definitely grew up over the course of the three years. I really went into it being a little bit – not really new, I've been [acting] a long time, but just personally being young. I got my driver's license, I bought a house – I stepped into the adult world. I left the kid world behind. I've done plays and films before, but a couple months and it's over. It's nothing like three seasons of a TV show. I've never had an experience like it. You really build relationships with the people you work with and you really come to know and love the character that you play. You don't feel that way a lot of times about your character. You like them, you play them and then you're done, you put them aside. But this you couldn't put aside. It really stuck with me. I was really lucky, I had a really good run on Buffy. ✛

> "AS MUCH AS I HATE THE FACT THAT SHE DIED, I THINK THAT IT WAS NEEDED. I KNOW THEY WERE REALLY WORRIED ABOUT MAKING PEOPLE UNHAPPY, BUT IT WAS THE ONLY WAY TO TAKE WILLOW TO ANOTHER LEVEL."

EPISODE SPOTLIGHT

"New Moon Rising"

First US airdate 02/05/00

First UK airdate 12/05/00

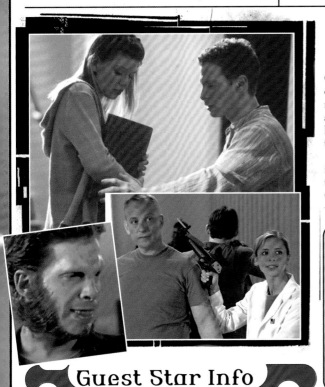

Synopsis

Oz is back in Sunnydale, and thanks to a visit to Tibet, seems to have learnt how to control the wolf in him. This used to be the moment Willow dreamt about – until she met Tara. Unfortunately, when Oz runs into Tara on campus, he senses Willow's scent all over her. He suddenly realises that he has a rival for Willow's affections, and the long dormant wolf takes control, heading off in hot pursuit of Tara. But Tara is saved thanks to the timely intervention of The Initiative, who capture Oz and lock him away.

When Riley realises that the wolf is Oz, he tries to prevent the Initiative from experimenting on him, but his rescue attempt fails. Eventually Buffy and the Scooby Gang turn up and manage to save Oz. Riley is forced to go AWOL when viewed as a traitor, Oz decides there's nothing for it but to leave Sunnydale, and Willow chooses to stay with the person she loves – Tara.

Trivia

- **The character of Oz** was based on a guy Joss Whedon knew in college.
- **When this episode** was originally broadcast in the US, actress Amber Benson received a pretty rough ride from fans because they felt that Tara was responsible for breaking up the Willow and Oz relationship.
- **The New York Daily News** referred to "New Moon Rising" as "a landmark in TV history." Something really significant happens at the end of this episode, although we don't see it because the scene plunges into darkness. However, the dialogue leading up to it makes the episode a landmark not just in *Buffy* but TV history: finally, Willow comes out and declares her feelings for Tara.

Guest Star Info

Amber Nicole Benson was born in Birmingham, Alabama on 8 January. As a young girl she studied singing, dancing and acting. Her family moved to LA so that she could pursue a career in acting. She's had roles in movies with Lindsay (Maggie Walsh) Crouse, Eliza (Faith) Dushku (*Bye Bye Love*) and Seth Green (*Can't Hardly Wait*).

In her spare time, Amber loves to read. Her favourite authors include J.K. Rowling and Ray Bradbury. Writing is another interest, so much so that she wrote a comic book based on the characters of Tara and Willow as part of the *Buffy* comic book series. Amber lives in LA with her mum, her dog Pennsylvania and her cat Benneton.

Memorable Dialogue

Oz: "It was stupid to think that you'd just be waiting."

Willow: "I was waiting. I feel like some part of me will always be waiting for you. Like if I'm old and blue-haired and I turn the corner in Istanbul and there you are, I won't be surprised."

Statistics

No. of times Buffy gets to kick ass: 2

No. of screams: 4

No. of deaths: 2
(Agent Willis and one HST)

No. of tear-jerking moments: 2

EPISODE CREDITS

Written by Marti Noxon
Directed by Nick Marck

Buffy Summers	Sarah Michelle Gellar
Xander Harris	Nicholas Brendon
Willow Rosenberg	Alyson Hannigan
Riley Finn	Marc Blucas
Rupert Giles	Anthony Stewart Head

Oz	Seth Green
Anya	Emma Caulfield
Spike	James Marsters
Forrest	Leonard Roberts
Graham	Bailey Chase
Adam	George Hertzberg
Colonel McNamara	Conor O'Farrell

Compiled by Kate Anderson

Dusk 'til Dawn

By Joe Nazzaro

Buffy has a sister? That was the reaction from many die-hard fans when it was unexpectedly revealed at the start of *Buffy*'s fifth season that the Slayer had a younger sibling. The reactions were mixed, from outrage about this new character who appeared without warning or explanation, to anticipation from viewers who wanted to see just what series creator Joss Whedon had up his sleeve.

As everyone soon discovered, Dawn was actually the key to an inter-dimensional gateway, disguised in human form and placed within Buffy's care for protection against the evil entity known as Glory (played by Clare Kramer).

"I'd say the biggest surprise – even though I'd always suspected it – was the fact that Michelle is one of the greatest actresses of our time," stated Whedon at the end of the show's sixth season. "Her scenes with Sarah elevated the show so much, and they really loved working together. That was really the big X-factor going in, because we basically designed Dawn to be the big emotional attachment of the year. If Michelle hadn't proved to have the acting chops she has, we could never have gone to the places we [have]."

Since joining the show, Michelle has seen her character going places she'd never anticipated. A first kiss in "All the Way" becomes an encounter with an older teen vampire. There was the memorable dance number in Whedon's critically acclaimed musical episode, "Once More, With Feeling." And in later episodes, Dawn's increasing sense of youthful alienation has led to acts of rebellion that may have painful consequences.

Buffy Magazine sat down with the actress during the show's sixth season to discuss the latest developments involving her character.

BUFFY MAGAZINE: LET'S START
BY TALKING ABOUT WHAT'S GOING
ON WITH DAWN THESE DAYS. SHE
SEEMS TO BE EXPERIENCING SOME
CLASSIC TEEN ANGST.

MICHELLE TRACHTENBERG: That can
be expected in any teenager. Teenagers in
America have so many things to deal with;
things that happen to them personally,
within their family and friends, so teenage
angst is something that's not uncommon.
But that's something that people don't
want to necessarily realize. Parents will say,
"Oh, he never went through that, we just
zoomed right through those years!" But in
reality, everyone has a certain amount of
issues that they have to deal with. This
year, Dawn's issues centre around, "Okay,
my sister was dead for a while, my mother
is dead, so I felt like I had no one, and all
of a sudden, my sister is back." So there's
this big part of Dawn that feels like she
wants to spend every second with her,
because God forbid she goes away again; a
demon can kill her at any time!

And also, Dawn is just trying to find a
place to fit in. She realizes she's not a little
goody two-shoes who loves school and
does everything that she's told, but she's
also not the extreme of the situation. She's
not one to go out and have excessive partying or do a bunch of crazy things. Basically,
this season is kind of her middle. She's tried
to go out without telling Buffy, which was
exciting to her in terms of doing something
she's never done before, which I think we're
all guilty of. We've all done something that's
not necessarily 100 per cent moral, but we
wanted to see how it went.

Please don't get me wrong – I'm not
talking about using substances like drugs

and alcohol. That's something that I would absolutely never do because it really screws up your mind and messes with your head. I'm talking about rebellion in the sense of not telling your parents where you're going, or not calling, or whatever. This is Dawn's year of screaming for attention, trying to fit in and trying to discover herself.

HOW DO YOU REGARD DAWN'S RELATIONSHIP WITH HER SISTER?

A couple of people have asked me, "Is Dawn jealous of Buffy?" But by no means is she jealous. In fact, she has a great admiration for Buffy, but mixed in with that admiration is the desire to be on equal terms. If you're in a class of 30 kids, and there's one person who has all-perfect grades all the time, if you're a goal-conscious person, then your desire may not necessarily be to surpass that student. But

Basically any time throughout the season where Dawn was not her goody-goody self. That was always exciting for me, because if a character stays in one mindset throughout a show's run, it gets very boring. The fact that Dawn is finally growing up and maturing is not only good for her as a person, but it's also great for me as an actress, because I get to experience different aspects of Dawn's personality.

I liked the Halloween episode, where Dawn doesn't tell Buffy she's going out but goes out and meets a whole of bunch of boys who turn out to be vampires. That was great for me, because in those scenes, Dawn was viewed as older than she was, or at least she wasn't seen as just the little sister. That was a real character growth process. There are a couple of scenes we filmed recently between Buffy and Dawn that are less, "Please look at me, please see me!" They're more along the lines of, "Here I am, choose if you want to look at me or not, but if you do look at me, here are the pros."

WHAT WAS YOUR REACTION WHEN JOSS ANNOUNCED THAT HE WANTED TO WRITE AND DIRECT A MUSICAL EPISODE OF *BUFFY*?

I was looking forward to the dancing part and dreading the singing part! Joss wanted to write me a full song and he wanted me to sing it, and I absolutely refused. Singing makes me too nervous. I feel I'm more vulnerable when I'm singing, so I didn't want to

{ **"THIS IS DAWN'S YEAR OF SCREAMING FOR ATTENTION, TRYING TO FIT IN AND TRYING TO DISCOVER HERSELF."** }

it might be to be on an even playing ground, and I think that's the way Dawn feels. She wants to be considered an equal to her sister, and she wants her sister to consider her an equal.

WHAT HAVE BEEN YOUR PERSONAL HIGHLIGHTS SO FAR THIS SEASON?

do a full-blown song, but I made an agreement with him that I'd do a dance number with whatever he wanted in there. Joss ended up sneaking in a couple of songs, which was very nerve-wracking, but he was there during the recording time. Even though I was very nervous going into it, he convinced me that it would be fine, so I sang, and it all worked out in the end.

WERE YOU NERVOUS ABOUT DOING A BIG DANCE NUMBER WITH HINTON BATTLE, A TONY AWARD-WINNING BROADWAY PERFORMER?

I love dancing so much that I wasn't nervous at all because he's just another guy who had this talent. When I get older – or even now – if I'm lucky enough to be working with some of the great actors like Dustin Hoffman or Al Pacino, just like dancing with Hinton Battle, there would

DID IT TAKE YOU LONG TO SETTLE INTO THE SERIES?

It was great knowing Sarah prior to being on the show, because we already had that foundation of a sisterly bond from *All My Children*. So it was easier for me than coming on to the set cold, but of course it still took a little time to click into the way things worked. I don't think it took very long, but I was mostly trying to figure out Dawn, and talking to Joss and Marti [Noxon] about the way they saw her and what kind of a

person she was. I didn't pay as close attention to making everything fit perfectly, because once I understood Dawn, I knew everything else would fall into place.

WERE YOU OFFERED THE ROLE RIGHT AWAY, OR DID YOU HAVE TO UNDERGO ONE OF THOSE UNCOMFORTABLE AUDITIONS WHERE YOU WALK INTO THE CASTING OFFICE AND THERE ARE 100 OTHER ACTRESSES SITTING THERE WHO LOOK LIKE YOU?

Actually, it's a yes and no to that. I did have to audition for Dawn, but when I was in the casting office, there was absolutely no one else there but me. That almost makes it worse because you're thinking, "Okay, maybe they've rejected everyone else, so what am I going to do?" I was very lucky, because the only people I had to audition for were Joss and Marti, so I just went to

them and they made the final decision. I don't know what other girls they were considering at the time, but I did speak to Joss afterwards about the casting process. I'm a very goal-conscious person and I've always imagined myself writing and directing and producing X number of years from now, and a big part of directing is the casting process. So I asked Joss, what was it about me, or about the other actors, that

convinced him that any of us would be perfect for the role?

He said (which was a help and not really a help) that you basically never really know until that person walks in, and all of a sudden, every single thing that they're doing is right. He told me that I walked in and the clothes that I was wearing were just like Willow's, kind of funky, because I was wearing a red T-shirt that was kind of glittery and sparkly and almost mysterious. And then he said my characteristics were very Buffy-esque as if she really were a sister of mine and I learned from her. So there were those two elements. And finally, he said, "And of course, you kind of could act!" He said when I started reading the scenes, "They absolutely didn't make sense. We just threw them together. There wasn't any relevance to anything." So that was a compliment to me, because he said I made them into part of the scenes from an episode.

{ "EVEN THOUGH I WAS VERY NERVOUS GOING INTO 'ONCE MORE, WITH FEELING', JOSS CONVINCED ME THAT IT WOULD BE FINE, SO I SANG, AND I GUESS IT ALL WORKED OUT IN THE END." }

be a certain amount of nervousness. But in the end, you have to realize that if this is something you love to do, then you love it and they love it too because they've been doing it for so long. So you just have to go out there and do it and hopefully it will be a great product.

DO YOU REMEMBER YOUR FIRST DAY ON THE SET?

It was funny, because the big scene in my first episode was the "Mom!" scene [in "Buffy Vs. Dracula"]. It was a longer day than any of the rest because it was just getting into the way things ran on the set, and getting into the groove of things. Everything was twice as long, from getting everything perfect on the make-up process to making sure everything was fitting right. But the second I was on the set, it was two or three takes and that was all. I said, "That's it?" and they said, "Okay, you have tomorrow off, because we're starting a different episode. You're not working the first day, but you're working the second day." So it was almost a false start, this little tiny scene, and then the real bulk of huge work came the day after that.

Buffy III

DID JOSS GIVE YOU A LOT OF INFORMATION ABOUT YOUR CHARACTER WHEN YOU WERE HIRED?

No, he didn't. My creative meeting at the beginning of the year consisted of "Hi,

the dialogue and the whole thing, and Joss made sure of that. I have a great admiration for him. I'm very lucky to be working with Joss because he's an absolute creative genius. He always knows the answer to creative things, and thinks them through so thoroughly. He could take a three year-old's random poem about their dog and make it into an epic story about this dog's journey from this end of the world to the other. That's the kind of thing he can do.

WHAT SORT OF REACTION HAVE YOU HAD FROM THE FANS?

with fan mail. But I hadn't really been acknowledged by fans like this, who specifically care about every single thing. They want to dive into every single part of the show, and understand this, and look for secrets here and read between the lines there. They're really devoted, so that was kind of fun to find out and see how they would react. But no one liked Dawn when she first came on the show. At first, they were like, "Oh, it's the cute factor; get her off, get her off!" Until they eventually began saying, "Right, I see it!" I think that was around the fifth episode, where they learned who Dawn really was.

ARE THERE ANY CHARACTER DEVELOPMENTS YOU PERSONALLY HAVE IN MIND FOR DAWN?

I think it's very important for an actor and a creator to collaborate in order to bring a

> "NO ONE LIKED DAWN WHEN SHE FIRST CAME ON THE SHOW. AT FIRST, THEY WERE LIKE, 'OH, IT'S THE CUTE FACTOR; GET HER OFF, GET HER OFF!' UNTIL THEY EVENTUALLY BEGAN SAYING, 'RIGHT, I SEE IT!'"

welcome to the show. You're playing Dawn. You're kind of Buffy's sister, and you're a key; have fun!" Thanks a lot! But Joss in his genius knew that was the only information I needed. If he told me more, it would have ruined everything, because I would have been like, "I'm the source of energy, so I have to act mystical here!" What he told me was perfect, and all I did in my scenes was just act like a regular teenager, because that's what he told me: "You're Buffy's sister; you're a regular teenager; you're a key – enjoy!"

HOW DID YOU FEEL ABOUT THE LARGE AMOUNT OF WORK REQUIRED OF YOU AT THE END OF SEASON FIVE?

It was great for me, because it was a challenge and I wanted to see if I could go there as an actress. I felt really comfortable with

It hasn't necessarily been overwhelming, because I've done other well-known projects before *Buffy*. So I'd had some experience

character together. I haven't had my meeting with Marti or Joss for next year to talk about Dawn's development yet, but it's forthcoming. I think it's very important, especially at this stage, because these are the most important years in Dawn's life. These are the years that she is discovering herself.

I'd just like to see Dawn maturing, and if that means getting a little more rebellious, then so be it; as long as she just finds herself a comfortable niche. One thing that I'm looking forward to is that instead of wearing sneakers, Dawn will be wearing heels next year, so that's my exciting point. As for the specific details of next year, we haven't really discussed them yet.

SO A REBEL WITH HEELS IS ALL WE KNOW AT THIS POINT.

I guess so. If you want to know any more info, that's a Joss and Marti question! ✦

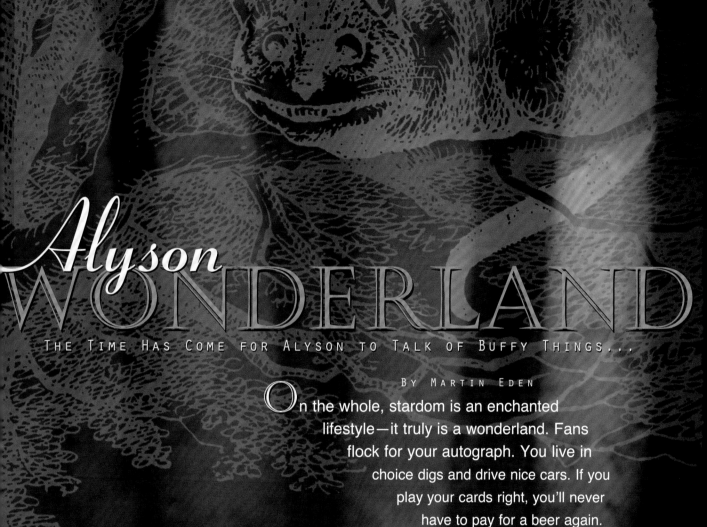

Alyson
WONDERLAND

THE TIME HAS COME FOR ALYSON TO TALK OF BUFFY THINGS...

BY MARTIN EDEN

On the whole, stardom is an enchanted lifestyle—it truly is a wonderland. Fans flock for your autograph. You live in choice digs and drive nice cars. If you play your cards right, you'll never have to pay for a beer again. But Alyson Hannigan learned the hard way that being famous enough to merit your own action figure doesn't mean you can get your hands on one. "There's this four-pack that I'm desperate to find," she says. "I begged and pleaded and couldn't get one. I saw it in Joss' office and said, 'You don't need that, do you?' He was like, 'There's no way you're stealing it!'"

Hannigan's had much more success in navigating her growing television and film career than she's had in nabbing that rare *Buffy* action figure box set—though if she's still jonesin' for it, she's welcome to negotiate for the one that proudly decorates the *Buffy* magazine offices. She's seen Willow through her darker days as one of Sunnydale High's least popular students and into a more challenging and accepting college lifestyle. College also brought with it some romantic changes—from a werewolf to a "witch," and from Oz to Tara.

After the fracture of the Scooby Gang and her break-up with Oz, it seems as though Willow has finally found some sense of peace in her life, just as Hannigan has found a burgeoning film career waiting for her while on hiatus from *Buffy*. With memorable supporting turns in 1999's monster hit *American Pie* and last summer's *Boys and Girls*, it looks as though the journey down Hollywood's rabbit hole is just beginning for Willow's alter-ego.

During a visit to Gilesland—a.k.a. Merry Olde England—Hannigan took time to chat with our UK correspondent, Martin Eden, before visiting a London store for a mobbed autograph session to promote the latest set of *Buffy* videos. Then it was off to visit Anthony Stewart Head before returning to the States. For anyone else, an amazing summer vacation—but for Hannigan, just another trip through the looking glass.

BUFFY MAGAZINE: LET'S START BY TALKING ABOUT THIS PAST SEASON OF BUFFY. IT SEEMED AS THOUGH WILLOW HAD A LOT OF CHARACTER DEVELOPMENT. ARE YOU PLEASED WITH HOW EVERYTHING TURNED OUT?
ALYSON HANNIGAN: Definitely. I think Willow probably got the best arcs of the season. Just by chance, too, with Seth [Green] leaving the show.

BTM: SO THAT WASN'T PLANNED FROM THE START OF THE SEASON?
AH: No, he was going to go away for probably six episodes to do a film. It was undecided whether or not he was going to come back, and I don't know what happened, but he chose not to. It's disappointing.

BTM: WERE THE FINAL EPISODES WITH HIM DIFFICULT TO FILM?
AH: They were, because I was dealing with the loss of Seth. I think that he and I had some really good scenes together, and we enjoy working with each other so much. We hadn't determined whether or not he was coming back at that point. We had hoped, but it's sort of like abandonment. "No, don't leave us! Come on!"

BTM: IT MUST HAVE BEEN NICE TO HAVE HIM BACK FOR AN EPISODE LATER IN THE SEASON.
AH: It was, but I knew that it was just the one, so it was a weird rollercoaster of emotions for me. On the one hand, I really loved working with him, but then it was also like a slap in the face, because we both know how well we work together. It was like, "Why do you want to leave? Couldn't you just stay for a couple more years?"

BTM: AFTER OZ, THOUGH, WILLOW FOUND TARA. HOW HAVE FANS REACTED TO THAT STORYLINE?
AH: It's been mixed. A lot of people completely support it, and are very into the way the show has handled it. I think the people who have a problem with it haven't even grasped what it is. They're still in the denial stage of, "Hey, wait, what's going on, how can you...You guys are always doing those spells." It's kind of weird, but the people who really understand the show completely get it and have seen the progression of the relationship. I don't personally think it matters that it's two girls at all. I think it's just two characters that are fond of each other who have fallen in love, and I think Joss is handling it so well. He's not trying to make it this big hoopla of, "We have two girls together on our show!" It's like any other relationship on our show. It just so happens that they're both female.

I was dealing with the loss of Seth, who is just wonderful to work with. I think that he and I had some really good scenes together, and we enjoy working with each other so much.

BTM: IT SEEMS LIKE THE COMING-OUT SCENE TO BUFFY MIGHT HAVE BEEN AN INTENSE ONE TO FILM. DID THAT GO SMOOTHLY?
AH: No, it didn't at all. Joss didn't seem happy with it, and it was just one of those that we had to get through. It was taking forever, and it was one of those long days.

BTM: IT'S DEFINITELY A SCENE THAT ANYONE WHO IS IN A SIMILAR SITUATION TO WILLOW'S COULD RELATE TO.
AH: Yeah, I know. I had hoped that it would be. On the page, it was great, but then doing it was like, "We're running behind, this set up's taking too long." And Joss was down there. He doesn't come down as much anymore because he's so busy—the poor guy's going to collapse if he doesn't slow down—but this was an important scene, and he didn't seem happy. When Joss doesn't seem happy, you just feel like, "Oh, man, I'm disappointed. Everybody in the world is going to hate this." But on the page it was lovely.

BTM: Did Joss have the Tara and Willow relationship in mind when the season began?

AH: I don't know if he had any idea that he was going to develop the relationship the way he did. He was very hands-on in the Willow and Tara scenes, so we got a clue about where it was headed, because he was always on the set. He wanted to develop it the way he saw it, and he only does that when he really cares. But then we started reading the stuff and it's like, "OK, this is clearly going beyond subtext here." And he tried to stick by the "No, no, it's just subtext" defense. Finally it was like "Oh come on, hit-yourself-over-the-head-with-it" text.

BTM: Is it fun to work with Amber Benson?

AH: She's wonderful. She's so sweet, and I've known her for a long time. I've never worked with her before, but I knew her through mutual people in the business. She's very down to earth.

know which one he's going to pick out of his brain.

BTM: It was kind of a shock to see the return of nerdy Willow.

AH: I thought Xander's dream was so cool, and Giles had such a great dream, but my dream was bunk.

BTM: You have to admit it was pretty scary, though, with all those things jumping out at you.

AH: I don't think I did very well, because it was confusing filming. You didn't exactly know what was going on. I don't think there was enough tension.

BTM: Maybe that's a good thing, because it seemed so surreal.

AH: That's what I was trying to do. I was trying to do the whole dream thing, and I don't know if it came across. But I thought that was a brilliant episode

I don't personally think it matters that it's two girls at all. I think it's just two characters that are fond of each other who have fallen in love, and I think Joss is handling it so well.

BTM: Do you have any clues yet about where season five is headed?

AH: I have absolutely no clue. I tried to pick Joss' brain, but he keeps stuff from us because he knows we're blabbermouths.

BTM: So it seems like you're almost as much in the dark about plots as the fans are. You don't really know what's going to happen until you get the script?

AH: Mostly. Occasionally we'll hear big things. Joss has so many ideas, you never

if you tuned in ten minutes into it, after my dream.

BTM: Did you get hurt at all when the ancient Slayer was trying to Cuisinart you?

AH: No, just dirt in the eyes and a couple of scratches, but nothing major.

BTM: Have you ever been injured while doing a stunt for *Buffy*?

AH: No, because our stunt people are incredible. They're amazing, and we'll get bruises, but I have a better chance of getting bruised walking into the trailer than I do on the set.

Seeing RED
WILLOW'S FINEST HOURS

I, Robot...You Jane, season 1, episode 8
When the mysterious Malcolm starts puttin' the cyber-moves on Willow, she falls for it...until she finds out he's really Moloch the demon.

Halloween, season 2, episode 6
She may have been turned into a ghost by Ethan Rayne, but she still saved the Scoobies when their costumes went haywire as well.

Phases, season 2, episode 15
Willow gets the male attention she deserves. And if it's from a werewolf, so be it...she's not much fun three days out of the month, either.

Becoming (part two), season 2, episode 22
Battling through serious injuries, Willow manages to use her newly minted witchcraft to restore Angel's soul—sadly, seconds too late.

Dead Man's Party, season 3, episode 2
It's Willow's angry reaction to Buffy's attempt to leave again that helps persuade her best friend that she's really still wanted in Sunnydale.

Lovers Walk, season 3, episode 8
Willow gets herself and Xander entangled in Spike's scheme to win Drusilla back, but that's the least of her problems, after Cordelia and Oz stumble upon the best friends making out.

Doppelgangland, season 3, episode 16
Willow vamps out and goes undercover as her evil twin to stop the doppelganger from wreaking havoc in Sunnydale.

Something Blue, season 4, episode 9
A miscast spell by Willow causes disaster for her friends and sends Buffy and Spike into the last place they want to be: each other's arms.

New Moon Rising, season 4, episode 19
Oz is back, and outraged by Willow's budding relationship with Tara, but Will stands her ground and remains with her new love.

Primeval, season 4, episode 21
Superpowers are all well and good, but Willow and her fellow Scoobies prove that the bonds of friendship can take out any evil imaginable.

BTM: WAS EVIL WILLOW FUN TO PLAY IN "THE WISH" AND "DOPPLEGANGLAND"?

AH: It was good for a little change of pace.

BTM: WAS IT ALREADY PLANNED TO BRING HER BACK A SECOND TIME, OR WAS THAT DONE AS A RESULT OF THE TREMENDOUS FAN REACTION?

AH: I think that while we were filming it, Joss was into having more fun with that side of things, so there was always that idea.

BTM: IT MUST HAVE BEEN FUN TO KILL CORDELIA.

AH: I remember that. That was fun.

BTM: HOW ARE THINGS WITH THE NEW CAST MEMBERS?

AH: Emma's the best. She's so cool. She and I have been hanging out a lot. We play Scrabble all the time. And Mark is just like a big old jock and he picks on me.

BTM: WHAT ABOUT JAMES MARSTERS? IS HE BELOVED BY THE LADIES ON SET?

AH: James is so sweet. He's just heaven. He's so happy to be there. I just adore Spike. He and I had that scene in season four where he's trying to bite me, and we just walked into that like, "This is the best scene, let's not screw it up." And we were so nervous, because when you read it, you're laughing out loud.

BTM: DO YOU MISS WORKING WITH CHARISMA CARPENTER AND DAVID BOREANAZ? DO YOU SEE THEM VERY OFTEN?

AH: David and I didn't have that many scenes together, so I probably see him more now than I did then. And he always made me laugh, which is not good when we're shooting, because he does thi little smirk thing when we're off camera. You think he's just about to bust up, so of course you bust up, then he plays it off like, "I wasn't smirking." And I never see Charisma anymore because she's so busy.

BTM: DO YOU ENJOY WATCHING ANGEL AS WELL?

AH: Yes, especially the latter half of the season, because I'm particularly fond of Wesley and he's a series regular now. Good for Alexis!

BTM: ARE YOU TWO AN ITEM NOW?

AH: [coyly] Why do you ask? Oh, it's out. He's the best.

BTM: HOW DID YOU FIND YOURSELF CAST ON BUFFY?

AH: Just through auditioning and auditioning, and I finally got it. It's never easy. It's nothing like, "Oh yeah, I was walking my dogs and somebody said I should try out for this," like David. His story is much better than mine. Mine's just the same old process. You audition and you either get it or you don't. Luckily, I did.

BTM: ARE YOU HAPPY WITH ALL THE BUFFY THE VAMPIRE SLAYER MERCHANDISE YOU'VE SEEN?

AH: It took forever for anything to come out, and now it's like we're seeing more things. Nobody tells us what's coming out. My cousin in Atlanta sent me a lollipop and I was like, "Oh my god, we have lollipops?" And then a few months later somebody was like, "Oh yeah, you have lollipops." We're on soda cans. There are going to be video games. But I want a pinball machine. There was a rumor that there's going to be a pinball machine for the show. Joss and I were thrilled because we go to the arcades together sometimes. Then somebody said that was just a rumor. But how cool would it be! That would be the one thing I would keep in my house.

BTM: EVEN THOUGH IT'S YOUR JOB, IT SEEMS LIKE IT MUST BE A REALLY FUN SET TO SPEND TIME ON. WHAT'S IT LIKE WORKING WITH SARAH MICHELLE GELLAR AND NICHOLAS BRENDON?

AH: She's a good laugher. Nick [Brendon] is funny; he's a funny guy. He cracks me up. He has the most sarcastic sense of humor, and he's just so witty.

> Sarah's a good laugher. Nick cracks me up. He has the most sarcastic sense of humor, and he's just so witty. Emma's the best. She's so cool. We play Scrabble all the time. And Mark is just like a big old jock and he picks on me.

BTM: YOU'VE ALSO FOUND A LOT OF SUCCESS OUTSIDE OF BUFFY. FOR EXAMPLE, NO ONE WILL SOON FORGET THE CHARACTER YOU PLAYED IN AMERICAN PIE. HOW WAS THE EXPERIENCE WORKING ON THAT FILM?

AH: Oh yeah, it was great. It is sort of difficult just because it's hard to find something that will work with the schedule, and we have such a small amount of time off. You sort of get desperate. It's just better to relax, and if there's nothing that's appealing to me, then I won't do it. I've just come into that. I've just finished a movie which I really loved, and it did really well, and it felt great, so I'm waiting for something that I really want to do. It's a lot of effort, and luckily I'm in a position where I don't have to work if I don't want to—nine months out of the year I have a job, which is wonderful as an actress. So I've been spoiled with American Pie and Buffy. I have wonderful scripts and wonderful people to work with.

BTM: NOW THE TOUGH QUESTION: HAS YOUR MOTHER SEEN THAT FILM YET?

AH: Yes. I warned her beforehand. "Ma, you might not be happy about this." ✛

IT'S BEEN A BUSY YEAR FOR
SPIKE. HE GOT HIS SOUL
BACK AND GOT RID OF THAT
PESKY CHIP – BUT WILL HE
GET BACK WITH BUFFY?
JAMES MARSTERS TALKS TO
ABBIE BERNSTEIN.

If you enjoy the character of Spike, the vampire anti-hero on *Buffy*, you've got company. James Marsters, who's been playing Spike for six years now, is very fond of him, too. "He's a Cadillac role," James enthuses.

Portraying a vampire on a TV show didn't sound promising at first to an actor with a substantial theatrical background, James admits. "I was a real snob. I always thought that if I did television, it would be more for the money than for getting artistic rocks off. And that has been the pleasant surprise of my *life*, that the highest-paying, the highest-profile [job] is also the most satisfying. I used to work at a place called A Contemporary Theater in Seattle that did only new plays

– some of them aren't good, because they're new. But [on *Buffy*], I'm in a process where it's always new work and the quality is always a modulation of 'great.'"

There have been a lot of variations in Spike's persona over six seasons, from villain, to comic relief when Spike's bloodlust is curtailed by a government chip in his brain, to Buffy's secret lover, to vampire with a soul –

who's required a lot of rescuing. "It's been Olive Oyl recently," James laughs. "I'm the damsel in distress!"

Which Spike does James like best? "There's the immediate gratification of playing the bad boy killer. But there's a deeper satisfaction of pursuing something that tries to reconcile that with redemption. Redemption is a theme that most writers shy away from, because it can seem sappy, but it's also wonderful if you could say something about

BLOND
ambition

woman. I dragged her across the stage by her hair, she dropped me off a 10-foot drop into a spa. That scene is the end of the play, and you get an emotional release [afterward]. If you do movies or plays, you choose what kind of projects you would be willing to do."

On a television series, however, actors are bound to perform the scripts as they come in. James now feels that it might have helped to discuss the scene further with Sarah prior to filming. "I think she probably tried [to talk about it]. It just terrified me. There was actually much less physical contact between Sarah and I than it looks like. We're playing with depth of field illusions, where the two

> "I, IN MY ARROGANCE, THINK [A SPIKE SPIN-OFF] WOULD BE A GREAT IDEA. BUT WHAT DO YOU CALL [A SPIKE SPIN-OFF] – NOT ANGEL? ANGEL'S A GREAT SHOW. YOU DON'T NEED TWO OF THEM."

redemption that's real, and it's very gratifying to be in on trying to do that. So in a way, I'm the most excited now. Spike is passing through all the guilt of really facing what he did when he was a killer. And he did some heinous stuff. I envisioned him remembering how he killed [each victim], how it felt, and having to really deal with that, trying to bring Spike into the moral universe that is *Buffy* without compromising the integrity of the show. I've never felt less secure artistically. This year is just all about letting it all hang out and risking everything."

When James came on board as Spike, he didn't realize the character was going to spend so much time in emotional pain. "I have to say, Method acting for series television can eat you alive. I don't think anybody who invented it was thinking in terms of submerging [in a character's emotions] that long. I may have learned a bit of a lesson there – trust the writing more and not put myself through so much. I suspect I'm instinctually pro-

tecting myself a little more from the work than I did before. I used to lay myself open to it, but I think I've learned that it can take weird turns unexpectedly in TV, and go places you never imagined very quickly."

James acknowledges that he never imagined when he signed on to play Spike that he'd wind up doing the attempted rape scene in "Seeing Red." "It still haunts me. I am artistically proud to have done it, but it was the hardest day of my career." Making it still more difficult, "Sarah [Michelle Gellar] is a friend of mine. I can't watch movies about women or children getting hurt. If anyone hits a woman, I want to kill the guy who played the role, I want to kill the guy who wrote it, the guy who filmed it, and it doesn't even matter if it's in a good movie. It's a completely irrational thing for me."

On stage, James has twice played men who are violent with women. "In *Voices in the Dark*, I played a serial killer [who has] a 10-minute fight scene with a

characters both move violently, and it looks like they're touching, but they're not. That scene, more than any other, was very carefully choreographed."

Unlike many screen sexual assaults, the scene was played not as though Spike's actions were premeditated or deliberately hostile, but rather as though he was too lost in his emotions to fully comprehend what he was doing until Buffy kicked him across the room. "It was written very carefully. But I was more freaked out about the scene than I should have been, and I think that freaked Sarah out, and then I, as the character, reacted to her freaking out and that dynamic kind of fed on itself. I think that it ended up being a much more aggressive and violent scene than we intended. I think there was an attempt to keep it from being that painful, but it played that way and so we have to deal with it. See, this is what happens when you are brave artistically. You set fires. And some of the fires burn hotter than you expected. *Buffy* is very brave about the risks we take, and that one burned us. At the same time, I'm kind of glad we did it. I was not glad that I *had* to do it, but it puts us in an interesting place."

The scene certainly put Spike in an interesting place, horrifying him so much that he takes the unheard-of step for a vampire of voluntarily getting a soul. "That's why the rape scene was there," James acknowledges. "Because how do you motivate him – how do you make him make a mistake that's so heart-rending that he'd be willing to do that?"

Even when Spike was soulless, James tried to hint that the character might not be *completely* bad. "When Spike thought the chip was inactive [in 'Smashed'], he went straight for a victim. [The writers] wanted to make that very clear. They gave me two [sets of] ellipses [in the speech to the intended victim], and I

Sunnydale's MOST WANTED!

DOES SPIKE DESERVE A STAKE? CHECK OUT TOM ROOT'S RUNDOWN OF SPIKE'S GREATEST HITS AND JUDGE FOR YOURSELF!

Now that he's got a soul, Buffy seems to have more or less forgiven Spike for the mayhem he's caused in the past. But for Pete's sake, this guy's done a lot of nasty things in his vampire career! Here's a list of some of the worst.

THE NAME GAME

When Spike first visits Sunnydale in Season Two, Buffy and the gang learn that the vampire, also known as "William the Bloody," goes by the name of Spike. Why? He earned the moniker because of his rather nasty trademark – torturing his victims with railroad spikes…

SLAYER HATER, PART 1

In Season Five's episode "Fool for Love," Buffy forces Spike to describe the Slayers he's killed in the past. The first was in China, during the Boxer Rebellion in 1900. The Slayer has Spike beaten and very nearly puts a stake in his heart when an explosion interrupts the proceedings. Spike sees his chance and puts his fangs in her. The dying Slayer's last words? "Tell my mother I'm sorry." Unfortunately, Spike doesn't speak Chinese…

SLAYER HATER, PART 2

The second Slayer-killing Spike describes during Season Five's "Fool for Love" takes place in 1977 New York, on a moving subway. Spike pins down the Slayer, breaks her neck, and takes her leather jacket. That's bad enough. The kicker? The Slayer is revealed in Season Seven to be Principal Wood's mother. Wow, not only was the poor gal fighting to save humanity, she was also someone's mom. Shame on you, Spike!

HERE COMES THE SUN

Even Spike's fellow baddies can't trust him. At the end of "School Hard," after a particularly unpleasant day in which he's thwarted by Buffy, Spike decides he's tired of listening to Collin, the Anointed One (the Master's successor), and hoists Collin's cage up into direct sunlight. The demonic child, whom Spike called "The Annoying One," is dusted.

UH-OH, IT'S MAGIC

Sunnydale had a magic shop long before Giles decided he'd give it a go. But in Season Three's "Lover's Walk," the store's original owner runs into trouble… in the form of Spike. Visiting the shop, angry at Angel and looking for the ingredients for a spell to put "dripping pustules" all over his rival's face, the shopping trip soon turns into a quick snack. Bye bye, shopkeeper.

HERE KITTY KITTY

In "Life Serial" from Season Six, a dejected Buffy accompanies Spike to a friendly game of poker. The other players are all demons, and when Clem tells everyone to ante up, it turns out the group is playing for kittens. Cute, mewling kittens. Now, we're not saying Spike would eat a kitten – although maybe he would – but the fact that he'd gamble kitties with a bunch of demons ready to gobble them down is bad enough. Guilt by association, man.

FOR BETTER OR VERSE

None of these atrocities measures up to Spike's biggest crime… his poetry. Spike's couplets were so miserable that he earned the nickname "William the Bloody" long before he ever became a vamp – for his "bloody awful" poetry. ✢

seized on that hesitancy. I'm always trying to play a little more soul than is written."

In Season Seven, Spike's soul taxes his sanity, especially in the first few episodes, where he's talking to himself in the school basement. "I kept saying, 'No, he's just really depressed,' I kept

about film, and someone proclaiming themselves in a room with only two people in it is just not that dramatic. And so Joss employed the great cinematic device of potential danger in the shadows. Spike went away into the shadows, and Buffy didn't know where he was, and that tension

scene. For years, he's said that if we see Spike's feet leave the ground, it's stunt double Steve Tartalia. However, that's really James doing the Spike vs. Bringer stunt in "Showtime." "I did a takedown that had everybody going crazy," he reveals happily. "Usually, we're fighting on cement, which is unforgiving for those kind of gags. But we were on a raised set that was really giving, so I did the footsweep. I'm like, 'Dude! It's WWF!' The reason I don't [usually] do those gags – first of all, Steve is an artist at doing that, but [also] on a cement floor, it's just brutal."

People often ask about a Spike spin-off. "I, in my arrogance, think that would be a great idea," James says. "I think that you could hold the audience's attention with the character. But what do you call [a Spike spin-off] – *Not Angel*? *Angel*'s a great show. You don't need two of them."

At press time, no one knows whether there will be any *Buffy* spin-offs. James says he would have been happy if *Buffy* had

"[THE RAPE SCENE] STILL HAUNTS ME. I AM ARTISTICALLY PROUD TO HAVE DONE IT, BUT IT WAS THE HARDEST DAY OF MY CAREER."

trying to save my dignity," James laughs. "And Joss [Whedon] would say, 'No. He's bonkers, his mind is absolutely shattered.'"

A prime example is the climax of "Beneath You", with a distraught Spike revealing to Buffy why he got the soul. Douglas Petrie scripted the episode, but Joss rewrote the final scene. "In the first [version]," James explains, "it was a lot more of Spike talking about what his experience was, which works really well on the stage. Both Doug and I come from the stage, and we were actually excited it was becoming theatrical. This is all hindsight, but I think [a soliloquy] is dramatic onstage because it's amazing for a person to stand in front of a group of people and be honest and open. But there's an implied privacy

held the scene while Spike talked about himself. Also, having me come in from the shadows allowed me to be more theatrical. Because you couldn't see my face, I could put more in the voice. Stage is hanging words in the air. Joss gave me a situation where we could get away with doing that on film."

Some of James' favorite *Buffy* scenes are early ones: "I remember the first fight scene with Sarah. It was a fairly long fight with a lot of moves and Sarah was rocking. And [in 'A New Man'], driving around and hearing Tony's [Head] voice, and looking over, and he's a demon. I just almost blew so many takes [laughing], it was so delightful."

James is also proud of a recent fight

kept going in its current form. "Anything that evolves this way, you only hope it can last this long. My character has better arcs than any character, except for a lead, has in any other project, movies or theater. And I'm not afraid of long-term projects. To tell you the truth, I'm not tired at *all*. We've got a lot of really great writers, great directors – I'm not afraid of going dry just yet. And I know that we could have continued to make good stories. Why would you want that to end?"

Although *Buffy* is drawing to a close, James says it doesn't feel like the end just yet: "I think it will later," he qualifies. "But right now, we're at war. The enemy is time and we're in the trenches, getting shot in the head by time. This is a long, sustained campaign, so you can't think about the future when you're in the middle of a season."

What can he tell us about the finale? James laughs: "For the first time, I know one thing that's going to happen and I don't want to blow it. The end of the season will be very romantic. The Buffy/Spike thing is gonna end very dramatically. It's both the coolest thing and the worst idea I've ever heard of in my life. It is the last thing I ever would have thought about doing, but when it was described to me, it almost seems inevitable. We are going to piss off people – oh, my God! But we're going to make them love more. It's amazing. I'm trying to think of another [creator] that's like [Joss], that takes you on really dark paths, but because you trust their heart, you know that they're talking about

but I'm an American.' And now I'm one of those actors I used to detest who could go get a stage job because I'm on some damn TV show. I've always felt I was good enough to do it, as every actor does, so hell, I'll use it!"

Plays James would like to do include Steven Berkoff's *Kvetch* and George Bernard Shaw's anti-war comedy *Arms and the Man*. However, there's no master plan. "I've never been one to set up a bunch of projects. I've always focused right on what I'm doing. I don't want to sound cocky, but I also feel very confident, because I had a career before *Buffy* in stage, that I can go back and have a career in stage again. A

love, probably, in the end of it, and that it's okay for them to take you through that dark journey and agitate you and make you afraid and angry and all of those things. I trust Joss, I trust Marti [Noxon] and I think our audience does, too. It's gonna [end beautifully]."

What does James see himself doing after *Buffy*? Besides continuing to perform with the band Ghost of the Robot, "I keep thinking of stage. I could get hired in New York, and I could get hired in London. I always thought, 'I'd love to break the West End,

stage actor has audience feedback right when he does something, so he knows when he's boring and when he's not boring. I know that I can be boring, but I also know that if I do my job correctly, I'm fairly successful in holding the

audience's attention. I have confidence that I do one thing well. I'm not a good carpenter. I don't know what's ahead, but I do know that I'm pretty well set to make my living acting for the foreseeable future."

Does James see acting any differently than he did when he started out? "I've become more ambitious, and I've become more specific about what I want out of storytelling. I have my own agenda now. [In] maybe my third play, *The Me That Nobody Knows*, I had a song and I was belting it out to this little audience in junior college in Modesto, and [got] that feeling of finding a way to let my light shine, and feeling like I found a home that night. I found a way that I could start to try to get at my best self. That's just a process of being very public about the things that we're normally very private about. Putting it on stage makes you consider it more and it makes you deal with your own issues. And that hasn't changed. I've moved on to having a list of plays that I want to produce, having ideas that I want to write about, knowing the kind of theater and television that I find valuable. But really, underneath it all, is just the joy of being able to express myself and learn that I'm not alone. Because that's what all artists are doing, is trying to get at something that is universal, because what happens when that's expressed is, whatever we're talking about, we all remember that we're really not alone." ✛

Angel Overview

Soul Man

DAVID BOREANAZ STEPS OUT OF THE SHADOWS TO DISCUSS PLAYING ANGEL, DODGING STAKES AND TO REVEAL WHO'S REALLY THE BADDEST BLOODSUCKER IN HOLLYWOOD.

BY MIKE STOKES

There are many ways to gauge the popularity of an actor. You can count the number of current magazines with his picture on the cover. You can take a stroll through Planet Hollywood to see whether his favourite jumpsuit is closer to the restroom or the bar. Or you can add up all the messages left by agents, interview requests and unread scripts piled up by his mailbox. There are so many ways, in fact, that the whole process can get quite complicated.

Then again, David Boreanaz just has to look at his dog. Chances are, if Bertha Blue is gaining weight, Boreanaz' star is on the rise. Incidentally, the black labrador hasn't been missing any meals lately.

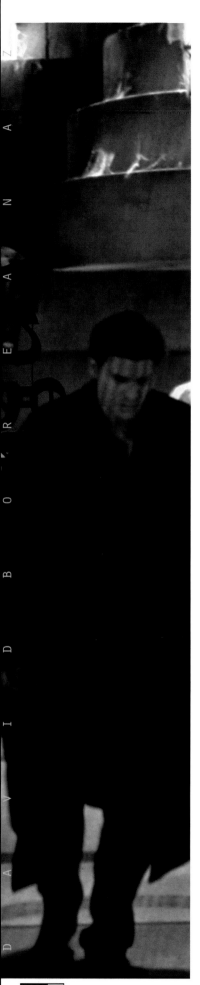

Boreanaz had been doing a lot of acting on stage and some sporadic work in commercials – both noble pursuits, but neither offered the job security to start buying the good canned stuff with any regularity.

When *Buffy the Vampire Slayer* debuted in 1997, it was just a matter of time before Boreanaz would emerge as a breakout star. In addition to his own talent, he was teamed with an excellent cast, outstanding writers, and let's face it – the guy's not going to be mistaken for Urkel in a lineup.

Introduced as a dark and mysterious stranger, Angel steadily developed into a complex character with a tortured soul who is capable of veering wildly across the line between good and evil. Whether he was saving humanity or plotting its extinction, Boreanaz proved he was up to the task of taking Angel in either direction. As *Buffy's* popularity soared over its first two seasons, there were suddenly too many stories for Joss Whedon to tell to be contained to one hour per week, so the idea for a spinoff was hatched. And Boreanaz, as Angel, was to anchor it.

So has this rapid success begun to spoil Boreanaz? Not a bit. Ask anyone who's worked with him, and they'll say he's, well, an angel. A self-described "old school" type of guy, talking to Boreanaz gives you the sense that he's one of the good guys. Gracious and with a good sense of humour, aside from his day job as a nightstalker, he seems to lead a pretty normal life. He lives in a house – not a mausoleum. He sleeps in a bed – not a coffin. And he likes to spend time digging around in the garden – not in a graveyard (and he even does it during the day with sunlight and everything).

Boreanaz talked about what was in store for the upcoming third season of *Buffy*, vampires in general and what drew the little kid with the raging imagination from upstate New York to the bright lights of Hollywood. Boreanaz' star is rising quickly, but he approaches his newfound celebrity with a blend of caution, confidence and savvy. He's willing to wait for the right projects to come along rather than striking while the iron is hot, and if he doesn't get what he wants right now, he's perfectly willing to wait.

By the time the interview was over, it became obvious that Boreanaz, like the character he plays, has a lot of heart and soul, and that after two years in the shadows, his story was just beginning.

BUFFY THE MAGAZINE: YOU LOOK PRETTY GOOD FOR BEING 242 YEARS OLD.
DAVID BOREANAZ: Pretty good lookin', huh? Angel ages well. He's 242 years old, but he's a vampire, so he has that immortal essence to him. That's a beauty.

BTM: ASIDE FROM THE OLD ADAGE THAT EVERY DAY ABOVE GROUND IS A GOOD DAY, WHAT EVENTS WOULD YOU HAVE LIKED TO HAVE BEEN AROUND FOR OVER THE PAST 200 YEARS?
DB: Probably Woodstock, or maybe seeing the '69 Mets would have been cool. The evening hours I enjoy to begin with, so I'd probably like to see a couple nice sunsets and sunrises.

BTM: WHEN WE LAST SAW ANGEL, HE WAS ON HIS WAY TO THE UNDERWORLD. HOW HAS HE BEEN HOLDING UP?
DB: Yeah, Angel got caught up in the vortex. Buffy sent him to the society of Hell, so he's been travelling. The time that he will have spent when he comes back is equivalent to about 100 years of torture on Earth, so he has some serious pain that he's going through right now. Angel will be a little messed up when he comes back.

BTM: SO WHEN BUFFY'S BOYFRIEND COMES BACK, IS SHE GONNA BE IN TROUBLE?
DB: I don't know exactly how Angel will be. That's a character choice that the writers are creating. I know a little bit about it, but I can't give that much away. I do know that it will be pretty crazy.

BTM: DID YOU EVER HAVE A GIRLFRIEND TRY TO KILL YOU WITH A WOODEN STAKE?
DB: All the time! [laughs] They're just thrown at me left and right. They don't want to stop. They just want to keep shoving stakes down my throat.

BTM: HOW IS IT TO BE WORKING SO CLOSELY WITH ONE OF *PEOPLE MAGAZINE'S* MOST BEAUTIFUL PEOPLE?
DB: Just like anyone else. Sarah [Michelle Gellar]'s a great girl to work with. I really love it. I really enjoy responding to her and working off her. We have a lot of fun. We play a lot and we get intense, so it goes full circle with the two of us. It's a lot of fun.

BTM: WHAT SETS *BUFFY* CREATOR JOSS WHEDON APART FROM OTHER GUYS IN HIS POSITION?

DB: What's great and unique and fortunate is that [the *Buffy* cast is] with someone who's climbing the ladder of storytelling and bringing television to a different genre. He's created an hour show that's unique and fun, and we're kind of along for the ride. It's exposed us and given us an opportunity to exercise our chops in more ways than we can imagine. He's a big jokester, but he's a serious guy as well. When he has to get a shot, there's no fooling around, and he gets what he wants because he's Joss Whedon, and because he's a creative genius... he's a super genius.

BTM: WHAT'S THE MOOD LIKE ON THE SET?

DB: Very loose. Not much tension. Joss keeps a very playful set. The fact that he's a producer who comes down to the set and actually partakes is a unique thing for a Hollywood television show. It's like an old-school thing. It's a lot of fun, people get along, and we're very close to the crew. They're one of the best crews—they're really

> # JOSS WHEDON GETS WHAT HE WANTS BECAUSE HE'S A CREATIVE GENIUS. HE'S A SUPER GENIUS.

responsive. Michael Gershman, who is the director of photography, is great to play with. Everyone from the props to the people in wardrobe are great, so it's a really fun atmosphere.

BTM: WHAT'S THE STRANGEST PART ABOUT GOING TO WORK?

DB: The make-up is probably the funniest part, because the different types of characters that come out of the makeup chair are pretty bizarre. You see demons and ghouls and spirits – yes, we do actually see spirits – and you'll be having normal conversations with them. Other people walk by and kind of do a doublecheck. You have to pinch them if they haven't been around,

but we take it for granted. Every day offers something that's kind of fun and exciting. Something's always coming out of the corners from the different creatures that are on the show each week.

BTM: GOOD ANGEL OR BAD ANGEL? WHICH IS YOUR FAVOURITE?

DB: Both. There's not really one that I prefer over the other. I think that there's a combination of the two of them that I really enjoy. I like the vulnerable side of him, and I also like the nasty side of him. Evil is more than likely what everybody says is better to play, but you don't really want to play it all the time.

BTM: HOW WAS THE PART OF ANGEL DESCRIBED TO YOU WHEN YOU FIRST AUDITIONED FOR THE ROLE?

DB: One of the lines I remember best about him is that he may get hit, but he'll always come back. He has the grace and movements of a boxer, and he's mysterious. That's all I really remember of it. When I went in and did the reading, [casting director] Marcia Shulman just told me not to be a "vampire," so to speak.

BTM: SHE DIDN'T WANT ANY THICK TRANSYLVANIAN ACCENTS?

DB: Exactly. None of this *"and God spoke"* crap.

BTM: IF YOU WEREN'T PLAYING THE ROLE OF ANGEL, WHO ON THE SHOW WOULD YOU LIKE TO BE?

DB: Joss Whedon, of course. Character-wise, I like Willow. Alyson [Hannigan] plays a really cool character. I like her sense of giddiness and happiness. She's also a very shy character.

BTM: DO YOU EVER WISH YOUR CHARACTER HAD A MORE OMINOUS-SOUNDING NAME?

DB: No. I think it's the perfect name for him, because it represents who he is, where his past was and how he is today. I have no problem with it at all. I mean, how can you say anything bad about an angel?

Highway to Hell

After only two seasons as Buffy's on-again, off-again vampire boyfriend, David Boreanaz had been cruising in the fast lane towards TV stardom. But long before Sarah Michelle Gellar shocked viewers by shoving a sword through Angel's heart to send him on the highway to Hell in the second season finale of Buffy the Vampire Slayer, Boreanaz' career was stuck in the parking lot.

"I used to valet park, and that was pretty bad," Boreanaz says. "It was a humbling experience, but it definitely gave me character."

While he got to meet a lot of big stars with nice cars, being a mechanic wasn't in the cards for Boreanaz. He soon found work in commercials and on stage at the Hudson Theater in Los Angeles. When he wasn't acting, Boreanaz tried to stay as close to the acting world as he could by working in a props department.

"I kind of immersed myself in the business rather than becoming a waiter – I never really understood that," he says. "I wanted to be around the business rather than distance myself from it."

His perseverance paid off. With viewers buzzing about the future of Angel, fans mobbing him at personal appearances and an Angel spin-off show due in 1999, he's working alongside the same people whose cars he used to speed through parking decks. But are there any lousy tippers or five-star jerks he remembers from the old days who he'd just as soon run over as rub elbows with?

"No response on that one," Boreanaz laughs. "I hear no evil, speak no evil."

Not unless he's just acting.

ESSENTIAL ANGEL

Angel's Top 10 Episodes with Bite

Welcome to the Hellmouth, season 1, episode 1
Popping up on the scene to warn Buffy of dangers ahead, the mysterious stranger tells her only that he's a friend – and not necessarily hers. Who can deny his charm? This mystery man's got style.

Angel, season 1, episode 7
Angel's real name, where he's from, how he feeds and whether he has any distinguishing marks are revealed. His romance with Buffy also heats up, but their first kiss reveals his vampire status and then he's framed for snacking on Buffy's mom.

Prophecy Girl, season 1, episode 12
The Master is getting stronger and Giles and Angel warn Buffy to head for the hills. Though Xander suspects Angel is eyeballing his jugular, the two rivals work together to save their beloved.

Reptile Boy, season 2, episode 5
Willow threatens to steal the show by uncharacter-istically reading Angel and Xander the riot act and then posing the question of how the non-reflective Angel shaves. Angel steals it back, however, as he vamps-out and prepares to kick some frat boy ass.

Lie to Me, season 2, episode 7
Angel reveals his dark past. "Things used to be pretty simple. One hundred years just hanging out, feeling guilty. I really honed my brooding skills – then she comes along." Watch out Bogart.

The Dark Age, season 2, episode 8
Angel not only saves Giles' life from Eyghon, but lets the demon jump into his own body to free Jenny Calendar of it's parasitic threat.

Innocence, season 2, episode 14
Angel is dead…long live Angelus! After experiencing true happiness with Buffy, Angel's soul goes on hiatus and the bloodthirsty killing machine is back. "She made me feel like a human being," he says. "That's just not the kind of thing you forgive."

Passion, season 2, episode 17
"Without passion, maybe we'd know some kind of peace," Angel says. That means no rest for the Slayer as he plots Buffy's demise.

I Only Have Eyes for You, season 2, episode 19
When the ghosts of a student-teacher affair that resulted in a 1955 murder-suicide reenact the scene through Buffy and Angel, the tortured spirits are freed, but Angel is left visibly shaken.

Becoming, part 2, season 2, episode 22
Willow restores Angel's soul just as he opens the portal to the Hellmouth, but it's too late. Buffy rams a sword through his heart, and a confused and hurt Angel is sucked into Hell's vortex.

BTM: Did you do any research when you found out you were going to play a vampire?

DB: It happened so fast. I'd read all the Anne Rice novels way beforehand, and I love the whole vampire lore and the whole romantic aura that it presents itself with, but I'm not a fiend about it. I don't go home and do sacrifices in the bathtub or roam the graveyards late at night.

BTM: Maybe you're just not putting your heart into it.

DB: I'll have to start doing that, I guess. Even though Angel gave Drusilla a heart once for Valentine's day. I like the whole genre, but I'm not overly obsessed by it. Our make-up artist, Todd McIntosh, is way into it. He loves it.

BTM: The character you play has hit the plateau where he's popular enough for his own show. What can fans expect from the Angel spinoff in 1999?

DB: It'll be a little bit more of a darker series. It's going to be more of an adult show. Angel's going to tap into the resources of everybody's minds in Los Angeles and fight their inner demons. It's kind of like a quest to save humanity. He's also going to be a character than can go bad or good – he'll take the soul or save the soul, depending upon the situation. The stories are going to be very strange. Of course, you have Joss running it and David Greenwalt – the two of them write these *Buffy* episodes together – it's going to be very unique and different. It's going to be a chronicle and kind of an extension of *Buffy*. It's moving on to a different level, a different look, and a different show, but the same kind of premises.

BTM: What do you think sets a successful spin-off like *Frasier* apart from a spinoff like *After M*A*S*H*?

DB: *After M*A*S*H*? What's *After M*A*S*H*?

BTM: Exactly.

DB: [Laughs] Right. *Frasier* is similar as far as inviting other characters (from *Cheers*) to the show – that *will* happen. But Frasier moved to Seattle. Angel is moving outside of Sunnydale, but still in California, so he's close in proximity. I think when you have something like that rather than having a totally new environment, it helps. Otherwise, it'd be harder for audience members to accept.

BTM: What do you think makes Angel such a cool character?

DB: Because he always wore the same outfit in the first season [laughs]. I think he just responds to people's inner mysteriousness – their passion for life, I guess. This is a character that's been well-developed by the writers and will continue to be well-developed. There's a deep sense of his past that we got exposed to, but that's just the tip of the iceberg. There's more to this character than there is on the surface. That's what's one of the best parts about playing it.

BTM: You only had one set of clothes the whole season?

DB: Just one, that was it. I just had one.

BTM: Did someone at least wash them?

DB: Yep, they had to wash it every night.

BTM: Including the guy who plays Ted in Bill & Ted's Excellent Adventure, who wins in a fight between Angel and any of the vampires in *The Lost Boys*?

DB: That's a good question. They wouldn't be able to wipe out the evil Angel, that's for sure. It'd probably be a draw. The good Angel would win, only because of his smarts. He'd have more of an edge.

[I DON'T WANT TO RUSH ANYTHING. THAT'S WHEN YOU BECOME SOMEONE WHO DID A ROLE AND IS NO LONGER WORKING, AND I DON'T WANT TO GO DOWN THAT PATH.]

BTM: COUNT DRACULA OR COUNT CHOCULA?
DB: Count Chocula. Definitely. I'm a big cereal guy.

BTM: WHAT KIND OF A KID WERE YOU GROWING UP?
DB: I was all over the place. I loved to go ride my bike, play in the woods. I was an adventurous kind of a kid. I got into trouble only because I let my imagination run wild. That's the only reason why I would get in trouble when I was a kid. Then as I grew older, I became very shy and inward. My high school years were pretty sad, but whose aren't? I was really kind of a misfit. I was bored with a lot of things. It wasn't until I got to college that I experienced life.

BTM: HOW DID YOUR HIGH SCHOOL COMPARE TO SUNNYDALE HIGH?
DB: I went to an all boys preparatory school in the Philadelphia suburbs, so I'd say it compared differently. I had Augustinian priests instead of demons running around, but in the same sense, they are demons [laughs]. If you want to look at it that way, it was the same.

BTM: WHAT WAS YOUR FIRST ACTING BREAK?
DB: It'd probably be a commercial when I came to Los Angeles. The third day I got here, I walked into a production office and there was a Foster's Beer commercial [being shot]. I wanted to work behind the camera, and they threw me in front of the camera.

BTM: YOU WERE A FILM STUDENT IN COLLEGE?
DB: Yeah, I went to Ithaca College in New York. I studied film there for three years. It's a really beautiful area.

BTM: DO YOU HAVE LONG-RANGE PLANS BEHIND THE CAMERA?
DB: Sometime in the future. Right now, I'm just having fun acting and playing different characters and personalities. I think it's a trip. I'm just starting to really get into it and get my feet wet in this business with acting. I did theatre in the past, and I'm in a position now where I can hopefully do some films down the line and continue to do more of *Buffy the Vampire Slayer*. I just want to learn from my work and continue to grow as an actor.

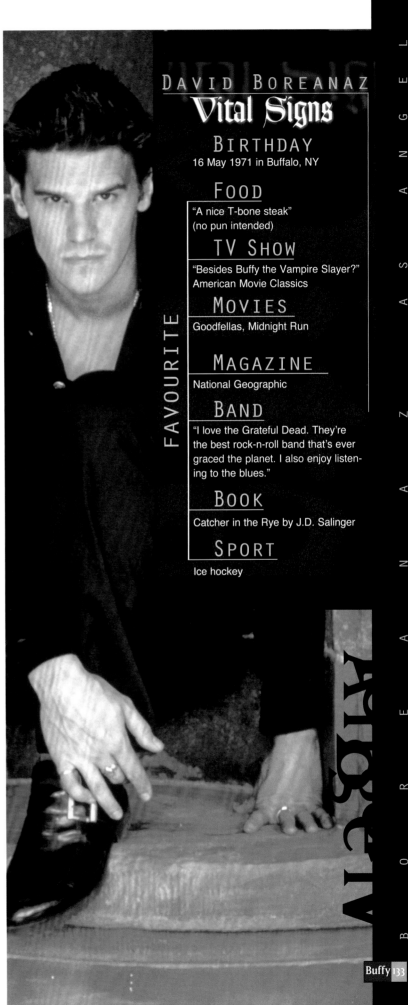

DAVID BOREANAZ
Vital Signs

BIRTHDAY
16 May 1971 in Buffalo, NY

FOOD
"A nice T-bone steak" (no pun intended)

TV SHOW
"Besides Buffy the Vampire Slayer?" American Movie Classics

MOVIES
Goodfellas, Midnight Run

MAGAZINE
National Geographic

BAND
"I love the Grateful Dead. They're the best rock-n-roll band that's ever graced the planet. I also enjoy listening to the blues."

BOOK
Catcher in the Rye by J.D. Salinger

SPORT
Ice hockey

FAVOURITE

> [I LOVE THE WHOLE
> VAMPIRE LORE, BUT
> I'M NOT A FIEND
> ABOUT IT. I DON'T
> ROAM GRAVEYARDS
> AT NIGHT.]

BTM: DO YOU GET RECOGNISED ON THE STREET A LOT NOW?

DB: Yeah, I do more and more. Of course living in LA, it's less, because everybody takes it for granted. They see stars every day. But New York's crazy. So is Chicago [and] Philadelphia. It gets kind of nuts.

BTM: I HEARD THERE WAS A PRETTY BIG INCIDENT IN NEW YORK CITY WHEN YOU MADE AN APPEARANCE TO LAUNCH THE *BUFFY* CLOTHING LINE.

DB: Yeah, it was pretty nuts. I was at the Warner Bros. store for an appearance to open up their clothing line, and fans were lined up for blocks. The cops came, and they had to shut me down 20 minutes into it, and I had to be ushered out and jump buildings. It was pretty scary. Pretty wild.

BTM: WHAT DO YOUR MUM AND DAD THINK OF YOUR NEW HEARTTHROB STATUS?

DB: My parents have always been supportive of whatever I wanted to do, so one of the best things is being able to see them enjoy it. Being able to have two great parents that can kind of chill out and hang and watch your success and be a part of it – that's one of the best things about being in this business.

BTM: WHAT'S NEXT FOR YOU?

DB: I want to just continue to work on my acting. Whatever comes, comes. I'm a patient person. I like to take baby steps. I don't want to rush anything. That's when you become someone who did a role and is no longer working, and I don't want to go down that path. I'd be more inclined to just do stuff that I really have love for, and that will come. In time, that will happen. ✢

in the Nic

WE CAUGHT UP
WITH NICK BRENDON
TO CHAT ABOUT
HIS FINAL DAYS
AS XANDER BEFORE
HE JETTED OFF TO
TORONTO TO WORK
ON HIS LATEST
PROJECT, ABC'S
FAMILY CHANNEL
MOVIE *CELESTE IN
THE CITY* – AND
WHILE HE WAS
RECOVERING FROM A
BOUT OF THE FLU...

BY TARA DILULLO

Over seven seasons in his role as Alexander 'Xander' Lavelle Harris on *Buffy the Vampire Slayer*, actor Nicholas Brendon has just about done it all. As part of the original core four characters, along with Buffy, Giles and Willow, Xander grew up before our eyes, maturing from wisecracking, awkward geek, to the steadfast and dependable rock upon which his friends could always rely. While he may not have had slayer strength or magical aptitude, Xander was always ready with the funnies and ever willing to jump into the fray to help save the world time after time. Sure, his dating record became a proverbial punchline as he displayed an unwitting penchant for demons (the Inca Mummy Girl, Lissa, Anya and, some might say, Cordelia), but that just made Xander all the more human and beloved in the hearts of the fans. Looking back over seven years, it may have been the Slayer's story that propelled the series, but watching the journey of Xander from kid to carpenter – so wonderfully portrayed by Nick Brendon – provided the series with much of its indelible heart.

It's been more than six months since Buffy looked off into the distance with the glint of hope in her eyes and the series faded to black. Since then, Nick has been moving forward with his career, working on new projects and enjoying time with his wife, actress and writer Tressa DiFiglia. But, as Nick reveals as he reminisces about the final season and his personal and professional growth over seven years on *Buffy*, the role of Xander isn't one that is easily packed away...

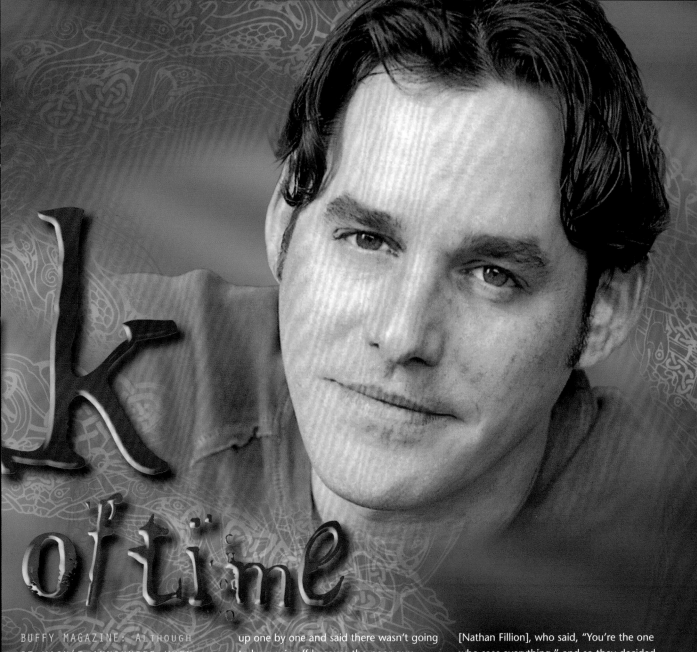

k of time

BUFFY MAGAZINE: ALTHOUGH IT WASN'T ANNOUNCED WHEN YOU STARTED WORKING ON SEASON SEVEN OF *BUFFY*, DID YOU HAVE A FEELING THAT IT WAS GOING TO BE THE SHOW'S LAST SEASON?
NICK BRENDON: We had a feeling. A few of us had a few more years on our contracts, but UPN only had the two years contracted. We knew something was different but we didn't necessarily believe it was going to be the last season until we read it on the front of *Entertainment Weekly*.

THAT MUST HAVE BEEN A SHOCK.
Yeah, yeah. The rumblings were rumbling a bit louder. [Laughs] Joss was talking about doing a spin-off, but he was just so exhausted at that point. Then he called us up one by one and said there wasn't going to be a spin-off because the poor guy needed some rest.

EVEN THOUGH SOME FANS COMPLAINED THAT THERE WEREN'T ENOUGH STORIES ABOUT XANDER IN THE FINAL SEASON, YOU STILL HAD SOME GREAT MOMENTS IN SEASON SEVEN. WHAT WERE SOME OF THE STANDOUT EPISODES FOR YOU?
I sure liked my left eye, so that was a problem! Joss had knocked around the idea of killing Xander, and then they decided that the fans would not have been happy with that. Xander was the 'eyes' of the group, and, being the carpenter, also the nails that held the group together. Then he had the whole thing with Caleb [Nathan Fillion], who said, "You're the one who sees everything," and so they decided to take an eye out. It's all fun and games until someone loses an eye. [Laughs]

HOW MUCH OF A CHALLENGE WAS IT FOR YOU AS AN ACTOR TO BE EYE IMPAIRED?
It was tough when I was wearing that big white turban, because I couldn't take it off for hours at a time. But when I finally had the eye-patch, it was a lot easier because I could just flip it up. But when I had it on for four or five hours, my vision was very askew. I would bump into things.

DID IT BOTHER YOU THAT XANDER TOOK SUCH A BEATING AT THE END?
It was sad because if they ever do a film,

I'm going to have to wear an eye patch [Laughs]. It was hard because I was with that kid for seven years and we've become very close, obviously. It was easy to act because I felt so deeply for the character.

THE BEAUTIFUL SPEECH YOU GAVE TO DAWN IN "POTENTIAL" ABOUT BEING SPECIAL WAS ONE OF XANDER'S BEST MOMENTS.

WAS THAT A DIFFICULT SCENE TO SHOOT?
Joss was directing. It was a Jim Contner episode, but on those important scenes, the director defers to Joss. I must have done that scene 20 times. It's a fairly long monologue, but Joss is like a maestro. Literally, the way Joss and I work is that on a specific line, he'll want me to tune it like half a pitch. He'll say on this line, "Go down half a pitch there." I was exhausted

at the end. We must have spent three hours just on my coverage for that scene alone. When you are shooting that kind of show in eight days that is a long time.

ANOTHER MEMORABLE SCENE WAS THE EMOTIONAL MOMENT BETWEEN XANDER AND WILLOW IN THE HOSPITAL IN "EMPTY PLACES."
Yeah. Alyson [Hannigan] and I work very well together, as do Michelle [Trachtenberg] and I, but I've been working with Aly for seven years. We did that scene in two or three takes. It was quite simple for us to get there, and then knowing that we weren't going to come back next year made it easier to get there.

OVERALL, WHAT ARE YOUR FINAL THOUGHTS ON *BUFFY* SEASON SEVEN?
I think it was a fantastic season. We did have a lot of slayers in the last six or seven episodes, so we were pretty much in that living room. It got really hot in there and it was problematic, but not a horrible thing. The way the season ended, most of us survived, so hopefully someday in the future we can come back and do something again.

WHAT, FOR YOU, WERE THE HIGHLIGHTS OF ACTING ON A SHOW LIKE *BUFFY*?
I always liked going on location. Like for the exterior of the winery, we were in the hills of Malibu. It was nice to leave work and think about what you did that day, take the

top ten xander moments

10. "The Harvest": Xander shows what he's made of
Ten minutes ago, Xander was quietly freaking over the whole idea of vampires. Now he's following Buffy into the sewers to rescue his friend Jesse from those same vampires, despite Buffy's orders and his own terror. "Jesse's my bud, okay? If I can help him out, that's what I gotta do. Besides," he adds, "it's this or chem class."

9. "Lovers Walk":
Cordelia breaks up with Xander He and Willow yield to their feelings and lock lips just as Cordelia and Oz arrive. Later, Xander brings a huge bouquet to Cordy in the hospital. Before he can even start an inarticulate apology, Cordy orders him, "Stay away from me!" Xander almost crawls from the room.

8. "Triangle": Xander defends Willow and Anya from Olaf the Troll
Xander fights well for a "tiny man" – in fact, he survives blows from Olaf's hammer that ought to kill a Slayer. To reward his valor, Olaf tells Xander to choose which of his women Olaf will kill. Xander's got this sort of dilemma handled. He refuses to choose between his girlfriend and his best friend, even when Olaf breaks his hand.

Pacific Coast Highway home and listen to some jazz, and to think about how lucky you were.

NOW THAT IT'S ALL OVER, ARE YOU ABLE TO LOOK BACK ON THE SEVEN SEASONS OF *BUFFY* AND PINPOINT A YEAR WHICH STOOD OUT FOR YOU AS A PERSONAL HIGHLIGHT?

Well, each one is so different. The first season, we were all just in shock, me in particular, because it was my first acting job. But I know the titles of all of those first 13 episodes. The show became a hit

> { "JOSS HAD KNOCKED AROUND THE IDEA OF KILLING XANDER, AND THEN THEY DECIDED THAT THE FANS WOULD NOT HAVE BEEN HAPPY WITH THAT." }

like to see what I did there and which take they used, how I reacted and whether I was listening, because you can learn from yourself, too. I like it all, but the drama seems easier. You can make your own beats where the comedy is ba-dum, ba-dum, ba-dum.

in the second season. But it's weird, because I remember them more for where I was emotionally. Season Three I met my wife; Season Five I got married. So it progresses on where I was emotionally.

WHAT ABOUT INDIVIDUAL EPISODES?

"Hush," "Once More, With Feeling," "Nightmares," "The Body," "The Zeppo," and "Halloween" stand out the most for me. I remember "Halloween" in particular because that was when Princess Diana died.

BUFFY WAS YOUR FIRST LONG-TERM JOB. WHAT HAS SURPRISED YOU MOST ABOUT YOURSELF IN THE SEVEN YEARS YOU'VE SPENT DEVELOPING YOUR CRAFT?

The fact that I realized I could act and [do] the comedy stuff! I was just watching the Dracula episode ["Buffy vs. Dracula"]. I *love* that episode, and Kelly, my twin brother, who can be really harsh, said, "Aw man you are good!" It's really something to hear that from your brother. I would watch myself too, and I know a lot of actors don't, but I

WAS THERE A PARTICULAR STORYLINE YOU WOULD HAVE LIKED TO HAVE EXPLORED IF YOU'D HAD THE CHANCE?

Sarah [Michelle Gellar] and I, at the end of Season Six, talked to Joss about entertaining the idea of Buffy and Xander getting together. Joss thought about it too, but it made a lot of sense with Spike instead, because Buffy is always going after things that she can't have.

TONY HEAD (GILES) ONCE MENTIONED HOW YOU WERE BOTH

top ten xander moments

7. "Into the Woods": Xander the romance expert

Xander forces Buffy to listen to him as he tells her just how badly she's treated Riley, and offers advice on what to do to save their romance before it's too late. As Buffy goes off to try and find Riley before he leaves Sunnydale – and her – behind, Xander goes home, sits Anya down, and tells her in the most heartfelt and honest speech we've ever heard him give, exactly why he loves her.

6. "Bewitched, Bothered and Bewildered": Xander the stud

Xander gets Amy to cast a spell to make Cordelia love him after she breaks up with him, but it backfires and he finds himself the object of every other woman in Sunnydale's desires. But being the most popular man alive proves a disaster when the women decide if they can't have him he must die!

5. "The Zeppo": Faith's boy toy

During a bizarre night that includes a 1957 Chevy and an undead gang, Xander ends up alone with the very horny Slayer. The poor Zeppo doesn't know whether to be embarrassed or excited as she pulls off his clothes, throws him on her bed and "steers him around the curves." Then she pushes him out of the room half naked with his clothes in a bundle.

ALWAYS ASKING JOSS TO MAKE YOU BAD. DO YOU STILL WISH YOU HAD TURNED EVIL?
I love that guy! Tony and I loved being bad, and that's why Joss wanted to kill me because he wanted me to come back as The First. I was evil with Alyson in "The Wish" and "The Pack," but Xander pretty much *is* Joss.

THE WRITERS HAVE OFTEN COMMENTED THAT THEY TOTALLY HEAR XANDER'S VOICE COMING FROM JOSS. DID YOU THINK THE SAME AND BASE ANY OF YOUR PERFORMANCE ON JOSS?
No, I really did it my way. The great writing staff would write him and I would just close my eyes and click my heels three times. [Laughs]

YOU AND EMMA [CAULFIELD], AS ANYA, HAD A WONDERFUL CHEMISTRY. DO YOU HAVE A FAVORITE SCENE OR EPISODE FEATURING THE COUPLE?
Our musical number was fantastic. I like ["Hells Bells"], where we flashed forward with me in my tuxedo and we've got the demon kids. I also like the scene in "Selfless" where we say goodbye for the last time and I just kind of walk away.

HAVING PLAYED XANDER FOR SEVEN YEARS, WHAT PARTS OF THE CHARACTER ARE SIMILAR TO YOU AND WHAT PARTS COULDN'T BE FARTHER AWAY FROM NICK?
I really don't know how to use any type

{ "WHEN I HAD THE EYE-PATCH ON FOR FOUR OR FIVE HOURS, MY VISION WAS VERY ASKEW. I WOULD BUMP INTO THINGS." }

of tool. I can hammer stuff into walls. I can hammer stuff into my hands. I can glue! [Laughs] Otherwise, our sense of humor – there is a dryness there and the sensitive side; those are the characteristics that are the most similar.

YOU WERE DOING A PILOT AND FINISHING BUFFY AROUND THE SAME TIME LAST SPRING. WAS THAT AN ODD THING, TO BE CLOSING A CHAPTER OF YOUR

LIFE AND POTENTIALLY STARTING A NEW PHASE AT THE SAME TIME?
Yeah. I did a sitcom pilot for Fox [*The Pool at Maddy Breakers*] that wasn't picked up, so I was back and forth so much on that last episode ["Chosen"]. I shot my last episode of *Buffy* on a Wednesday and then I shot my sitcom on the following Thursday. I had to say goodbye to two casts on back-to-back days. It was amazing that I had something to go on to, but I

top ten xander moments

4. "Go Fish": Xander in Speedos
Xander's total buffness makes Buffy, Willow and Cordy – and the entire female audience – just about lose their eyeballs gawking. When he sees the girls looking, he abandons studly coolness, grabs a concealing kickboard, and stammers, "I'm under cover." "Not under much!" giggles Buffy.

3. "Hell's Bells": Xander leaves Anya at the altar
Even when he learns that the horrible futures he foresaw were all demon delusions, Xander can't see past his own parents' misery. "If this is a mistake, it's forever," he tearfully tells Anya. "I don't want to hurt you. Not that way. I am so sorry." Like he could do any more damage than abandoning her at the altar!

was prolonging the inevitable. I was going to cry even if the show was picked up, and I was working on it already. Then it was my birthday and summer was coming. Then I dislocated my shoulder and I couldn't move, so it kind of all hit me later on.

HOW IS THE TRANSITION FOR YOU NOW?

It's a slow process, and I knew it would be and so did my wife. I was trying to prepare myself for it but it's really hard. We just got back from Alyson's wedding last month and that was nice to see them all. If you include the presentation pilot, which I have never seen, *Buffy* ran for eight years. It was eight Christmases, eight Thanksgivings, eight Halloweens and eight birthdays. That's a long time. I'm still healing. It was a fantastic show; there was pretty much no weakness on that show.

YOU MADE IT OUT OF THE HELLMOUTH ALIVE. WOULD REVISITING XANDER IN THE FUTURE BE SOMETHING THAT WOULD INTEREST YOU?

Oh completely! That's why I was happy Joss didn't kill me! I would have done it one more year, but there was a higher power. Now we'll take a couple of years off and then hopefully have us all come together again. We'll all have kids running around the set... actually, I'm scared and terribly frightened of that!

ON A PERSONAL FRONT, YOU ARE STILL CONTINUING YOUR WORK AS THE NATIONAL SPOKESMAN FOR THE STUTTERING FOUNDATION.

I'm on for the third year in a row. It's getting a pretty awesome response. I get a bunch of mail from kids who have gotten a lot of help from it and are so appreciative. It makes me cry. When you have a stutter and you have trouble communicating, you feel like you're alone, and hopefully I've helped the cause. I'll continue to do it as long as they ask me.

ASIDE FROM THAT WORK, WHAT ELSE ARE YOU FOCUSING ON?

I want to be involved in a longterm show, but I also want to do a sitcom. A one-hour drama is a lot of work and I commend Sarah – that little strumpet worked her ass off! I never thought that I would do an hour-long show. That's why I did the sitcom for Fox and I'm doing an ABC Family Channel movie, *Celeste in the City*. We leave soon for Toronto and shoot that until Christmas. It's a flamboyantly gay character, which will be a lot of fun. Otherwise, we've been taking a lot of meetings to get something hooked up for next fall. ✦

top ten xander moments

**2. "The Replacement":
The two Xanders bond**
Once persuaded they're both the real Xander, they start goofing over a railroad nickel and old *Star Trek* jokes. Giles mutters, "He's definitely a bad influence on himself," while Anya demands that she be allowed to take "the boys" home and have sex with them.

1. "Grave": Xander saves the world
Xander gets in the way of Evil Willow's apocalyptic energy bolts. "You've been my best friend my whole life," he says. "I love crayon breaky Willow and I love scary veiny Willow. So if you wanna kill the world, start with me. I've earned that." Every time she zaps him down, he gets up and tells her he loves her, until she can't zap anymore, and falls into his hug, weeping her heart out.

D. B. Woodside didn't realize when he signed on for *Buffy the Vampire Slayer* that the show's previous principals – namely Flutie and Snyder – had a bizarre habit of dying gruesome, premature deaths. "I didn't know until a few weeks into it, when I was working and Sarah [Michelle Gellar] happened to tell me," says D.B., who plays Principal Robin Wood, son of a Slayer and Buffy's boss at Sunnydale High. "She said, 'Do you realize what happened to the other principals in this school?' And it was very, very funny, but so far, that fate hasn't cut the legs out from underneath my character."

D.B. Woodside also didn't know much – anything at all, actually – about *Buffy*

the Vampire Slayer before he joined the cast effective with "Lessons", Season Seven's first episode. "It's kind of a funny story and I'm a little bit embarrassed to admit this, but they had called, I guess, my agent and my manager for me to come in for this recurring role on *Buffy*, to play the new principal," he recalls. "They weren't exactly sure which way they wanted to take the character and I had really never watched the show. I just think maybe because of the title of the show and because actors can sometimes take our craft and ourselves a little bit too seriously, I thought, 'Oh, I don't really want to do *Buffy the Vampire Slayer*. I don't really want to.' So, at first I passed on it, and then they called back and said, 'You know, you really should go in for this. It's going to be something really interesting and you're going to be playing opposite Sarah, who's great.' So then I reconsidered and I went back in. They offered it to me and I decided to do it, and that was really it. And I ended up falling in love with the show, like everyone else."

Principal Wood started out as something of an enigma, a man who lurked around a basement wielding a shovel. Through such episodes as "Help", "Bring on the Night" and particularly "First Date", "Get It Done", "Storyteller" and "Lies My Parents Told Me", Robin Wood continued to evolve into a fully formed person. He went on a date with Buffy, discovered, courtesy of The First,

that Spike killed his mother, and even ended up fighting by Spike's side as the Scooby Gang battled to protect the Potential Slayers. "What drives Principal Wood?" D.B. asks, repeating the question just posed to him. "I'm sure that Joss [Whedon] might give you a different answer. For me, as the actor playing this character, the fact that he lost his mother so young and was raised by his mother's Watcher, I think that there's a lot of rage that propels this character forward. I think that he's a smart man and gifted, but I think that he's really driven by his

A MATTER OF PRINCIPA

INTERVIEW BY IAN SPELLING

As if things didn't get hellish enough for Buffy in Season Seven, she also had to deal with the dark secrets of Sunnydale High's new principal, Robin Wood. *Buffy Magazine* caught up with actor D.B. Woodside as filming on Season Seven headed toward its conclusion.

L WOOD

rage and being abandoned, unfortunately, at such a young age.

"From that list of episodes you just read off, my favorite for my character was the one where Sarah and I, Buffy and Wood, went out on their first date. That was my favorite episode with my character. I feel like the audience discovered what his real story was, for one. Two, I got a chance to work with Sarah in a different way, which was nice. You saw them, character to character, and in a different setting. I think that you saw a softer side of both of their characters, a romantic side, which I don't think that we really got before that episode.

Let me amend what I actually said about a minute earlier. My favorite episode is 'Lies My Parents Told Me'. What I loved about the episode was that you got a chance to really see what propels this character forward. You got a sense of his vengeance, his rage, his vulnerability, his strength, and even his grace. I feel like so much of that was in the writing, and then, David Fury, who was the director and also the co-writer of 'Lies My Parents Told Me', was wonderful to work with

because he really put a lot of faith in me. If there was something I felt wasn't working or that I thought was something I could switch up to make it more my own, David was open to that all the time. Most of my stuff in that episode was with Spike, with James, who I just adore."

This interview with D.B. Woodside took place a week after series creator and executive producer Joss Whedon officially announced that the current season would be *Buffy the Vampire Slayer*'s last. Joss' statement came on the heels of Sarah Michelle Gellar going public with her decision not to stay on for an eighth year. Such timing meant that seven or so episodes remained in the show's run and that four or five hours had yet to be filmed, thus providing Joss and his team an opportunity to properly close out the saga. As a result, D.B. could shed some light on scenarios to come and also touched on his own ideas about Principal Wood's possible future activities. "I think they have plans to align Faith and Principal Wood," the actor says. "They have a few things in common. I think their upbringings were very similar, in that they've always felt like they've been the outsiders. So they have that in common. I was glad to finally get a scene in with

Eliza. We did our first scene together last week. I think she's great. It doesn't hurt that I find her absolutely gorgeous. She's a gorgeous woman and an actress who overflows with talent.

"I don't think you'll get to see any more of the [Buffy/Wood] romance. I think that that's a case of first date, last date. From my character's point of view, Buffy betrayed him in the next episode in that he could see that Buffy and Spike still had barely suppressed feelings for each other. I think that for Wood the romantic feelings ceased. He continues to respect her and like her as a person, but I think he probably sees that she's somewhat unavailable to him in the way that he would like her to be. And, of course, Angel is coming back for the finale. So far as what I personally would like to explore, I don't know what it is that I'd necessarily do, as in, 'This is what I want to find out about Principal Wood.' He is a dark character,

dark and brooding, and I think that he's in a lot of pain. Maybe I could be wrong here, but I don't think that story arc is ever going to be resolved given that *Buffy* is ending this year and there are only a few more episodes to shoot. But I see him as a

television movie [about the legendary Motown singing group]," he says. "I'd probably say they should check out *Romeo Must Die*, which was a feature with Jet Li and Aaliyah. I had this great guest-starring role on *The Practice* a little while back that I'm very proud of. And I would also have them check out the second season of Steven Bochco's series *Murder One*."

And where does *Buffy* fit into the mix? "It's been a great experience," D.B. enthuses. "I don't know for sure what people think of the character. I'm one of those actors who doesn't follow the websites because I don't really like to know what people are thinking. But I've heard things. I've heard that people really love Principal Wood. I've heard that people think the character can stand on his own, and I agree, because I think that Joss and [co-executive producer] Marti [Noxon] have created an amazing character. That's a testament to their genius, that people find the character fascinating. They've given me so much to play that people are really

spin-off?' That's really none of my business. That's her life and her world, and that's that. As far as I know, the whole idea of a spin-off is pretty much dead. I think Joss might consider bringing some of those characters in for feature films later on, but as far as a spin-off, I don't think that's going to happen at all."

D.B. Woodside, like all good actors, is ready to play the gypsy and move on to his next big gig. In fact, he's got his first post-*Buffy the Vampire Slayer* endeavor well in the works. "I'm going to be going up to San Francisco to shoot a pilot for a television show," he reveals. "It's called 'The Untitled Danny Glover Project' right now. I'm going to be playing his son. We'll see how that goes. I have aspirations to be more of a filmmaker than an actor. I'm writing and I want to start getting into directing and trying that avenue eventually. But right now, my priority is this show with Danny Glover [of *Lethal Weapon* fame]. He plays an ex-cop who went to prison for a number of years. We come

{ "I THINK THAT [PRINCIPAL WOOD IS] A SMART MAN AND GIFTED, BUT I THINK THAT HE'S REALLY DRIVEN BY HIS RAGE AND BEING ABANDONED, UNFORTUNATELY, AT SUCH A YOUNG AGE." }

character that's in a lot of pain and has a lot of anger. I'd like to see that resolved, but not in a fairy tale, Hollywood happy ending sort of way."

Buffy the Vampire Slayer represents only the latest achievement for David Bryan Woodside. Born and raised in and around New York City, D.B. Woodside decided early on that acting was for him. Since relocating to the Los Angeles area six years ago, he's amassed an impressive array of stage, television and film credits. D.B., in fact, proudly rattles off a few performances that he'd recommend to anyone who has discovered him as a result of his stint on *Buffy the Vampire Slayer*. "I would probably have them go check out *The Temptations*, which was a made-for-

digging the character. As far as the fans and just D.B.'s world, they've been very sweet. I can't say anything other than that. They're very sweet and loyal."

No one knows for sure at this point what will happen to the *Buffy*verse once the show wraps production. D.B. is quick to acknowledge that he's among those eager to see what Joss Whedon will do next with the franchise. "I'm as interested as you are," he notes. "As far as I know, when *Buffy* ends this year, that is it for everything. That's as far as I know. That's coming from the articles I've read and things I've heard. I've never sat down and had a conversation with Sarah about it. I've never asked, 'Are you going to come back and do a few episodes if there's a

into the story at a point when Danny has started his own private investigation firm and it's not doing so well. I'm his successful son, who is a lawyer, and we don't have the best relationship in the world."

Buffy the Vampire Slayer isn't quite over for D.B. Woodside yet, however, who, at time of speaking, has yet to film the final episodes. However, he has a stab at predicting Robin Wood's future. "I'm going to go out on a limb here and say that I believe this character will live to see another day," D.B. declares. "I don't know how the season will end, but I'm guessing that this character will go off somewhere and continue to fight demons and vampires until he works through his issues." ✛

AFTER HER SHOCKING EXIT FROM THE SHOW IN SEASON FIVE, IT'S BEEN GREAT TO SEE JOYCE SUMMERS' SUBSEQUENT REAPPEARANCES IN SEASON SEVEN — IN WHICHEVER FORMS THEY HAVE TAKEN. ACTRESS KRISTINE SUTHERLAND DISCUSSES HER MOST RECENT WORK ON *BUFFY*.

K ristine Sutherland had an inkling. "It's going to sound strange, but it doesn't surprise me that we're still talking about *Buffy the Vampire Slayer* after all these years," says the actress, who plays the title character's mother, Joyce Summers. "I don't know why, but I always sort of had a gut instinct. It just felt that way. It wasn't a rational thing, where you go, 'This show is about such and such, and it's time has come and this will hit a nerve.' It wasn't like that. It was just a gut feeling that this was a really special show. So in a strange way, to be honest, I never doubted that it would keep going for so long."

And keep going it did. For seven years – a long time for any TV show. And Kristine has kept going too. Even after series creator Joss Whedon killed Joyce off, he brought her back from time to time, and more so lately. Though there's never been a question that Buffy is the show's lead, Joyce/Kristine was always the matriarch. "I think oftentimes parents on television are more stereotypical cardboard cut-outs. It's not an easy thing to be someone's parent on a show when the focus isn't on the parents.

THE MUMMY RETURNS

INTERVIEW BY IAN SPELLING

The adolescents – I certainly can't say children – on *Buffy* are the focus. But I've enjoyed playing Joyce because I felt like she was a real, live person who was there as a parent, who made mistakes. I've also liked that she's been a single parent. She's never been a sitcom widow. Joyce was a real person struggling to make it on her own and struggling to make sense out of her relationship with her teenager. Their relationship went through a lot of changes over the years. It was a pretty amazing thing, as an actress, to be able to play that all out over a period of time. It's not been like a film, where everything that happens to the characters is condensed into a roughly two-hour period. The relationship between Joyce and Buffy was played out over the course of almost real time.

Everyone got older in life as well as on screen, and I think that added even more depth to it."

Kristine enjoyed the work so much that she wanted more. She'd be lying if she said anything other than, "Of course... not," when asked if the actress in her got enough to do on the show. "What actor or actress worth his or her salt wouldn't want more?" Kristine asks. "Especially on a show like *Buffy the Vampire Slayer*. But, as we were saying, I do understand that the show is called *Buffy the Vampire Slayer*. There are times, though, when I wish they'd explored other aspects of [Joyce]. I would have liked to have explored Joyce as a single mom more. She was a single mom who supported the family, and I'd like to have seen how she did it, how hard it was for her. The writers kept going, 'Ah, we just never do that, do we? We kept meaning to get into that art gallery.' And they never did. I think it would have been nice to have seen her more as a working woman."

Joss Whedon told Kristine two years in advance that he intended to bring about Joyce's demise, and he delivered on his promise with "The Body" (although some fans might argue that the deed was actually done in "I Was Made to Love You").

6 DEGREES OF...
JOYCE SUMMERS!

You'll be surprised how Joyce Summers links up with the movie world! Tom Root plays the "Six Degrees of Separation" game with Kristine Sutherland!

ORSON WELLES
Kristine can reach the *Citizen Kane* legend in just three steps!
1. Orson Welles was in 1984's *In Our Hands* with Holly Near
2. Holly Near was in 1998's *Heartwood* with Matt Frewer
3. Matt Frewer was in 1989's *Honey, I Shrunk the Kids* with Kristine!

MARILYN MONROE
The blonde bombshell is only three steps away!
1. Marilyn Monroe was in 1962's *Something's Got to Give* with Grady Sutton
2. Grady Sutton was in 1966's *The Chase* with Robert Redford
3. Robert Redford was in *Legal Eagles* with Kristine!

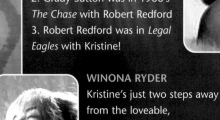

WINONA RYDER
Kristine's just two steps away from the loveable, light-fingered waif!
1. Winona was in 1990's *Welcome Home, Roxy Carmichael* with Thomas Wilson Brown
2. Thomas Wilson Brown was in 1989's *Honey, I Shrunk the Kids* with Kristine!

GARY COLEMAN
We were expecting a much more convoluted path to link Kristine with the *Diff'rent Strokes* star, but check it out – only two steps!
1. Gary Coleman was in 1994's *S.F.W.* with Amber Benson
2. Amber was in *Buffy* (natch) with Kristine!

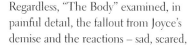

Regardless, "The Body" examined, in painful detail, the fallout from Joyce's demise and the reactions – sad, scared, and lost – of those who loved her. "I thought 'The Body' was an incredible episode," Kristine says. "It had a lot of personal reverberations for me because I lost my father when I was in my late 20s. At that time, if you're in that situation, you're probably one of the few people you know who's lost a parent. So it's a very, very lonely journey and you have all these incredibly intense feelings about it. Death just isn't that big a part of your landscape when you're that age, so you go on this journey very much alone.

"Only as you get older, much older, and your friends' parents start dying do you feel you can talk with somebody about it. But even then it's different, because you've already experienced it and already been on the journey alone. So I had a lot of personal feelings invested in how 'The Body' played out and in what Joss was trying to do. It was amazing to me because I remember when my father died, trying to figure out what I was going to wear to the funeral. I was at such a loss that I painted my nails hot pink and wore a pale blue flower dress. It was just the only way I could deal with it, going against the grain. I felt so raw and far too young to go out and buy some black dress. That was my reaction to death, bringing in bright colors. It was my rebellion against death. So when I read 'The Body' and

Willow just gets herself completely overwrought because she doesn't know what to wear to the funeral, I was like, 'Oh my God!' It just rang so true with me. That's not the kind of thing you think about if you're over 30. You're thinking about other things. You get out your black outfit, put it on and go to the funeral. And at the funeral you're thinking about a lot of different things. But when it happened to me I wasn't 30, and so I didn't know what to think, didn't know what was appropriate or how to behave. You don't know the rules yet. My parents were divorced and my mother was ill at the time, so like it was for Buffy, my journey was very lonely. There were no adults around to sort of tell me what to do. So that episode hit home for me and I think it hit home for a lot of people, probably each in his or her own way."

Given that Joss Whedon told Kristine in advance that Joyce would perish, it seems fair to ask if he informed her during Season Five that she'd be back in Seasons Six and Seven. Kristine laughs knowingly. "No, we didn't get that far!" the actress admits. "Nobody worries too much about death in Sunnydale." Sure enough, Joyce turned up in Season Six in "Normal Again" and this year in "Conversations with Dead People" and "Bring on the Night." "I thought that 'Conversations with Dead People' was a great episode," Kristine enthuses. "It was

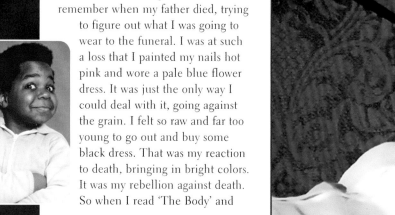

JEAN-CLAUDE VAN DAMME
As a testament to Kristine's omnipresence in Hollywood, she's connected to the 'Muscles from Brussels' in just two steps!
1. Jean-Claude Van Damme was in 1990's *Death Warrant* with Armin Shimerman
2. Armin Shimerman was in *Buffy* with Kristine!

JAMES DEAN
It takes four steps to hook up Kristine with the 'Rebel Without a Cause'.
1. James Dean was in 1953's *Trouble Along the Way* with Dabbs Greer
2. Dabbs Greer was in 1997's *Con Air* with Chris Ellis
3. Chris Ellis was in 2002's *Beyond the City Limits* with Alyson Hannigan
4. Alyson, Kristine, *Buffy*... you know the drill.

JOHN RITTER
Kristine is only... er, whoops, he played her android boyfriend once. Never mind!

JENNIFER LOPEZ
Jenny from the block, meet Joyce from Sunnydale. Two steps!
1. J-Lo was in 2002's *Enough* with Bruce French
2. Bruce French was in *Legal Eagles* with Kristine!

EMINEM
You probably won't see them hanging out together too often, but Eminem and Kristine aren't too far removed.
1. Eminem was in 2001's *The Wash* with Tommy Chong
2. Tommy Chong was in 1995's *Senior Trip* with Matt Frewer
3. Matt Frewer was in *Honey, I Shrunk the Kids* with Kristine!

KEVIN BACON
Naturally, we had to try this one on for size! Kristine makes the grade in just two steps.
1. Kevin was in 1991's *JFK* with Brian Doyle-Murray
2. Brian Doyle-Murray was in *Legal Eagles* with Kristine! ✣

really terrifying and Michelle [Trachtenberg] did a great job of being in the center of all that and really creating the terror of that situation. For me as an actress it was just sort of strange being a ghost. That's when you're not quite sure who you are. I knew that I was mom, but I also knew that The First, the evil one, was speaking through me. It also felt kind of brief, because we did it with me in front of a green screen. So I was standing there alone with these enormous lights shining on me. It was strange to do, but I know a lot of people really like that episode, so I was pleased. And 'Bring on the Night' was interesting, too. Buffy just sort of went into a dream state, but it happens so subtly that you're

not even aware until afterwards that that's what's happening. Joyce was bopping around like good old mom is back at home. 'Can I get you some tea? How was work today?' They were these little brief blips of passing through as the old Joyce.

"Going back to last season, I liked 'Normal Again,' Kristine adds. "I loved the conceit of that episode, and it was really fun to play. It was interesting to explore, even mentally through the whole process of shooting, the idea of this alternate reality and what it meant. It was brilliant. Joyce would be a totally different person, in a way, if she had stayed married and if this had happened to her daughter, if her daughter was mentally disturbed rather than really a Slayer. It's totally different to be the mother of a young, ripe superpower than the mother of a child who's institutionalized."

So what does the foreseeable future hold? Will Joyce be back for more in Season Seven? "I don't know," replies Kristine, who spends her off-time with her family and pursuing a passion for photography. "Joss isn't one to write a million episodes ahead. But I'd imagine I will be back. It doesn't seem like they're quite finished with Joyce yet, but where it will go and how it will take place, I don't know. I can only say that whatever I think it will be I know it won't be, because Joss never does what anyone would expect him to do." ✣

WATCH

THE WATCHERS HAVE ALWAYS BEEN AN INTEGRAL PART OF THE SLAYER TRADITION — ALMOST AS IMPORTANT AS THE SLAYER HERSELF! FOR EVERY CHOSEN ONE, EVERY POTENTIAL, THERE IS A WATCHER READY TO TRAIN THEM, LOOK AFTER THEM AND GUIDE THEM. THINGS MAY HAVE CHANGED A BIT SINCE THE COUNCIL WAS BLOWN UP AND MOST OF ITS EMPLOYEES KILLED, BUT HISTORY TELLS US YOU CAN'T KEEP A GOOD WATCHER DOWN FOR LONG. *BUFFY MAGAZINE* TAKES A CLOSER LOOK AT THE WATCHER'S COUNCIL, AND THE MYSTERIOUS MEN AND WOMEN WHO MAKE UP ITS MEMBERS… AND ASKS THE QUESTION, JUST WHERE WOULD A SLAYER BE WITHOUT HER WATCHER?

BY K. STODDARD HAYES

ERS, INC.

WOLFRA
ATTO

Giles: "A Slayer slays, a Watcher –"
Buffy: " – Watches?"
Giles: "Yes – no! He trains her, he prepares her."
Buffy: "Prepares me for what? For getting kicked out of school? For losing all of my friends? For having to spend all of my time fighting for my life and never getting to tell anyone because I might endanger them? Go ahead. Prepare me!"
Giles: "Damn!"

With this heated exchange in "Welcome to the Hellmouth," Buffy and Giles introduce the Slayer's greatest ally, supporter and teacher, the Watcher. Watchers and their governing body, the Watchers' Council, seek out Potential Slayers throughout the world, and assign a trained Watcher to every Potential they find. When a Potential is called to become the Slayer, she is prepared for the job, thanks to her Watcher; and she also has the resources and knowledge of the Watchers' Council to support her. At least, that's the ideal. What happens in the real world can be an entirely different matter.

The Council has been training Watchers for centuries, and most Watchers live up to their training and their purpose as mentors of the Slayers. The two Watchers whom we know best, Giles and Wesley, both have extraordinary learning as the foundation of their education. Between them, they read dozens of demonic languages, have studied thousands of texts and can even wield powerful forces of magic in casting spells. For this alone, the Watchers are indispensable to the Slayer, who can't possibly learn all that she needs to know about the supernatural in the short years that she has to prepare for her calling. Giles is Buffy's never-failing source of specialized knowledge and insight into the shadowy worlds where she does battle. And if he doesn't know something

himself, he knows where to find the information, whether it's a prophecy about the Master or a spell to contain a demon or a god.

The Watchers must also be good mentors and guides for the young girls in their charge; hence we can guess they must have some training in education, psychology, and the emotional issues of bringing up a Potential Slayer. Kendra was raised by her Watcher, and Faith seems to have been fairly attached to her murdered Watcher; while Giles becomes the ideal Watcher, mentor and father figure for Buffy. Wesley, though young and immature when he is first assigned as a Watcher, always had the potential to become the same kind of mentor, if he chose to return to the Council.

A Watcher's training of a Slayer, as described by Kendra in "What's My Line?" contains three main elements. First, there's rigorous physical training in many fighting skills. Giles puts Buffy through combat training in many episodes, taking more than his share of bruises along the way. Second is heavy hitting of books, so that the Slayer can learn as much as possible about vampires, demons and other supernatural forces. Kendra has a great time talking academics with Giles; as for Buffy – one out of three is a good start! The third discipline a Watcher requires of his Slayer is a personal regimen far more restrictive than monastic life. No friends, no boys, no family except one's

POST'S — MARK

While most Watchers can be a bit stuffy and pompous, it would often seem that, generally, they have their Slayer's best interests at heart. But all that changed when the very strict Gwendolyn Post arrived in Sunnydale, claiming to be Faith's new Watcher – but having something far more sinister in mind. *Buffy Magazine* caught up with Serena Scott Thomas, the actress behind the memorable Rogue Watcher, to reflect on her time on the show…

Nearly six years have passed since Serena, the younger sister of Oscar-nominated actress Kristin Scott Thomas, turned up on the set of Season Three's "Revelations" for her *Buffy the Vampire Slayer* outing. Ms. Post arrived in Sunnydale unexpectedly, and promptly announced that she was Faith's new Watcher, sent by the Watchers Council to train her and keep an eye on Giles and his charge, Buffy, who was getting a bit of a reputation for

herself back at the Council's HQ. After much blood-letting, attempted stakings and attacks with shovels, it was revealed that Ms. Post was an ex-Watcher out to possess the Glove of Myhnegon, a mystical and powerful artifact. Ms. Post went down in a blaze of glory – first, glass dismembered her arm and then a bolt of lightning blasted her to nothingness.

"It doesn't matter what else I do, people will always recognize me for *Buffy the Vampire Slayer*," the actress marvels. "I was just talking with somebody about this yesterday.

Watcher; and no time off for dancing, going to the mall, or just kicking back. Kendra's Watcher taught her that personal relationships and social activities are a dangerous distraction from the pure focus and discipline of the Slayer. Clearly, a Watcher has considerable discretion here. Giles makes no attempt to enforce this regimen on Buffy, and it's obvious that Faith's Watcher never tried to make her stay home and hit the books, either.

The Watchers do much more than watch and train. They are the keepers of Slayer tradition. Preservation of the Slayer heritage and lore may be the most important function of the Watchers' Council. Its vast library on all aspects of the Slayers' history has helped to preserve that tradition for centuries (one of its rituals, the Cruciamentum, is over a thousand years old). And the Council's library doesn't stop there; it also extends to information on the enemy. The Council's accumulated learning about vampires, demons, dark magic and all matters supernatural is unparalleled anywhere on Earth (except, perhaps, at Wolfram & Hart, which has the advantage of being far older and also interdimensional). When Buffy and Giles can't identify Glory by themselves, they seek help from the Council, who

REAL WATCHERS DRINK TEA

Most of the Watchers we have seen are English: Giles, Quentin, Wesley and his father, Gwendolyn Post. The Watchers' Council Headquarters is (or was) in London. And when Ms. Post tells Giles he has come under the Council's scrutiny because he has become "too American," he believes the threat. This implies that English culture and values have come to completely dominate the Watchers' Council, to the exclusion of all others.

How realistic is this? Not at all. If Potentials can come from all over the world, there's every reason why the population of Watchers should be international as well. Even Buffy and Giles sometimes had trouble with the culture gap between English and American, while the relationship between Giles and the Chinese Potential should be a dire warning for any Watcher opposed to multiculturalism!

This narrow culture could be another reason why the Watchers' Council failed in the crisis. It had clearly become completely insular, believing that its own conservative and monolithic culture was the only acceptable perspective.

The post-apocalypse generation of Watchers seems to be on the path of diversity. While Giles – and possibly Wesley's father – are involved in the rebirth of the tradition, so is Andrew. Though he may be an Anglophile, Andrew will never be an Englishman – but it's a start!

disclose Glory's divine nature (after they try to put Buffy in her place, and she smacks them back into theirs). The Council's knowledge also proves invaluable in defeating the First Evil. Not because the Council is forthcoming with it, but because Giles steals the few relevant texts from the Watcher library, just days before the First Evil blows up the Council's headquarters.

For most of their long history, the Watchers and the Council seem to have served their purpose well. They kept the Slayer tradition alive, trained large

numbers of Watchers and located most Potentials to train them before they were called (both Faith and Kendra had Watchers before they were called as Slayers, as far as we know). The Council also had systems in place for dealing with rogue Slayers and rogue Watchers, and a whole tradition of tests, like the Cruciamentum, to help develop the Slayer's abilities.

However, during Buffy's reign as Slayer (and perhaps for years before) the Council completely lost touch with the realities of the Slayer's life. The first hint that their rules and practices are no longer working is Kendra's mention of the Slayer handbook, in "What's My Line, Part Two." Buffy has never heard of it, and questions Giles about it. Giles explains: "After meeting you, Buffy, I realized that the Slayer handbook would

If you're not the kind of person who gets into these cult-y things it's amazing when you meet people who are. It's to the point of religious, almost. I never knew that existed. I get people who come up to me all the time and say, 'You played Gwendolyn Post.' And they recognize me even though my hair is a completely different color and I look completely different. They still recognize me and they know exactly who I am, which character I played, what episode I did, what season it ran. It's amazing."

Back in 1998, when "Revelations" aired, Serena was best known for her role as Princess Diana in the American TV movie, *Diana: Her True Story*, as well as for a guest shot on *She-Wolf of London*, her work in the mini-series *Nostromo* and a steady role on the Don Johnson series, *Nash Bridges*. Serena won the role of the rogue Watcher the old-fashioned way, by auditioning. "I went in there in my grey tweed skirt and my pearl earrings and did Gwendolyn Post," she recalls. "And I talked just like my grandmother. I actually did model her on my grandmother. It was great fun to be the bad guy. I loved it. Nobody really told me anything about the role. They just sort of let you get on with it, which is always rather terrifying because you have to jump

in and do what you think it should be. I guess I was lucky; I don't know. Grandma came through for me!

"It was fun to do. I had a great scene with Eliza Dushku. She's a very, very cool actress. I did a little bit with David Boreanaz and also with Anthony Stewart Head. Tony was great. We shared a common interest in horses, so we talked long and hard about horses when we were doing the scene where Gwendolyn and Giles had tea together. Sadly, I didn't have very much interaction at all with Sarah Michelle Gellar. But they were all terrific and so amazingly young and self-confident and happy. I remember that everybody was very happy to be doing that show. There was a great atmosphere, a lot of laughter. And the writing was great. It's always a pleasure to do a show when the writing is great. I loved the bursting into flames at the end and that sort of maniacal laughter. People still ask me about how they had me burning at the end. I don't really know how they did it. I just stood there and they said, 'We'll take care of the rest.' I also loved having the prosthetic arm. I just really enjoyed the experience. It was a far cry from Princess Diana."

Lots of characters that died on *Buffy* went on to return to the show in one form or another. Gwendolyn Post, however, never did – not that Serena ever expected to reprise her role. "It never really occurred to me," the actress explains. "When you self-immolate you sort of figure, 'I'm done.' I know they killed off lots of characters and brought them back later, but I never thought they'd do that with me."

Not long after her *Buffy* appearance, Serena was showcased as a Bond girl in the 007 adventure *The World Is Not Enough*. She played the memorably monickered Dr. Molly Warmflash opposite Pierce Brosnan's legendary British spy. She returned to genre television in 2001, co-starring as Dr. Nicole De Brae in the short-lived series *All Souls*. The show followed the be of no use in your case."

Giles is quick to recognize that if he wants to be of service to his Slayer, he will have to adapt and change his Watcher training. Other Watchers, adhering more closely to the Council's values, are not so flexible. Kendra's Watcher and Wesley, following their own training, encourage their Slayers to be dependent on the Watchers' judgment and authority. Kendra has been taught to return to her Watcher for instruction in each new situation, and Wesley also expects Buffy and Faith to do as he tells them. Giles, in contrast, allows Buffy to take the lead. While he offers advice, he lets her make the decisions. Unlike the Council, he recognizes that she should be in charge, as she's the one who is actually fighting the battles. So committed is he to her growth and independence that in "Once More, With Feeling," he decides that he must leave her, so that she will grow up and stand on her own.

Clinging to outdated approaches and values isn't the Council's worst problem. By the time Buffy turns 18, the Council has completely lost sight of the Watcher's primary purpose to train and prepare the Slayer for battle. The Slayer's coming-of-age ritual, the Cruciamentum, is supposed to be a test of the Slayer's

courage and fighting instincts. Giles, observing Buffy's distress, concludes that making her think she has lost her powers is a cruel and pointless exercise, and so he reveals the test to her. The Council fires him, alleging that his fatherly feelings toward Buffy disqualify him for the job of her Watcher, as he can no longer be detached towards her. This, at least, is the claim of Council leader Quentin

Travers, who warns him to have no further contact with the Slayer, even though he knows Giles will never obey his orders.

The truth is that Giles' actions prove his loyalty is to the Slayer, not to the Council – and the Council cannot tolerate this. All their insistence on making the Slayer obedient to her Watcher has little to do with discipline, and a lot to do with keeping the Slayer dependent on the Council and under control. In this context, even the Council's desire to keep Potentials like Kendra completely isolated from all relationships except with her Watcher, begins to look rather like suppression. The whole set-up might be designed to keep the Slayer believing she is dependent on her Watcher and the Council, so that she won't discover how powerful she really is.

The Watcher chosen to replace Giles is another proof that control, not the good of the Slayer, is the real goal. Since only one Watcher can be assigned to the Council's most important "client," the Slayer, naturally, you'd expect the Council to send their best. And for Buffy's previous Watcher, they did. It's hard to imagine a better choice than Giles, who combines a vast amount of learning with extensive field experience;

who's mature enough to be an authority, and accessible enough to become a respected friend and mentor to teenagers (Slayers are usually teenagers; those who reach adulthood, like Buffy and Robin's mother, Nikki, are rare).

Giles may be ideal from the Slayer's perspective, but from the Council's perspective he's a liability from the moment he puts Buffy's best interests ahead of the Council's rules. They can't allow the Slayer to have a Watcher who "doesn't give a rat's ass" for their authority. They need a Watcher who will follow their rules and obey them. They choose Wesley Wyndam-Pryce.

A young man with no field experience, no tact in relationships with teenagers, and an inflated idea of his own knowledge, is hardly an ideal choice to mentor the Slayer. He's even more unsuited for the unusual circumstance of having two Slayers to manage, both with difficult case histories. But helping the Slayers is not the job the Council wants Wesley to do. The job is to bring the Slayers back under their control. Wesley has nothing to recommend him except a family tradition of being Watchers; an education nearly as extensive as Giles', and – the critical factor – his complete devotion to the Council. They can

beleaguered and creeped-out staff at All Souls Hospital, a haunted medical facility in Boston. Unfortunately, despite generally favorable reviews and a talented cast that included 24's Reiko Aylesworth, Roswell's Adam Rodriguez, Mutant X's Karen Cliché and Daniel Rodriguez, who shared the screen with David Boreanaz in the horror-thriller Valentine, few viewers tuned in and UPN quickly axed the show. "I'm just an actor," Serena says with a sigh. "I don't understand the politics and machinations of the networks and the studios. When things like that happen I just try to mind my own business, keep doing my job and move on to the next thing. It can be very disappointing. It was a good show and different and interesting. And they just had Stephen Kings' Kingdom Hospital, which was very similar in the style and everything. Maybe we were a little ahead of the times with All Souls; I don't know."

Looking to the future, Serena is now excited about her new movies. "Hostage and Haven are my two big projects, and I'm very excited about them," she enthuses. "I play the wife of Bruce Willis in Hostage. We're an estranged couple and I get kidnapped, and he has to recover this disk from a house that's under siege. And I probably shouldn't be telling you the whole story. But in order to save myself and our daughter he has to recover the disk. So it's this big psychological thing for him because he's had this trauma of losing a boy in a hostage situation before. It's a very emotional film and Bruce is amazing in it, amazing. Most of my scenes in it were with Bruce and our daughter is played by his daughter with Demi Moore, Rumer. Rumer is the best. She is so great. It's also got Jonathan Tucker and Ben Foster [as well as Glenn Morshower, who played Mr. Newton in the Buffy the Vampire Slayer episode "Help"]. I couldn't have

wished for nicer people to work with. And even though I had a gag in my mouth and a burlap sack over my head most of the time, I still had fun.

"Haven was great, too," Serena continues, referring to the upcoming crime drama that also stars Orlando Bloom, Stephen Dillane and Bill Paxton. "We shot that on the Cayman Islands and [writer-director] Frank E. Flowers is probably one of the most energetic, positive, optimistic people ever. He has this incredible energy that is just absolutely infectious. Everybody was just having a blast. I play the wife of Stephen Dillane, who was in The Hours. He's a great actor. So I've had a couple of wonderful roles opposite these great guys who are also terrific actors. I've been very happy lately. It's very nice."

For Serena, it's now a case of waiting for Haven and Hostage – as well as The Brothel, a supernatural drama that she filmed in 2003 – to reach movie theaters worldwide. In the meantime, she's living at home in Los Angeles and visits family and friends back in England a couple of times a year, usually at Christmas and during the summer. So far as the future, she's open to anything, anywhere. In fact, Serena totally concurs when it's pointed out to her that she's a true acting Gypsy, appearing in big projects and small ones, in films and on television, and in American and British productions. "I basically do whatever life throws at me at this point," she notes. "It does look like I sit back and think about the strange range of things I've done, but I've really not. I just love doing them all. I've done radio plays to James Bond. I just enjoy every facet of performing. If I get to go to the Cayman Islands for a film, well, bring it on. That's all I can say. I've been very lucky. I've been to some great places. I've gotten to work with some great actors and directors. And right now I'm just pounding the streets again, trying to get another job." ✛

control him, and through him, they assume they can control the Slayers.

They're wrong, of course. All they accomplish through Wesley is to alienate both Slayers. Under his authority, Faith becomes a rogue Slayer, while Buffy virtually ignores him while he is present, and continues to ignore the Council once he is gone. When the Council try to blackmail Buffy into knuckling under again, in return for information about Glory, Buffy finally figures out who has the real power: she does. She is the Slayer, without whom the Watchers' Council and the Watchers have no function at all. She tells the Council to reinstate Giles, give her what information she needs whenever she needs it, and otherwise, to stay out of her way.

The Council's alienation from the Slayer probably results in their downfall. Cut off from the Slayer and the front lines of the struggle against the First Evil, they act too late, and too slowly. They're mired in the bureaucracy which has already driven Giles to simply rob their library of what he needs. Before the Council can even prepare themselves for battle, their part of the battle is over in one catastrophic explosion, when the First blows up their headquarters.

The old Watchers' Council may be gone, but fortunately for the Slayer heritage, the Watchers and the Slayers endure. Willow's spell creates hundreds of new Slayers, all awaiting guidance and training, so Buffy, Giles and the Scoobies will have to create a new Watcher tradition, making changes which go far beyond merely recruiting people like Andrew from outside the Watcher heritage.

The biggest change is established during the final struggle against the First, when the Slayer herself takes charge of training the Potentials. The Watchers are no longer the only keepers of the Slayer's knowledge, no longer the only bridge between each dead Slayer and her lone successor. The Slayers will now hand on their lore, training and tradition to each other, directly from Slayer to Slayer, and start a brand new order.

It's a new world. ✢

FAMOUS AND INFAMOUS WATCHERS

Rupert Giles Surrogate father, mentor, scholar, friend and champion in his own right, he's the paragon of Watchers. So naturally, the Council fires him, thus alienating not only their best man, but the Slayer herself. The re-formed Council couldn't do better than to have Giles write a new Slayers' Handbook to replace their hidebound rules.

Wesley Wyndam-Pryce Trained in the Watcher tradition from childhood, Wes might have become a fine Watcher if the Council hadn't ruined him by first giving him a job far beyond his ability (taking charge of Buffy and Faith) then breaking him for failing in that job. Another example of the Council's ability to rid itself of its finest people.

Kendra's Watcher (Sam Zabuto) A traditional Watcher, he raised her from the time she was five, and indoctrinated her completely into the discipline and tradition of the Slayer. Allowing her no personal life whatsoever, all her time and energy was focused on study, training and obedience.

Faith's First Watcher All we know of Faith's first Watcher, a woman, is that she was killed in a particularly horrible fashion by the demon Kakistos.

Gwendolyn Post A rogue Watcher with plenty of learning and ability, and an unfortunate and fatal ambition to control a mystical Glove.

Roger Wyndam-Pryce Wesley's father, whose cyborg clone gives us a glimpse of the real man, a learned Watcher and an ego-crushing father (like we didn't already know that from Wesley's hang-ups).

Collins, Weatherby and Smith Watcher assassins who show up whenever a rogue Slayer, like Faith, has to be contained. They'd kill a prisoner, or even let their prisoner kill a hostage, before they'd let her go. With the Council, it's always about control.

Quentin Travers Head of the Watchers' Council, he may once have been a fine Watcher himself, but the desire for power reduces him to a rigid, doublespeaking bureaucrat. Make that "*dead* rigid, doublespeaking bureaucrat."

Andrew The former supervillain wannabe has a lot to learn (and he may never get over being a geek), but his heart is in the right place; he's got Giles and Buffy to train him; and he's even learned to stand up for his Slayer, as he shows when taking the insane Slayer Dana away from Angel.

EPISODE SPOTLIGHT

"A NEW MAN"

Who's that demon?

SEASON 4 EPISODE TWELVE

First US airdate
25/1/00

First UK airdate
24/3/00

Synopsis

Happy birthday Buffy! She's 19 – but poor old Giles is feeling a bit left out. He feels that he's been kept in the dark about Buffy's new boyfriend, Riley, and the Initiative. And the reappearance of one-time old friend turned-nemesis Ethan Rayne does nothing to raise his spirits. In fact, things get decidedly worse!

While Professor Walsh talks to Buffy about joining the Initiative, Giles, Willow and Xander have a much more pressing problem to deal with: the rise of the Demon Prince Barvain. Whilst staking out his crypt, Giles is shocked to bump into Ethan, who negotiates his way out of a beating by warning Giles of an impending danger.

During a heavy drinking session, Ethan tells Giles that all the demons are running scared of something called '314'. The next morning, Giles wakes up with much more than a hangover – he's been turned into a hideous-looking Fyarl demon, complete with huge horns and enormous strength. Ethan, it seems, has been up to his old tricks again!

After trashing his house in a panic (well, wouldn't you?), Giles is forced to turn to an unlikely source for help – Spike – whilst being hunted by Buffy and the Initiative...

Ratings for "A New Man": UK= 740,000 viewers (Sky One): US= 3.9 (Nielsen Ratings, 1 point equals one million households)

Trivia

Long before *Buffy the Vampire Slayer* burst onto our screens and into our hearts, Anthony Stewart Head was perhaps best known for his role in a series of hugely popular coffee ads. Between 1987 and 1997, Head played the smooth, sophisticated male lead in the ads which charted, soap-opera style, the budding romance between two neighbours who shared the same love of a particular brand. Coffee ads have never been quite the same since!

Guest Star Info

Robin Sachs: The British born, Shakespearean-trained Sachs has appeared in such BBC TV classics as *Upstairs, Downstairs* and *Brideshead Revisited*. But sci-fi fans will probably know him best for his work on *Babylon 5* and in movies like *The Lost World: Jurassic Park* and *Galaxy Quest*. His upcoming movie projects include *Crush Depth* and *Megalodon*.

Memorable Dialogue:

Prof. Walsh: "We use the latest in scientific technology, and state-of-the-art weaponry, and you, if I understand correctly, poke them with a sharp stick."

Buffy: "Well, it's more effective than it sounds." ✛

Giles (to Ethan)**:** "This is what gets me. 20 years I've been fighting demons. Maggie Walsh and her nancy ninja boys come in and six months later, the demons are p*****g themselves with fear. They never even noticed me." ✛

Statistics

No. of times Buffy gets to kick ass: **2** (Riley & Giles)

No. of unbelievably scary sights: **2** (Ethan attempting to chat up a waitress and Spike's driving)

No. of people scared by Giles (as a demon): **2** (Xander & Professor Walsh)

No. of snogs: **1** (Buffy and Riley)

Compiled by Kate Anderson

Episode Credits

Written by	Jane Espenson	Directed by	Michael Gershman
Buffy Summers	Sarah Michelle Gellar	Riley Finn	Marc Blucas
Xander Harris	Nicholas Brendon	Anya	Emma Caulfield
Willow Rosenberg	Alyson Hannigan	Tara	Amber Benson
Rupert Giles	Anthony Stewart Head	Ethan Rayne	Robin Sachs
Spike	James Marsters	Professor Walsh	Lindsay Crouse

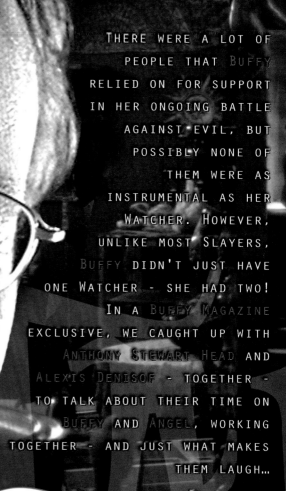

THERE WERE A LOT OF
PEOPLE THAT BUFFY
RELIED ON FOR SUPPORT
IN HER ONGOING BATTLE
AGAINST EVIL, BUT
POSSIBLY NONE OF
THEM WERE AS
INSTRUMENTAL AS HER
WATCHER. HOWEVER,
UNLIKE MOST SLAYERS,
BUFFY DIDN'T JUST HAVE
ONE WATCHER - SHE HAD TWO!
IN A BUFFY MAGAZINE
EXCLUSIVE, WE CAUGHT UP WITH
ANTHONY STEWART HEAD AND
ALEXIS DENISOF - TOGETHER -
TO TALK ABOUT THEIR TIME ON
BUFFY AND ANGEL, WORKING
TOGETHER - AND JUST WHAT MAKES
THEM LAUGH...

A TAL
TWO WATC

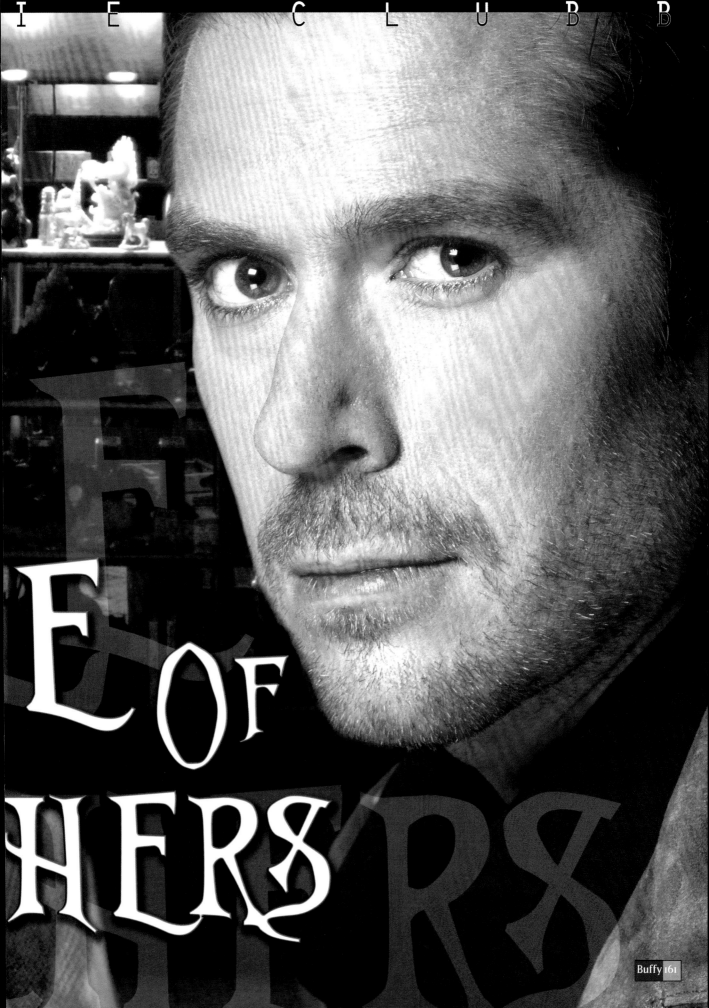

> "Giles and Wesley are sort of founded in jealousy – fear of losing something to the other person – so that made for great comedy." Alexis

HOW HAVE YOU ENJOYED THE COLLECTORMANIA CONVENTION SO FAR?

TONY HEAD: It's excellent. I mean, I've done this one before and it's very full on. But it's extremely efficiently run and I've done a few now and I must admit it's one of the more relaxing ones. I was a bit scared at one point that I wasn't going to make it and get through everyone, but I did!

ALEXIS DENISOF: It's a lot of people and there's always the dilemma when you're a guest they've come to see, do you sign quickly so that more people get the chance to say hello, or slow down and give them a little bit of time so they feel they've had an experience? So we've always got to make a strict judgment about that,

based on how many people we take. And at this one, there are a lot of people waiting, so we end up going quite quickly, but I think it works out. So I think, you know, try to meet as many as you can, so they've not wasted their journey.

ARE YOU EVER SURPRISED BY THE LONGEVITY OF THE SHOW AND ITS ABILITY TO CAPTURE PEOPLES' IMAGINATIONS, EVEN THOUGH IT'S BEEN OFF THE AIR FOR A LONG TIME NOW?

AD: Yeah. I mean, you can never predict that sort of thing going into it. Obviously, by the time I joined *Buffy* it was well under way and the phenomenon was established.

TH: I mean, I said to Joss right at the beginning, I'd already done one show for Fox that didn't go beyond 12 episodes, which I thought was a sure hit. So I said, "Look, I don't know, is this going to be a hit?" [and he said] "Yeah, yeah, yeah." He said, "the studio don't get it, the network certainly don't get it and none of the executives seem to get it, but ultimately, yes, it's going to be a huge hit. It's not going to be an overnight success, but it will grow and be handed from one viewer to another." And because of that, because of its critical success as well as being a cult success, people really love it and it's not just like any old sci-fi

show, it's got such a heart that it's not a surprise to me at all.
AD: It's very difficult to get a good show on the air. You'd be surprised – I mean the television industry is actually quite flawed, and how and why programmes make it to the air…
TH: On both sides…
AD: On both sides, yeah, it's not an exact science and, what's the expression? There are a lot of chefs and

the soup can be rescued, so credit to Joss, that his vision is what really carried the shows.
TH: And the fact that at 19, he tried to get it made as a movie and basically, it was taken out of his hands and it was made into a movie but not his original concept. It was fine, it did its thing, but it wasn't Joss' concept. He actually pursued it down the line and said,

"Well, you know, it'd make a good TV show," and 10 years later he was able to prove that he was right.

IS THERE ANY POSSIBILITY OF *RIPPER*, OR A WATCHER SPIN-OFF OF SOME SORT, STILL HAPPENING?
TH: We should do Wesley and Giles….
AD: The dancing Watchers!
TH: I don't know, to be

Opposite: Alexis met his wife, Alyson Hannigan (Willow) on the set of *Buffy*.
(Photo: Albert Ortega)

Opposite Bottom: The dance scene from "The Prom" proved to be a source of amusement for Tony and Alexis.

Left: *Buffy Magazine* editor Natalie interviews Tony and Alexis at the Collectormania convention.
Photo: Dan-ee Scudamore

honest. I communicated with Joss a couple of times recently, and it hasn't been mentioned, but up until that point, he would regularly come up with new ideas for how it would happen. I really have no idea. I heard a rumor that he was directing *Wonder Woman* or something, is that true?

AD: True, true.

TH: So probably, it's going to be in a while, if it happens at all. And it would be lovely to do it. The bottom line is, the story that he pitched to me went from being a series, which he announced to the press, and I was like, "Let's make sure we're serious before we announce it to the press." It was very nice because we've talked about it lots. But it's gone from, like, being a series to a two-hour movie, that might be part of a series of DVDs that we were talking about doing for the different characters from the shows. I don't know – it's got a lovely story, and I hope he does something wonderful with it.

YOU WERE BOTH INTEGRAL TO THE PLOTS OF *BUFFY* AND *ANGEL*. WHAT WAS THE MOST CHALLENGING STORYLINE THAT YOU PERSONALLY HAD?

AD: The whole thing was challenging. The stuff with the dad, that was difficult, and when Fred/ llyria was dying – that was a tough day. I remember that day very clearly, and me and Joss kind

of huddled on the set to go through all these scenes in the bedroom where she dies. You know, that was tough – but in a good way, definitely.

TH: What about the one where you took your trousers off?

AD: There was so many of those I wouldn't remember, but yes, this seems to be haunting me – the fact I got so bored with all the scenes at the desk, that I eventually did all those scenes with my trousers around my ankles, just to keep it interesting for me. But eventually people caught on and the other actors would be in the scene, looking over and seeing if I had any clothes on. There's a lot in Seasons Two and Three, and if I'm sitting at the desk, smirking a secret smile, you'll know why.

TH: Challenging? "Hush" was great, because we all had to do it without talking, so that was a bit of a challenge. That was fun. I mean most of the challenges always were fun – [like] the episode I got to do, when I got to [be] a demon. I was told like, a week before, by the second assistant. He came up to me and said, "You're a demon next week." And I said "really? Fantastic. All this time I've really wanted to be a demon or the bad guy." And then he said, "You're really funny." But it was cool with the make-up thing, I really enjoyed it.

AD: We had a lot of trouble, Tony and I, keeping a straight

face. That was quite challenging, because he would make me giggle a lot, and then once Tony giggles, it's very infectious, as you can see. As soon as Tony would giggle in a scene, then I would giggle, and it wouldn't be long before everybody was giggling.

YOU BOTH HAD A LOT OF ASPECTS TO YOUR CHARACTERS – BOTH COMEDIC AND VERY DARK. WHICH SIDE DID YOU PREFER?

AD: To be honest, I really love both aspects of the character. Wesley was a tremendous buffoon on *Buffy*, so when Joss talked about going on to *Angel*, we had a meeting about what we had to do to toughen him up – knock some of the ridiculous out of him. I think early on, I loved how silly he was, then I sort of wanted him to be tougher, and so I loved it when he was. And he was so serious, so when we got to go back and do ["Spin the Bottle"] it was a joy to recapture that.

TH: The same for me – the joy was you got to do so much. The great thing about *Buffy* and *Angel* was every action had a repercussion, it had a knock-on effect, and even if it didn't happen immediately, somewhere down the line, your character would

This page: Tony and Alexis were a huge hit with the fans when they attended the U.K. Collectormania event.

Photos: Dan-ee Scudamore

suffer miserably for something that you had done.

I loved the fact that there were both aspects to him, that Giles was a buffoon and the fact that he did have a dark side – that he killed [Ben] at the end. The entrance [in "Grave"] basically, coming back in to a scene when Willow had been kicking butt all over the place, all I've got to do is open the door and then get beaten up. Joss got to do this stuff he pioneered. You can have tragedy and comedy and all the histrionics all rolled into one in a show. You can turn emotions on a dice and it really makes it right.

OVERALL, WERE YOU BOTH HAPPY WITH THE DIRECTION OF YOUR CHARACTERS THROUGHOUT THE RUN OF THE SHOW, OR WOULD YOU RATHER THEY HAD FINISHED DIFFERENTLY?
AD: Well, we never really got together to have it off [laughs] which I think was a real shame, so other than the heartbreak of Wesley and Giles…
TH: I always wanted to be bad, you know. I remember right from the beginning of the first season, I'd go to the local Tex-Mex with Nicky [Brendon] and we'd say, "So what we going to do next season?" "Oh, I don't know, there's going to be a bad guy. I can be it!" "Yeah, that could be really cool." "Yeah, I can be really bad!"

There was a point when, I think in Season Four, I

remember saying to Joss, "I'm feeling kind of out of the league a bit here, now that I've burnt the library up and I'm no longer a Watcher. That's ended, what am I doing here? Why am I here? Why don't I go back to England and be with my family?" So that's when the "New Man" thing came in and Giles is having a mid-life crisis and feels out of the loop. You have to be very careful about what you say to Joss, about your emotions or what you're doing in life – you find it very mirrored. [Laughs]

DO YOU WISH THAT THERE HAD BEEN MORE OF AN OPPORTUNITY TO CROSS OVER BETWEEN THE TWO SHOWS?
TH: That would have been nice. I have to admit, I did have conversations with two or three people about, "Hey, wouldn't it be cool if Giles came over?" Just ask and I'll be there. But I think the problem was pretty much shoe-horning me in there. If it had occurred to Joss that it was something that we could really do, I think it would have been done in a flash. The real reason why the musical took six years to get on is he never ever wanted it to look like we'd run out of ideas so were doing a musical instead, [as with Giles appearing on Angel, it had to be a case of] purely when the time was right and the line fitted. That's why I think the musical is such a great episode; Joss broke three major storylines in music and lyrics.
AD: The other thing is, when

Angel was starting, Joss was anxious not to have Angel as the second hour of Buffy, but to really make the world go on and I think that he succeeded. [The shows were] related, but they're clearly different fields and different things are explored, and so the crossovers were used when they were really necessary and important, but not abused to the extent where you sort of have someone wandering back and forth between L.A. and Sunnydale. And the other thing, on a practical level, is that it's up to the network, they have to sign off. When you do a crossover, they have to do a lot of advertising and extra money for actors to be in both places – it effects their filming schedule if they've lost one person to another show on another set.

YOU'VE OBVIOUSLY GOT A GOOD RAPPORT WITH EACH OTHER. SPEAKING FOR YOUR CHARACTERS, WHAT WERE YOUR FAVORITE ASPECTS OF THE GILES AND WESLEY RELATIONSHIP WHEN YOU WERE ON BUFFY

> "As soon as Tony would giggle in a scene, then I would giggle, and it wouldn't be long before everybody was giggling. Alexis

TOGETHER, AND WAS THERE ANYTHING YOU WOULD LIKE TO HAVE DONE THAT YOU DIDN'T GET A CHANCE TO DO PLOT-WISE?

AD: [*Laughter*] I always wanted more scenes with Tony. I mean A) I love him as a person and I love acting with him, so I was always anxious for there to be more of that, but quite frankly, I'm sure we would have just gone on and on and on. But what I liked was the fractiousness with each other, that they were just very temperamental with one another and they really – when Giles was annoying Wesley, Giles really had no idea of it, and when Wesley was annoying Giles, Wesley really had no idea of it, and that always tickled me enormously, that Giles would be getting so petulant, and Wesley would be oblivious and vice versa. That's one of the things I liked about their relationship. Giles and Wesley are sort of founded in jealousy – fear of losing something to the other person – so that made for great comedy.

WERE THERE ANY PARTICULAR MOMENTS, REALLY FUNNY MOMENTS, THAT STAND OUT?

TH: I'm trying to remember the moment in the graduation ball, and there was actually a line that Alexis had about something that he did in his school days...

AD: That's what it was. I was attributing that to Cordelia and it wasn't. It was talking about Wesley being tortured as a school boy...

TH: [*Laughs*] And basically being spanked, I think. But basically, Alexis was just sort of running on [*laughing*] and once I had the image in my head I found it very difficult to complete the scene. It was the fact that he said it with such candor. It's one of those things, when someone says to you, "You know when we were at school and we used to do that thing and..."

AD: And it's not something you should really admit to. "Remember that time we were lighting our farts?!" [laughs]. You just don't really say that out loud, do you?

TH: It was just very cute and it tickled me something rotten.

HAVE YOU GOT ANY NEW PROJECTS THAT YOU'D LIKE TO TALK ABOUT AT ALL?

AD: I wish I had. I've been reading some plays, I'd like to go back to the theater at some point, but I don't want to say too much because we're just talking about it right now.

TH: I've got a charity project. We're trying to get a documentary... It's called The Gambia Horse & Donkey Trust. Basically, it's a charity that I've become involved in. It's two women that have got this charity, a tiny charity in the Gambia, and the idea is that they're taking saddlers and ferriers, and vets. They've done it in tandem with the International League of the Protection of Horses, and they've been recognized and endorsed by Make Poverty History, and that campaign has allowed them to produce a white rosette which we're selling. But ultimately, I want to go out there with Sarah, my partner, and she will teach and I'll sort of hover and do the celeb thing [*laughs*].

There's a movie that I did last year called *Click*, and that's coming out as well.

TONY, ALEXIS – THANKS VERY MUCH FOR TAKING THE TIME TO TALK TO US!

AD: Well, we like being together.

TH: We do, in fact we're going to spend this evening together, aren't we?

AD: Yes, well, part of it. [*Laughs*]. Steady on! ✛

THANK YOU TO EVERYONE AT SHOWMASTERS AND COLLECTORMANIA WHO MADE THIS INTERVIEW POSSIBLE

ALEXIS, HOW FAR INTO THE LAST SEASON OF ANGEL DID YOU KNOW THAT IT WAS GOING TO BE CANCELED, AND DID THAT CHANGE THE STORYLINE IN ANY WAY?

AD: YES, IT DID. IT WAS JUST AFTER CHRISTMAS, I THINK, JOSS LET EVERYBODY KNOW – AND THAT WAS SAD. HE RANG ONE DAY AS FAR AS STORY CHANGES GO, AND HE SAID THAT HE'D HAD A REALLY GOOD IDEA, BUT I MAY NOT THINK IT WAS SO GREAT, AND IT WOULD INVOLVE DYING AND HOW DID I FEEL ABOUT THAT? AND THEN HE SAID A LITTLE ABOUT HOW IT WAS GOING TO HAPPEN, AND I THOUGHT IT WAS SUCH A GOOD STORY I COULDN'T SAY NO TO IT. HE'S VERY SWEET, WITH THINGS LIKE THAT. HE ALWAYS GOES TO ACTORS AND SAYS 'LOOK, YOU'RE GOING IN THIS DIRECTION WITH THIS STORY, ARE YOU ON BOARD, AND IF YOU'RE NOT THEN HE'LL CHANGE DIRECTION WHEN IT'S WORTH IT. THERE WERE PLANS IN TERMS OF CHANGING THE STORY, THE ILLYRIA, FRED, WESLEY THING WOULD HAVE BECOME MORE INVOLVED IN SEASON SIX, AND THERE WERE SOME OTHER THINGS WITH ANGEL AND NINA THAT WERE ON THE CARDS THAT NEVER GOT PUT OUT THERE. IT ALL TOOK PLACE, BUT IT WAS ALL TOTALLY COMPRESSED INTO THE LAST SIX EPISODES, WHERE HE JUST TRIED TO TOUCH ON ALL THE THINGS HE WANTED TO EXPLORE FOR A LONG TIME, WHICH HE'S SUCH A GENIUS AT. ✛

Opposite: Tony and his horse, Otto, displaying the White Rosettes that are part of the Make Poverty History Campaign. For more details on these, and The Gambia Horse & Donkey Trust. visit www.anthonyhead.org/gambiatrust (picture © Sarah Fisher)

The BUFFY AND ANGEL GUIDE TO:
BEING A WATCHER

With the entire Watchers Council headquarters having
been blown up by minions working for that nasty old
First Evil, not surprisingly, Watchers have become a bit thin
on the ground. With Giles left trying to re-establish the ancient
organization, the Council is currently seeking to recruit and train a
new generation of Watchers. So, to find out if you've got what it takes
to become the next Rupert Giles or Wesley Wyndam-Pryce, have a read of
our handy guide to being a Watcher. But don't worry; the Council can't
afford to be too fussy when it comes to recruiting new blood. After
all, who'd have ever thought Andrew Wells was Watcher material?!

By Kate Anderson

🏛 Tip#1 It helps to be, er… English

Although not all Watchers are English, it does however seem to be something of a contributing factor. Rupert Giles, Wesley Wyndam-Pryce and Gwendolyn Post are just three of the British Watchers to have descended on Sunnydale. In some instances, being a Watcher is something of a family affair, with several generations of a family undertaking the role. Both Giles and Wesley came from families of Watchers. In Giles' case, both his father and grandmother were Watchers. Although young Giles had aspirations to be a fighter pilot or a grocer, being a Watcher was what was expected of him. And after rebelling and dabbling in the black arts, Giles eventually accepted his destiny. Similarly, Wesley also followed in the footsteps of his father, Roger Wyndam-Pryce.

Tip #2 Knowledge is power

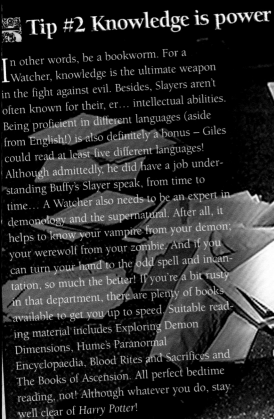

In other words, be a bookworm. For a Watcher, knowledge is the ultimate weapon in the fight against evil. Besides, Slayers aren't often known for their, er… intellectual abilities. Being proficient in different languages (aside from English!) is also definitely a bonus – Giles could read at least five different languages! Although admittedly, he did have a job understanding Buffy's Slayer speak, from time to time… A Watcher also needs to be an expert in demonology and the supernatural. After all, it helps to know your vampire from your demon; your werewolf from your zombie. And if you can turn your hand to the odd spell and incantation, so much the better! If you're a bit rusty in that department, there are plenty of books available to get you up to speed. Suitable reading material includes Exploring Demon Dimensions, Hume's Paranormal Encyclopaedia, Blood Rites and Sacrifices and The Books of Ascension. All perfect bedtime reading, not! Although whatever you do, stay well clear of Harry Potter!

 ## Rule #3 Don't be a cry baby

As a Watcher, you're going to come across all kinds of nastiness – from fish men to horned demons, snake-monsters and giant praying mantis'. So, having a strong stomach goes a long way. If you faint at the mere sight of blood, then Watcher material you are not! But above all, 'don't panic' is the golden rule – even if you get up one morning and discover that an evil old chum has somehow managed to turn you into a Fyarl demon.

In the past, training to become a Watcher was all about books and theories. Now, it's much more hands on; more field work. Even going so far as to face vampires – albeit in controlled circumstances – before you enter the field of combat. Furthermore, you'll quickly discover that being a cry baby is a definite no-no for a Watcher. Although perhaps someone should have pointed that out to Wesley – when he first arrived in Sunnydale, he didn't exactly come across as Captain Courageous! Giles, on the other hand, certainly proved just how physically resilient he was, right from day one. After all, it's not exactly pleasant being tortured by Angelus or facing off against Dark Willow. Sometimes you may even be called upon to undertake some really nasty jobs; things that even your Slayer won't do – just as Giles suffocated mortal Ben, in order to finally defeat Glory. However you look at it, being a Watcher isn't a job for a wimp!

Rule #4 Don't get too attached to your charge

Watchers have been known to lose their charges, from time to time. So on reflection, it would probably be best not to get too attached to your Slayer. However, try telling that to the likes of Rupert Giles or Bernard Crowley! Giles has always had a rather unique relationship with his Slayer, but it was his open and honest relationship with Buffy that ultimately led to his dismissal by the Watchers Council. His affection for his charge – said to resemble a father's love for a child – was apparently clouding his judgement, thus making him incapable of being impartial. But by the same admission, the close bond the two shared undoubtedly made them both stronger, and it could also be said, a more effective Watcher and Slayer. Of course, robbing your charge of her powers and putting her up against a loony-tune vampire in the name of some ancient test on Council orders, isn't going to put you in her good books!

Rule #5 Look good in tweed

When it comes to being a Watcher, there are certain traditions that must be followed. For starters, tweed. No one looked better in tweed than Giles – with perhaps the exception of Spike/Randy! Unlike Buffy and all her killer outfits, Giles' wardrobe predominantly seemed to consist of shirts, ties and the same tweed jacket. It seems that to cut it as a Watcher, it helps to look good in tweed. Even Watcher-in-Training, Andrew, turned up in Los Angeles sporting a rather fetching tweed wardrobe – not to mention a shaggy new hair do and pipe! Tweed doesn't just belong to royalty or the country set. Other British traditions to follow include always maintaining a stiff upper lip, not to mention being a tad on the stuffy, maybe even a bit pompous, side. Oh, and having humor as dry as a slice of toast. And drinking lots of tea. And looking good in glasses.

Rule #6 Avoid any sort of social life

Being responsible for a Slayer isn't a nine to five job. As a Watcher, you are charged with the care of your Slayer 24/7. And that means you are always on call, night and day. Consequently, you won't find maintaining any kind of a social life that easy. Which is perfect, if you're the quiet, loner type who prefers to keep yourself to yourself. But if you're something of a social butterfly, then you may have quite a battle on your hands to balance your Watcher duties with a personal life. In fact, dating may seem even more perilous than facing off against all those creatures of the night and dastardly demons! Unless, of course, you can find yourself a nice lass or lad who matches your own intellect and has an interest in the occult.

Rule #7 Keep a diary

If you ever kept a secret diary as a kid, then you should find keeping a Watcher's Diary a breeze. Just so long as you don't leave it around for your little bro or sis to get their hands on! The Watchers Diaries are an essential source of information. Not only are they used to record a Slayer's progress, the diaries are the way present day Watchers research how situations were solved in the past. They also provide valuable information on all the demons Watchers and Slayers have come up against. In fact, it was thanks to old Watcher Diaries that Giles was able to source information regarding the exploits of Angel and Spike.

Rule #8 Be a bit bossy

Ultimately, to be a good Watcher, you have to have a bossy streak. After all, mentoring a Slayer is a very responsible job. You'll be required to discipline your charge and, if she's a 16 year old school girl, that may not be particularly easy! After all, hanging out at the mall with your chums is bound to be far more appealing than training, training and more training! But if all else fails, saying please and giving your Slayer a cookie before sending her out on patrol has been known to work in the past. Occasionally.

Rule #9 Don't mention the C-word

Whatever you do, don't mention the Cruciamentum! Especially if your Slayer is about to turn 18.

Watching
the Watchers

Whether it's Giles getting sacked, Gwendolyn Post going psycho, or Wesley and Cordelia locking lips – badly – Sunnydale's Watchers have given us many a memorable moment. Here are just a few of them...

"The Dark Age" Giles faces off against the demon Eyghon. And Giles and Jenny share their first kiss.

"Becoming, Part Two" That nasty Angelus tortures poor old Giles.

"Passion" – After Angelus murders Jenny, Giles goes all "Ripper" and tries to kill the vampire.

"Band Candy" Giles and Joyce getting it on!

"Helpless" The Watchers Council tests Buffy's skills. And Giles gets fired.

"Revelations" Faith's new Watcher, Gwendolyn Post, has a very dangerous fashion accessory: the Glove of Myhnegon.

"Graduation Day, Part Two" Wesley and Cordelia snog. Very badly!

"Checkpoint" The Watchers Council is back in Sunnydale. And Giles gets reinstated.

"The Gift" Giles is back in full Ripper mode, murdering Ben.

OTHER GREAT TV TIE-IN COMPANIONS FROM TITAN

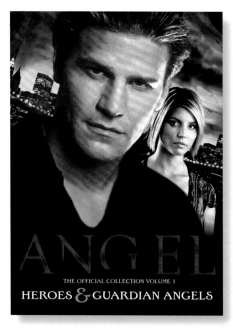

Angel - The Official Collection Volume 1
On sale November 23, 2015
ISBN 9781782763680

The X-Files - The Official Collection Volume 1
On sale January 5, 2016
ISBN 9781782763710

COMING SOON...

The Slayer Collection Volume 2 - Monsters & Villains
On sale March 29, 2016
ISBN 9781782763659

For more information visit www.titan-comics.com

TITANCOMICS